A Man Called
PETER

Anniversary Edition

A Man Called
PETER

THE STORY OF
PETER MARSHALL

Catherine Marshall

Chosen Books

A Division of Baker Book House Co
Grand Rapids, Michigan 49516

To
Mother and Dad
who took Peter into their hearts as a son

© 1951 by Catherine Marshall

Published by Chosen Books
a division of Baker Book House Company
P.O. Box 6287, Grand Rapids, MI 49516-6287
www.bakerbooks.com

Second printing, November 2003

Printed in the United States of America

New paperback edition published 2002

Library of Congress Cataloging-in-Publication Data
Marshall, Catherine, 1914–1983
    A man called Peter : the story of Peter Marshall / Catherine
Marshall. — New pbk. ed.
        p.   cm.
    Originally published: 1998.
    Includes bibliographical references.
    ISBN 0-8007-9311-0
    1. Marshall, Peter, 1902–1949. 2. Presbyterian Church—United
States—Clergy—Biography. 3. Immigrants—Biography. 4. Scottish
Americans—Biography. 5. United States. Congress—Chaplains—
Biography. I. Title.
BX9225.M352 M3   2002
285'.1'092—dc21
[B]   20001055285

In the back of this book you will find an offer for some original audio recordings of Dr. Peter Marshall's sermons.

CONTENTS

5

ᲤOREWORD

*M*y favorite place on Cape Cod, where I live, is Nauset Beach, in our town of Orleans. Recently, I was walking on the beach, watching the seagulls skimming the greenish-blue Atlantic surf as it crashed in on the shore, and thinking about writing this foreword to the new edition of *A Man Called Peter*. And then I suddenly remembered that my father, Dr. Peter Marshall, knew this spot well, and realized I had found another bond that ties us together. Dad loved the sea. And he especially loved Cape Cod, surrounded as it is by saltwater, with its fogs that reminded him of his native Scotland.

When I was a small boy, he was the senior pastor of New York Avenue Presbyterian Church, in Washington, D.C., where I was born and raised. He and Mom bought our Cape Cod cottage, "Waverley," in the town of West Harwich in 1943, and thereafter the three of us would spend Dad's summer vacation weeks away from the church on Cape Cod. Sometimes he would drive over to Nauset Beach at sunset to surfcast for striped bass. Though I don't share his passion for fishing, I have certainly inherited his love for the sea.

My father died at the age of forty-six, when I was just nine years old, and I sorely missed not having him to teach me things—how to play baseball, the history of the Scottish regiments, and much more. Yet, in spite of my sorrow in growing up without my father, I know beyond a doubt that God used my loss to motivate me in my own ministry. In the years I have spent researching American history, I have found that famous fathers were often strong motivators for their sons. Would John Quincy Adams have been as great a statesman without John Adams (and Abigail) showing him the way? I have long prayed that the old saying about the acorn falling close to the tree will also prove to be true in my case.

My father's legacy has been a tough one to live up to. Yet as I approach sixty, having been in the ministry for over thirty years, I have lately had a definite sense of picking up where he left off. I'm absolutely certain that were Dad still alive and in the ministry today we would both be preaching the same things—calling America back to God.

It seems hard to believe that half a century has passed since that cold January morning when Dad went home to be with the Master whom he helped so many people meet. What incredible changes the world has seen in those intervening years! The Korean and Vietnam conflicts, rock 'n' roll and the sexual revolution, the dawning of the computer age, the first human steps on the moon, the collapse of Soviet communism, and the end of the Cold War . . .

So much has changed, one might wonder why a new edition of *A Man Called Peter* should be published. Will people today be interested in reading about the life and ministry of a preacher who has been dead for fifty years?

But some things never change. The deepest issues of life are the same for us as they were for our parents and grandparents before us. We have the same types of fears and anxieties, hopes and dreams as they did. We too worry about how our children will turn out, about whether there will be enough money to pay the bills, how to properly take care of our aging parents.

My father was uniquely gifted by God to preach to people's hearts about those issues. With near perfect diction, and a Churchillian mastery of the English language, Dad nonetheless communicated in such a down-to-earth way that even first-time visitors in the pews felt that he knew them personally and understood their problems. As he once told seminarians preparing for the ministry:

"You must root your preaching in reality, remembering that the people before you have problems
    doubts
        fears
            and anxieties
                gnawing at their faith . . .

If, when you write your sermons, you can see the gleaming knuckles of a clenched fist . . .
    the lip that is bitten to keep back tears . . .
        the troubled heart that is suffering because it cannot

forgive . . .
    the spirit that has no joy because it has no love . . .

If you can see the big tears that run down a mother's face . . .
If you can see these things—preach them . . .
    preach for them—and get down deep."

Dad did get down deep in his preaching—so much so that during the anxious years of World War II, and even afterward, news photographers would record lines of people waiting in freezing rain (or oppressive humidity) to get into the church in Washington, D.C., to hear him preach. Those waiting in line came from all walks of life—young men and women in military uniform, government workers, members of congressional staffs, university professors, gas station attendants, bus drivers, and U.S. senators.

Throughout the years of my traveling ministry I have had hundreds of older people in every area of the country tell me that they heard Dad preach in the 1930s and 1940s, either in the capital or in their hometown. What is even more astonishing is that they can remember whole sections of one of his sermons—fifty or even sixty years later! (Most of us preachers are fortunate if our listeners have not forgotten our sermons by the following Sunday!)

Even when his words were preached "secondhand" by Richard Todd, the English actor who superbly played Dad in the movie version of *A Man Called Peter*, they had an amazing effect on people. I have met scores of ministers across the country who have personally told me that they received their call to the gospel ministry sitting in a theater in 1955 watching that movie. They said that when they came out of the movie they *knew* that the Lord had called them to preach!

For my father, as for me, the Christian faith was always about the reality of Jesus Christ, and His desire to draw each and every one of us into a personal relationship with Him as Savior and Lord. That was what Dad lived for in his preaching and ministry, to make Jesus real to people. He succeeded. When he preached about Jesus, as one woman put it, "We seemed actually to *feel* Christ beside us, to hear the rustling of His robes."

9

A prominent judge once wrote my father a note after a service: "I never attended a communion service that I *enjoyed* so much as this one this morning. Christ and His life must be very real to you; otherwise you could not make Him so real to others."

In the first edition of *A Man Called Peter*, my mother chose six of Dad's sermons that reveal how much he made Christ real to others. For this anniversary edition, I wanted to include some material that had never been published, so I exchanged one of those sermons for one of his wartime ones, entitled "If." It was preached on January 24, 1943.

The same Lord Jesus Christ whom my father preached so eloquently is still desperately needed by all of us today. And He is just as available to us through the pages of this book, as He was when Dad preached about Him in the 1930s and 1940s. It is my prayer that you will find the reality of Christ in a fresh and new way for your life as you read.

Reverend Peter John Marshall
Orleans, Cape Cod, Massachusetts
March 1998

REFACE

$\mathcal{S}$ince Peter Marshall left us to be at home in our Father's house, I have often dreamed of him. But one dream was different from all the rest. It had the feel of reality about it. I dreamed that I was allowed to visit Peter briefly, to see him in his new setting. I found him working in a rose garden, surrounded by those perfect hybrid tea roses he always wanted to grow.

After a while, he said playfully, "I know perfectly well what you've been doing, Catherine. You're writing a book. Now, now— no exposés! What you're doing to me shouldn't happen to a dog!"

Then in a more serious vein, "It's all right, Kate. Go ahead and write it. Tell it all, if it will prove to people *that a man can love the Lord and not be a sissy. . . .* "

So, in the months since then, I have written it. Reliving and recording parts of the life that Peter and I shared has been a joyous task. The Presence of Christ has shed glory on even the hard-to-bear parts of it.

I hope that you will enjoy it, and that by the time you have come to the last page, you will know that if God can do so much for a man called Peter, he can do as much for you.

C. M.
Washington, D.C.
April 29, 1951

⍺CKNOWLEDGMENTS

No man lives to himself or dies to himself—or writes a book by himself. To a host of friends, all the way from Washington to South Africa, who have patiently answered many questions and have joyously reminisced of their association with Peter Marshall, I owe a great debt of gratitude.

Specifically, I offer my appreciation to Miss Alma Deane Fuller, who has listened patiently and often and counseled wisely; to Miss Sara Leslie for her editorial work; to Miss Ruth Welty, Mr. Miles Clark, Judge J. Russell Leech, and Mr. Robert Ingraham for their constructive criticism; to Dr. Richard Lee Silvester who checked chapter 14 from the physician's standpoint; to Mr. John D. Rhodes, the Chief of the Official Reporters of Debates in the United States Senate, for his suggestions on chapter 18; to Dr. George Docherty, who checked on Scottish geography and customs; to my secretary, Mrs. William D. Redding, who has typed with her heart as well as her hands, and who has staunchly sought to preserve some shreds of my reputation by correcting my capricious spelling; to Peter John Marshall, who has given up many an evening's fun for "Mommy's book."

Since Dr. Marshall had no idea that a book of his sermons would ever be published, the sermon manuscripts which he left behind were not completely annotated. Often he gave informal oral credit to others from the pulpit. Such statements were not always incorporated in his manuscripts. Thus the task of uncovering all sources of indebtedness to others has been a difficult one.

In preparing the present volume I have undertaken the most careful and conscientious research, and in footnotes throughout the book have given proper credit in each instance in which I was able to discover that quoted material had been used. It is possible, how-

Acknowledgments

ever, that I have not been able to identify every single instance of this kind. If, therefore, there should remain any unacknowledged quotation in the sermons or the sermon excerpts in this book, I shall welcome information to that effect and shall be glad to credit such material to the proper source in future editions of the book.

one

ABOVE TIME AND CIRCUMSTANCE

For ye shall go out with joy . . . and it shall be to the Lord
for a name, for an everlasting sign that shall not be cut off.
Isaiah 55:12–13

The morning was bleak and cold. A damp penetrating wind ruffled the steel-gray waters of the Potomac, chased bits of paper and debris down the broad roped-off expanse of Pennsylvania Avenue, and whistled around the dome of the Capitol.

Everywhere Washington wore an air of expectancy. The hillocks of lumber, which had been piled for weeks along the Avenue, had finally been fashioned into grandstand and bleachers. Every street corner was garnished with the navy blue of District policemen. The gray lampposts were decorated with small American flags and pictures of Truman and Barkley. Red, white, and blue bunting was everywhere. In a few hours, forty thousand marchers and more than forty floats would form a column seven miles long in honor of the President of the United States. It was Inauguration Day, January 20, 1949.

Before the stately Capitol building with its wide-spreading wings, I sat with 120,000 other people on crudely built benches watching the dignitaries taking their places on the special platform before us.

Radio, television, and motion-picture technicians scurried up and down their newly built platforms, adjusting and testing their equipment. At twelve noon, the eyes and ears of most Americans would be centered on this scene.

I knew that in the old Senate Chamber, with its plum-colored leather seats and green-carpeted aisles, Peter Marshall, the Senate Chaplain, called by many a reporter the "conscience of the Senate," was at that moment praying. His simple, sincere, down-to-earth prayers had been having an increasingly profound effect on the Senators. But it was an intimate thing—not the kind of thing a man talks about readily.

I could picture the scene, as I had often seen it—the sudden hush, the way the men reverently dropped their heads as Peter prayed:

God of our fathers in Whom we trust and by Whose guidance and grace this nation was born, bless the Senators of these United States at this important time in history and give them all things needful to the faithful discharge of their responsibilities.

We pray especially today for our President, and also for him who will preside over this chamber.

Give to them good health for the physical strains of their office, good judgment for the decisions they must make, wisdom beyond their own, and clear understanding for the problems of this difficult hour.

We thank Thee for their humble reliance upon Thee. May they go often to the throne of grace as we commend them both to Thy loving care and Thy guiding hand.

Through Jesus Christ our Lord. AMEN.

Soon I spied Peter marching, hat in hand, with the Senators, into the seats provided for them to the left of the inaugural stand. He was between Senator Lucas and Senator Vandenberg. The expression on his face suggested that he was particularly pleased about something.

From where I was sitting, I could just see Peter and the Senators well enough to guess that much quiet camaraderie was going on in that section of the stand.

Peter had then been Chaplain of the Senate for two years. He had not sought the job, nor wanted it at first. In the beginning he had found it hard to believe that the Senators regarded his opening prayer as more than a necessary gesture.

Time and a closer acquaintance between him and the men had changed that. The Senators were men of the world, not easily impressed with preachers. Yet Peter had earned their respect and the deep affection of the members on both sides of the aisle.

Elected by a Republican majority in 1947, he had been unanimously reelected by the Democrats on December 31, 1948. On that day, Peter had telephoned me from the church office to tell me the news. There was exultation in his voice. "I'm glad, Catherine. At least it shows I convinced them that I have no politics."

The affection the Senators felt for their chaplain was reflected in the way Senator Arthur Vandenberg, who presided as president pro tempore of the Senate in the absence of a vice-president, always called Peter "Dominie," the Dutch word for "parson."

"To know Peter is to love him," Senator Vandenberg said. "My chaplain is my intimate and priceless friend."

Indeed many an astute observer on Capitol Hill felt that Senator Vandenberg's unobtrusive spiritual partnership with Peter Marshall had undergirded the increasing stature of his statesmanship, as he rose to become the architect of the United Nations and of America's first bipartisan foreign policy in many years.

On that Inauguration Day, the vista of an ever-growing and deepening ministry among all those men opened out before Peter. Long ago he had been "tapped on the shoulder" by "the Chief" as he loved to call his Lord. Twenty-two years before he had landed at Ellis Island—an immigrant boy. God had sent him into strange places to preach His message. It seemed to Peter that the old Senate Chamber was almost the strangest of all. Yet, there in the highest legislative hall in the nation, the Risen Christ and the wisdom of Almighty God were surely needed. It thrilled Peter to have the chance to be Christ's representative in that place.

The uncertain Washington sun broke through the heavy clouds as Harry S. Truman took the oath of office as President of the United States of America. His left hand was resting on two Bibles, a Gutenberg Bible and the White House Bible. His outstretched fingers covered passages from the Sermon on the Mount and the Ten Commandments as he intoned the solemn words:

I do solemnly swear that I will faithfully execute the office of President of the United States, and will, to the best of my ability, preserve, protect, and defend the Constitution. . . .

The sky umbrella of planes was already forming for the inaugural parade as I made my way through the crush of people back to our parked car. It was quite a while before my husband joined me. His rugged face was beaming.

"Guess *what*, Catherine," he said as he opened the car door. The joy of a small boy was in his voice.

"What? What's happened?"

"Senator Vandenberg called me 'Peter' today!"

It was a small thing. But it represented the outstretched hand of friendship—the open door to a man's heart.

A long and dramatic train of events had led Peter Marshall to that memorable day. The story has about it the feel of a Biblical saga; yet, it is the story of a modern man, a warmly human man.

As I write I see a procession of vivid mental pictures: A boy walking through a Scottish lane lined with rhododendron, trying to hear God's call; a ship plowing through the cold waters of the North Atlantic; a blast furnace in New Jersey; a boy on a train going south to Birmingham. There are traces of wistfulness in the story, and a procession of the haunted hearts of men and women. There is much laughter—and sometimes a sob.

The story begins some thirty years ago in a grimy industrial city in Scotland.

two

*U*NDER SEALED ORDERS

Now the Lord had said . . . , Get thee out of thy country, and from thy kindred . . . unto a land that I will shew thee . . . and I will bless thee . . . and thou shalt be a blessing.

Genesis 12:1–2

eter Marshall did not grow up wanting to be a minister. That was God's idea—not his. In fact, it took quite a lot of divine persuasion to get him to accept that plan.

Peter's first adolescent ambition was to become a deck apprentice in the British Mercantile Marine and, of course, eventually rise to nothing less than an admiral.

He was born in Coatbridge, Scotland—a city of 45,000, nicknamed "The Iron Burgh" because it was the chief center of the Scottish iron trade. Since Coatbridge was only nine miles east of Glasgow, the sea and the famous Clyde shipyards were never far away. When Peter was very young, he fell under the spell of all the color and romance of British Navy tradition.

Whenever he got the chance, the young boy would stand and watch the ships as they warped into the Glasgow wharves or as they put out to sea for distant and romantic ports. From the time Peter began to read, he devoured tales of the sea. Many a time he would stop in his reading to turn his thoughts adrift, to imagine himself walking the deck of his proud ship, displaying his immaculate uniform with all its gold braid, licking imaginary brine from his lips. With pen and pencil and water colors, he sketched and scribbled, and always of ships. How he longed to run off to sea and escape what he regarded as his drab and uninteresting life!

Undoubtedly, in Peter's case, it was escape he sought, romanticized in the glamour and glory of the sea.

His father had been the Prudential Insurance Company's field superintendent for the Bellshill and Coatbridge area. He had been a Mason and the leader of the kirk choir. As a small boy, Peter had loved him with all the warmth of his affectionate nature. But his father had died when Peter was only four and when his sister Chris was only a few months old. The little boy vividly remembered the scene around his father's deathbed; the day of the funeral, when he had stood—numbed and stricken outside their home on Kildonan Street—watching the funeral cortege from a distance. He remembered that there was a handsome horse-drawn brake, bearing his father's fellow Masons.

As the little boy grew up, his adoration for his father and for his memory increased. All of his life it showed itself in a deep hunger to learn everything possible about him. Whenever, through the years, he encountered anyone who had known the first Peter Marshall, he always eagerly questioned him for every possible detail.

With all of this, it was not strange that, when, a few years after his father's death, his mother married Mr. Peter Findlay, the little boy was filled with emotional opposition. Admittedly, it would not have been an easy situation for any man to handle. Thus as a boy, a growing dissatisfaction with his life fed in Peter a secret, consuming desire to escape to sea.

At that time, the British Navy signed boys at fifteen years and nine months. Soon after Peter's fourteenth birthday, he decided that he would conveniently age a year and nine months overnight. So he said farewell to his friends at school, informing them that he was joining the Navy. At dawn the next day he slipped away from home to the recruiting station, and proceeded to apply for enlistment, saying that he was the required age. For a year or more he had been doing violent stretching exercises to acquire the proper height.

His navy "career" lasted but two days; his enlistment papers were discovered. Since he was actually only fourteen, his parents refused to give their consent, and a very eager A.B. was lost to Jellicoe's fleet. A bitterly disappointed and crestfallen boy secretly sobbed himself to sleep that night.

Peter did not understand it then, but this was the first big step in God's guidance for his life. Often God has to shut a door in our face, so that He can subsequently open the door through which He wants us to go. People today wonder about this matter of God having a detailed plan, a blueprint, for each individual in the universe. "If there is really a God," they ask, "and if He is interested in *me*, how do I go about getting in touch with Him? *How* does He talk to people today?"

Peter Marshall's story answers these questions out of one man's rich experience. I can imagine God saying: "There is a boy down in Lanarkshire. I have a plan for him. He is to go to America, in order to enter the ministry. He will spend almost half his life in the United States. His life and his ministry will bless thousands of people. I have all the circumstances planned and all my helpers designated, to make sure that my plan does not go awry." So the hand that firmly shut the door to a career in the Royal Navy, in order to open the way into the ministry, was really God's—not man's.

Peter, however, like most of his countrymen, was born doggedly resolute. He would not easily give up his cherished ambition. Having told his high-school friends that he was leaving to join the Royal Navy, a boyish pride made him unwilling to go back and face possible ridicule. The only alternative was to begin working. By day, he started as an office boy with a firm of civil engineers, and four nights a week, from seven to ten, he went to the Coatbridge Technical School, where he studied mechanical engineering. At home, in any spare minutes left, he studied semaphore and Morse, and stewed over trig problems, feverishly working against the day when he might get another try at the Navy. So thoroughly did he learn the International Code of flag signals that all his life he could read much of the colored bunting fluttering from the halyards of ships entering and leaving port.

It seemed as if even Peter's friends were ordered by God. In one of his evening classes at the Technical School, he met Robert P. Hunter of Airdrie and David R. Wood of Coatbridge. The three boys became close companions. They studied and played together. They were all members of the Garturk Cricket Club. Soon they became known to friends in Coatbridge as "The Three Musketeers." The strands of their lives were destined to cross and recross in other years and on other continents.

Bob Hunter and Dave Wood fell in love with two sisters—Margaret and Tillie Christie of Gartsherrie. But in October 1923, the Christie family emigrated to the United States. Three years later both boys followed their sweethearts—all the way to Birmingham, Alabama. Peter, the lone musketeer left in Coatbridge, had no thought that he would ever see his friends again.

When Peter was seventeen, through a little notice in a church magazine called *The Congregationalist,* he tracked down his half brother. He had not seen William Marshall since the day of his father's funeral. Willie was his father's child by an earlier marriage. As it turned out, he lived only thirty miles away, in Dumbarton. One Saturday afternoon Peter took John Neil, one of his best friends, with him, and they went to Dumbarton. When the brothers met and shook hands, they were so filled with emotion that neither could speak. That was in August. Some correspondence followed between them, as Willie tried to help the young boy achieve his ambition to get to sea.

Dumbarton

My dear Peter,

I must apologize for not replying sooner . . . I am taking the liberty of enclosing two letters of introduction to the McLay, McIntyre Shipping Co., 21 Bothwell Street, Glasgow, should you still want to go to sea. You could easily do that business on a Wednesday afternoon, and if arranged, I could meet you in the evening, by 6 oc. . . .

Hoping to hear from you soon again, I remain,

Yours affectionately,
Willie

This letter was dated November 10, 1919. Peter *did* still wish to go to sea. He wished it passionately. But four days after the letter was written, William met with a serious accident. The next time Peter saw him, he was dead.

In the absence of the regular sexton of the local kirk, Willie Marshall had offered to fire the furnace. The night of November 14 was bitterly cold, freezing. The furnace exploded; Willie's legs were shattered. Subsequently they had to be amputated. He died on November 29, without seeing Peter again. Thus it came about that Willie's efforts to help his young brother achieve his heart's desire and get off to sea were fruitless.

Later, Peter tried again and applied for a berth as a cadet navigating officer. But by then ships were scarce and even experienced men were hunting jobs. Again God said "No."

By 1923, he had become a machinist in Stewarts and Lloyds Imperial Tube Works. If he were fortunate enough to work full time, nine hours a day, he earned thirty-eight shillings a week. As part of the aftermath of World War I, Great Britain was then undergoing a severe depression. Unemployment had reached staggering figures; suffering was acute; bread lines were everywhere.

Although Peter was now approaching his twenty-first birthday, he was still restless and dissatisfied at home. Eventually the time arrived when he decided that it was best for him to leave the family circle and strike out for himself.

His mother was sympathetic and helpful. She had supplied a steadying hand throughout his uneasy childhood. As she helped him gather together his few possessions and pack them in his tin trunk, they talked over his financial situation. It seemed critical. He had given his mother his pay envelope each payday, and so had not been able to save any money. The thirty-eight shillings a week from the Tube Works could not possibly provide decent food and lodging and leave anything at all for night school.

To this crisis, his mother brought her strong homespun faith. Often, as a young girl, she and her seven sisters and three brothers had faced dire economic necessity. She, herself, had started work as a weaver when she was very young. Her trust in God was real and warm and alive, because it had been nurtured through those early years of hardship.

Peter watched his mother as she folded and packed the warm clothing which she had carefully mended. Her naturally curly hair was already turning white, but her pink cheeks and sprightly understanding blue eyes gave her a perpetually youthful appearance. It seemed to him that her hands were very beautiful. True, they were red. Some of the finger tips were rough with household care, but how many times the warmth of her heart had flowed through those hands to smooth away his boyhood sorrows during all those troubled years!

When the trunk was all packed, she walked to the little iron gate with him. It was when her heart dictated affection, which a reserve deep inside her would not let her lips express, that she lapsed into the "braid Scots" of her childhood. It sprang naturally to her lips at this moment.

"Dinna forget your verse, my laddie," she said. "Seek ye first the kingdom of God and his righteousness, and all these things shall be added unto you."[1] Her blue eyes smiled reassuringly at him. "Long ago I pit ye in the Lord's hands, and I'll no be takin' ye awa noo. He will tak' care o' you. Dinna worry."

That was on a Friday. The next Monday morning, after Peter had been at his machine for two and a half hours, a grimy hand tapped him on the shoulder. "Ye're wanted in the office of the manager, Marshall."

As he walked toward the office and stood hesitantly outside the door on which was printed CAPTAIN J. WILSON, MANAGER, Peter wondered whether he was about to be reprimanded, or perhaps even laid off. Many men were being dismissed every day. Finally, he tapped on the door.

"Come on in, Marshall," a voice said. "I thought it would be you."

On Captain Wilson's desk Peter recognized a drawing for a suggested machine improvement which he had made and turned in months earlier.

The manager struck a match and relit his pipe. "This suggestion you've made is good, Marshall. Our engineers think it has possibilities and may save us money. I've been keeping my eye on you." He sucked on his pipe reflectively. "How'd you like to have a try at being charge hand?"

A few minutes later Peter left the captain's office. There was a new lift to his shoulders. Everything was arranged. Before ten o'clock that morning, his transfer from the Screwing Section to the Poles and Derricks Section had been completed, with a salary that would double his paycheck and provide abundantly for his augmented needs. He could hardly wait to tell his mother how quickly and how generously God had answered their prayer for financial help.

Since Peter was now rooming in a house in another part of Coatbridge, as a rule he saw his mother only on Sundays, when they met in the little Buchanan Street Evangelical Union Congregational Kirk. There, where his father had once been choirmaster, Peter was very active.

He taught in the Sunday School, was leader of the Junior Choir, and became a Scoutmaster. Often there were hikes or camping trips with his Cub Scouts away from the industrial atmosphere of Coatbridge; away from the smoke and soot, the roar and rattle of machinery, the dull glow of its blast furnaces on the midnight sky.

Often the boys went to the Sholto Douglas Estate, the shores of Loch Lomond, or more rarely, as far as the Trossachs. Once Peter took his Cubs for a week's camping trip to his uncle's farm "Cassingray" near Largo, in Fifeshire. The young Scoutmaster was a tall, slender boy with a shock of blond, curly hair, who wore kilts of the Gordon tartan, with the regulation khaki jacket.

Tramping the bare hills and the heatherswept moors, climbing the tors and the bens, whose heads were often circled with mist or crowned with clouds, exploring the loch sides in the sunshine or the rain, Peter acquired a love for his native countryside that no years of exile could ever dim.

Sometimes he took his Scouts to the tiny village of Luss, whose one narrow street winds down to the shores of Loch Lomond. There, in the summertime, the casement windows of the little stone houses look out on the profusion of climbing roses that seem to cover everything. From there, the boys would take one of the excursion steamers that regularly ply the loch's twenty-eight miles of clear blue water. This was a favorite outing in order to enjoy the scenery, with Ben Lomond always standing sentinel in the background, to explore some of the beautiful green islands that dot the loch.

On other days the boys would wade through knee-high bracken to trace to its source some little burn cascading down a mountainside, and would stop to drink of its crystal-clear, icy-cold water. Sometimes they fished for trout in the brown shadows of a secluded stream, and afterward cooked the fish outdoors, eating them with homemade scones and cups of steaming tea.

Peter learned to love the music of the Gaelic tongue, the undying beauty of Scottish melodies that have been handed down from generation to generation, the poignant, pulse-quickening wail of the bagpipes. He was unconsciously accumulating from these years pictures that would never fade, sounds that would never die away.

Peter's last four years in Scotland were filled with a great variety of interests and activities. He played soccer on the Dunbeth YMCA team. Their jerseys were crimson and gold.

Soccer is played in Scotland from August through April. No winter weather is considered too severe, if the players can stay on their feet at all. Only a pea-soup fog holds up the game. Peter was customarily the goalkeeper.

He kept several newspaper accounts of those Saturday matches.

> Woodilee v. Dunbeth YMCA. The match was played in cold weather, and on very hard ground. . . . The YMCA forward quintette were as slippery as eels, keeping their opponents' defence on tenterhooks. . . . With twenty minutes to go, both teams strove hard. Campbell burst through and almost scored a third, Marshall saving. . . .

The boys on the Dunbeth team were part of a group of about twenty young people who went around together. They also played cricket and at times became a dance band, in which Peter played the drums. The girls in the group had a winter hockey team. In the summer they played tennis together and went on picnics.

In 1925, one of their number, Bert Paterson, received his medical degree from the University of Glasgow and went out to Sulenkama, Cape Province, South Africa, to establish a Scottish Presbyterian Medical Mission. Because the village was so primitive, with nothing but native grass huts, Bert was forced to leave Nessie, his bride of a few months, at home in Scotland.

Bert sent back desperate letters. He badly needed a dispensary and hospital, but he had no money. He had gone out like a happy warrior to tramp the highroad of service and sacrifice, and the group of young people felt that they could not let him down. The question was: How could twenty of them raise five or six thousand dollars?

Nessie Knight Paterson was a tiny girl with a towering spirit. She knew that whatever they did would have to be done in a big way. Under her direction, the gang formed themselves into a dramatic club and proceeded to produce and act two of Sir James Barrie's plays—*Quality Street* and *Dear Brutus*. On faith and a kind of

God-inspired madness, they hired the Athenaeum, one of Glasgow's downtown theaters, for a full week.

Sir James Barrie liked the sound of the wholly crazy venture. He presented them with an autographed copy of each of the plays to auction off. Horace Fellowes, first violinist and leader of the Scottish Orchestra, heard of what they were doing and not only agreed to let the orchestra play but came himself to conduct for the opening night. The Glasgow newspapers picked up the story and played it up under the title "Pilgrims of the Lonely Way." The group sold tickets feverishly. They had more fun than they had ever had on the dance floor or the football field.

The Athenaeum was packed to the doors every night. The cast acted as if inspired. Many of Glasgow's million and a quarter citizens caught something of the group's spirit of joyous abandon and adventurous faith. When it was all over, Nessie was able to join her husband in Africa, taking with her almost seven thousand dollars.

The Nessie Knight Hospital at Sulenkama is still there, ministering to the patient blacks in the jungle. Bert and Nessie kept in touch with Peter through subsequent years. Now they have a hospital with a hundred beds, a church, a school, and at least fourteen outstations. It all began with the vision of a group of youngsters.

Another very strong influence on Peter during these most impressionable years was his intense admiration for Eric Liddell. Eric was Scotland's greatest and best-loved athlete, a divinity student who planned to be a missionary. He was a Rugby Internationalist, playing center three-quarters. In addition, he was a sprinter, the British record holder for the 100 yards.

In 1924 he was chosen to run in the Paris Olympics. But he electrified Britons by refusing unequivocally to run the 100 meter, when he discovered that the "heats" were to be run off on a Sunday. At great sacrifice, he decided to train for the 400 meter.

In Paris, on Friday, July 11, 1924, Liddell had to compete with two men, a Swiss and a Swede, who had both broken world records that same week in the 400-meter semifinals.

Just before the start of the race, a band of Cameron Highlanders played in the stadium—always a blood-stirring experience for any Scotsman. As they finished, a man slipped up to Liddell and put a piece of paper in his hand. On it was written these words, "Them that honour me will I honour" (1 Samuel 2:30).

Exactly 47.6 seconds later the unknown friend's prophecy was fulfilled. Eric had established a new world's record for the 400 meter and a reputation for the greatest quarter-miler yet seen.

Peter Marshall, along with thousands more young people in Scotland, followed every detail of all this. To them Eric was a hero, not just because of his great athletic ability, but also because of his modesty, his undeniable charm, the great strength of his Christian witness. His influence on Peter's life can scarcely be measured.

One summer Peter spent working in the English village of Bamburgh, sixteen miles southeast of the Scottish border. The village, which had only about four hundred inhabitants, had a charm all its own. Red-roofed nineteenth-century stone cottages, vine-covered, were set on the edge of the cold, misty North Sea. Around the village was a spacious countryside of wheat and barley fields, pasture, and moorland where black-faced sheep roamed. It was dominated to the west by the desolate, heathery height of Chalton Moor, and had been built in the sheltering lee of Bamburgh Castle. The hoary natural fortress, whose foundations went deep into solid basalt, with outer walls hewn from whinstone quarried nearby, had dominated the countryside since the twelfth century.

That Northumberland countryside was noted for its good workable limestone. There were alternations of whinstone (the local name for limestone), shale, and coal, with the whin often eighty to one hundred feet thick. Craggy Ridge, Spindleston, and Belford Crags overlooked the lofty, bleak moorlands of Rayheaugh and Roseborough.

Walking back from a nearby village to Bamburgh one dark, starless night, Peter struck out across the moors, thinking he would take a short cut. He knew that there was a deep deserted limestone quarry close by the Glororum Road, but he thought he could avoid that danger spot. The night was inky black, eerie. There was only the sound of the wind through the heather-strained moorland, the noisy clamor of wild muir fowl as his footsteps disturbed them, the occasional far-off bleating of a sheep.

Suddenly he heard someone call, *"Peter! . . ."* There was great urgency in the voice.

He stopped. "Yes, who is it? What do you want?"

For a second he listened, but there was no response, only the sound of the wind. The moor seemed completely deserted.

Thinking he must have been mistaken, he walked on a few paces. Then he heard it again, even more urgently:

"*Peter!* . . ."

He stopped dead still, trying to peer into that impenetrable darkness, but suddenly stumbled and fell to his knees. Putting out his hand to catch himself, he found nothing there. As he cautiously investigated, feeling around in a semicircle, he found himself to be on the very brink of an abandoned stone quarry. Just one step more would have sent him plummeting into space to certain death.

This incident made an unforgettable impression on Peter. There was never any doubt in his mind about the source of that Voice. He felt that God must have some great purpose for his life to have intervened so specifically. Through subsequent years there were other close brushes with death, times when he was spared while others around him were hurt or killed. Once an automobile killed a friend walking at his side; once fire broke out in a tiny boat ten miles out at sea; once an airplane he had just missed, crashed. God's hand was very evidently on his life. This gave him a sense of destiny and of purposefulness.

Out of his experiences during these years, Peter coined the phrase "God's nugatory influences." During this early part of his life, however, God's influence often seemed more determined than merely nugatory. God's next step in channeling his life toward the one goal of the ministry now became evident.

That fall, a missionary returned from China spoke to the young people in the Buchanan Street Kirk. He came as a representative of the London Missionary Society, and was not seeking money, but recruits—volunteers for life for the mission fields.

Peter was deeply touched by this appeal. He knew that his own father had once offered his life as a missionary, but for some reason which Peter was never able to ascertain, had been turned down. In addition, Eric Liddell had just announced that he was going to China as a missionary under the auspices of the Congregational Church. Peter longed to follow in his hero's steps.

At any rate, whatever the influences, from that moment Peter knew that his call was for full-time Christian service. That afternoon, at the close of the meeting, he stood up and stated publicly that he accepted the missionary's challenge.

"I have determined," he said, "to give my life to God for Him to use me wherever He wants me."

As often happens, there was a sharp disillusionment in the contrast between the adventurous spirit in which he sought to invest his life and in the negotiations that followed. Correspondence with the London Missionary Society revealed that in order to go to China it would be necessary to receive training at Mansfield College, Oxford. But scholarships were not available. Bursaries were very limited. He could expect no financial help from home. It was as if God said through circumstances, "You were right in offering your life, but China is not the place."

Said the Home Missionary Society in Edinburgh, "Since the door to the foreign mission field seems closed, why not consider home missions?"

About this time he received a letter from the Reverend T. Hywel Hughes, principal of the Scottish Congregational College in Edinburgh.

> *29 Hope Terrace*
> *Edinburgh*
> *Oct. 16, 1924*
>
> *Dear Mr. Marshall,*
>
> *As I told you on Monday, the Committee accepted you as a student of the College and gave you permission to do the first year's work at home, with a view to passing the Preliminary Examinations of the Scottish University, so that you may then go on for your M.A. degree.*
>
> *I would suggest your joining Skerry's College in Glasgow, and preparing to pass the Preliminary in March next in English and French. You would then take Higher Math, and one other subject afterwards. . . . Then you might, if you can find time, begin a little Greek. . . .*
>
> *Let me know how you get on.*
>
> > *With kind regards,*
> > *T. Hywel Hughes*

So Peter started going into Glasgow to Skerry's College three nights a week. He did not "get on" too well. The standard for the Preliminaries in English and French were very stiff. At least seven hundred students usually sat the English examination alone. If four hundred were allowed in, that was considered generous.

Peter found it hard to concentrate on classwork at night, after nine hours' work in the Tube Mill. Since on class nights he got home shortly before midnight and had to go to work at six in the morning, there was hardly any spare time for Greek. Moreover, it was impossible to save any money for further study. Living expenses, books, fees for classes and examinations, and traveling back and forth to Glasgow ate up everything. Full-time Christian work of any kind looked hopeless, impossibly far away.

At this juncture, James Broadbent, a cousin who had emigrated to the United States, came back to Scotland on a visit. Though Jim had arrived at Ellis Island with even less than the minimum amount of money required by the immigration authorities, he had subsequently been most successful in America. He was an engineer for the M. W. Kellogg Company in New York. He had made a quick trip over to Scotland from Swansea, Wales, where he was doing a job for the Anglo-Iranian Oil Company.

Jim carefully inquired about his cousin Peter. When he found out where Peter was employed, he sought him out at the Tube Mill. A Mr. Ash was then one of the head men at Stewarts and Lloyds. Jim knew him well.

"What section is Peter Marshall in?" he inquired.

"Poles and Derricks," Mr. Ash answered promptly. "Go on down and see him, if you like."

In the Poles and Derricks Section, Jim encountered a little gaffer, the foreman. He was wearing the usual bowler hat, the distinguishing mark of a foreman in Scotland.

"Could I speak with Peter Marshall?" asked Jim.

"Aye, help yoursel'. He's richt over there."

A glad reunion followed. "Look," Jim said finally, "I won't be in town long. How about takin' the rest of the day off? Then we could really have time to talk?"

Peter was trying to get a bit of steel filing out of his finger. He looked up amazed. "Why Jim! No chance of that. We get off when the whistle blows, *not before.*"

Jim smiled knowingly. He had learned a few things in the United States. "Mind if *I* ask for you?"

"No, of course not. Go ahead," said Peter.

Jim sauntered over to the gaffer. Quickly he sized the man up. His bowler hat looked very new. ("Probably *just* been promoted to a foreman," thought Jim. "Feels his oats—down to the last oat.")

"Look. I'm only in town briefly. I'd like to have a talk with my cousin here. How about letting him off for the rest of the day?"

The little man with the bowler hat drew himself up to his full five feet five. He spoke through his teeth. "Yer cousin'll get off when the whistle blows."

"But suppose I got Mr. Ash's permission?" Jim persisted.

"Aye . . . Aye, thot's what it wud tak all richt." The gaffer's tone said plainly, "That's a bluff. *You* don't even *know* Mr. Ash."

Jim walked into the adjoining office and telephoned his friend. Peter and the foreman both stood in the doorway with quite undisguised incredulity on their faces, listening to Jim's side of the conversation.

"Sure, Jim," said Mr. Ash. "Put the foreman on. I'll fix it."

A few minutes later the two men were heading toward Peter's boardinghouse on Laird Street.

While Peter was washing up and getting out of his overalls, Jim Broadbent looked curiously around the room. It was a little attic room with dormer windows. A simple iron bed was against one wall. There were several chairs and many books. On one wall was a large old-fashioned clock; hanging under it, on a peg, were Peter's kilts. Jim was busy looking at Peter's books when he came back.

"I don't understand this, Peter," he said. "What on earth is an engineer doing with *these* books—beginning Greek, Hebrew—of all things, all this theology and stuff?"

Peter flushed slightly. "Well, you see—Jim, I want to be a minister. It's rough going, though."

With little encouragement from Jim, the whole story poured out—all of the developments, difficulties, and disappointments of the last years.

Jim looked very thoughtful. "You know, my early life was remarkably like yours. My father died when I was very young, just as your father, my Uncle Peter, did. I too had a stepfather. I too had to fetch for myself. I was awfu' fond of Uncle Peter. I'd do almost anything for his son. Look, Peter, why don't you go to America to enter the ministry?"

"But Jim, I don't want to go to America. *Why should I?* Besides, I haven't any money for passage."

"Never mind that. Look, we've got just as many sinners in the United States as Scotland ever had. It's easier to get on over there. If you want to go, I'll gladly stake you to the United States."

Jim then pointed out that it was possible to work one's way through school in the United States, and that many generous scholarships were available. But though he painted a rosy picture of all the opportunities in the New World, even the opportunities in the American ministry, Peter still had no desire to go. In fact, going to the United States seemed to him the last thing he wanted to do. He agreed to pray about it though, to ask God if this could possibly be part of His plan, and to let Jim know his decision.

"I have to leave tonight for London," explained Jim. "But I'm due to be back in Paisley for a business conference on Monday. Tell you what—why don't you have dinner with me Monday night, say at the Central Station Hotel in Glasgow. Bring your girl along. We'll talk some more about it then."

But on Monday night, when the three of them met, Peter was still not able to give Jim a definite answer.

Peter prayed about it for three weeks, but no answer came. Then one Sunday afternoon, as he was walking through the rhododendron-lined lane in the Sholto Douglas Estate, suddenly "the Chief" gave him his marching orders.

"It would be hard to describe to anyone how God can make His will so plain to a man at times," Peter said later. "I was walking along that lane puzzling over the decision before me, weighing this factor against that, as one does at such a time, when all at once, *I knew.* The answer was just a clear-cut strong inner conviction, quite unmistakable, that God wanted me in the United States of America."

Now that the next step was plain, one might think that difficulties and obstacles would melt away. Such was not the case. The United States had stringent immigration laws. The quota allotment each year from the British Isles was very small. It took a year and a half to get a visa.

When finally Peter could sail, his cousin Jim was in Poland on business. All alone he boarded the *Cameronia.* All alone he watched the hills of Scotland sink into the cold waters of the North Atlantic. He felt lonely and frightened.

Let Peter tell it in his own words in the sermon "Under Sealed Orders" which he wrote in 1933:

> I do not know what picture the phrase "Under Sealed Orders" suggests to you. In these terrible days, it may have several connotations. . . .
>
> To me, it recalls very vividly a scene form the First World War, when I was a little boy, spending vacations at a Scottish seaport.
>
> I saw a gray destroyer slipping hurriedly from port in response to urgent orders . . .
> I watched the crew hurry their preparations for sailing,
> watched them cast off the mooring hawsers . . .
> Saw the sleek ship get under way, as she rose to meet the lazy ground swell of a summer evening . . .
> with her Morse lamp winking on the control bridge aft . . .
> Watched her until she was lost in the mists of the North Sea.
>
> She was a mystery vessel.
> She had sailed "under sealed orders."
> Not even her officers knew her destination or the point of rendezvous.
>
> So, in like manner, all the pioneers of faith have gone out—and all the explorers . . .
> Abraham, of old
>> Columbus
>>> the Cabots
>>>> Magellan
>>>>> Balboa
>>>>>> John Smith
>>>>>>> Peary
>>>>>>>> MacMillan
>>>>>>>>> Scott
>>>>>>>>>> Lindbergh
>>>>>>>>>>> Byrd.
>
> They all went out in faith, not knowing what lay ahead.
> Sometimes this going out in obedience to God's command is more dramatic than at other times . . .

sometimes more spectacular . . .
    sometimes more brave . . .
but always it is a venture into the unknown.

I know something of what it means to go out like that for I have experienced it in my own life.
Well do I remember on the 19th of March, 1927, standing on the aft deck of the *Cameronia*,
    watching, with strangely moist eyes, the purple hills of the Mull of
    Kintyre sinking beneath the screw-thrashed waters of the Atlantic,
when every turn of the propeller was driving me farther from the land of my birth—from all I knew and loved.

And then—I walked slowly and wonderingly for'ard until I was leaning over the prow.
I stood looking into the west,
wondering what lay behind that tumbling horizon—
wondering what that unknown tomorrow held for me.

I, too, was going out in faith, "not knowing whither I went."
I was leaving the machine shops, where I had been working in a tube mill.
I was coming to the United States to enter the ministry, because I believed, with all my heart, that those were my orders from my Chief.
But I did not know how
    or when
or where.

I could not foresee the wonderful way in which God would open doors of opportunity.

I could never have imagined the romantic, thrilling way in which God was to arrange my life . . .
order my ways
    guide my steps
        provide for all my needs
            give me wonderful friends, generous helpers
until, at last, I would achieve His plan for me, and be ordained a minister of the Gospel. . . .

But as Peter stood that day on the aft deck of the *Cameronia*, there were still difficulties ahead for him. In his heart was a stanch and stubborn faith—a faith which was to be tested.

In his pocket he carried a letter in triplicate that read:

> *Imperial Tube Works*
> *17th March, 1927*
>
> *To Whom It May Concern:*
> *The bearer, Peter Marshall, of Laird Street, Coatbridge, has been in our services for six years, and leaves now of his own accord, to emigrate.*
>
> *He was primarily a machinist in our Screwing Section and latterly was charge hand in Poles and Derricks Section. We have found him a steady, reliable, and good workman and wish him success.*
> *For Stewarts and Lloyds, Limited*
> *W. S. Dewey*

This letter was a strange key with which to unlock the door into the ministry.

three

$\mathcal{S}$INGING IN THE RAIN

But seek ye first the kingdom of God, and his righteousness;
and all these things shall be added unto you.

Matthew 6:33

On April 5, 1927, Peter arrived at the battery off Ellis Island, with just enough money in his worn brown leather billfold to last two weeks. He kept this particular wallet ever afterward as a souvenir of the months that followed. Indeed, it became a sort of symbol of the next big lesson that God wanted to teach him. That April day he landed, the wallet contained—as it still does—three clippings of soccer games in which Peter had been goalkeeper, a few calling cards, two Tuck's picture post cards of Highland scenery, and various letters of recommendation.

To many people, their pocketbook represents the real proving ground for Christianity. Most people either finally accept or reject God on the question of whether religion is practical enough to descend from the stained-glass window level to the pocketbook level. "Can God feed a starving man? If you need an overcoat, can He provide one? Can He find an unemployed man a job? If not, then where is His power?" So many a man reasons.

If a preacher is to be effective, he has to be convinced that Christ is Lord of the street corner and the marketplace as well as of the cathedral. God had every intention of making Peter Marshall into an effective preacher; so He lost no opportunity to demonstrate His ability to deal with any problem the brown leather wallet could present.

Since all incoming immigrants have to have a specific destination, Peter was tagged, as if he were a bale of cotton, to the home of an aunt, Mrs. J. Twaddle in Elizabeth, New Jersey, where he planned to room.

Though the young immigrant's immediate concern was that of getting a job as quickly as possible, he first joined the New Jersey National Guard, Company D, 114th Infantry. He thought this move would help him to get and to keep a job. Instead, it was not long before it made him lose one.

Before he had left Scotland, Jim Broadbent had given Peter some specific advice about getting a job in the United States.

"Peter, I'm giving you a letter of recommendation to the chief engineer of my outfit in New York, the M. W. Kellogg Company. That man's a good friend of mine, a fine fellow, a Presbyterian elder. He would do right by you.

"But, lad, I advise you not even to try for a desk job. You want to be a preacher. Maybe manual labor, work with your hands, will be the best preparation you'll ever get for the ministry. The trouble with most preachers is that they don't know how the other half lives. Here's the letter. But my advice is—put it away, don't even use it unless you have to."

Peter thought there was good common sense in the advice Jim had given him. Just how good it was he could never have guessed. Years later, even in the halls of the United States Congress, it would be one of his most appealing qualities—that he *had* worked with his hands and had never lost touch with working people.

That was how it came about that Peter began digging his way across the state of New Jersey for the Public Service Essex Gas and Electric Company. Public Service was putting down four-inch conduits across the Hudson Tubes through Kearny and into West New York. It was necessary for Peter to get up at four A.M. in order to be on the job by seven. Because of the distance and the heavy traffic, it would be eight at night by the time he got back to Elizabeth. He never forgot either the feel or the smell of the territory through which he worked.

His next position was doing work on the construction of a golf course. By this time, summer had struck, and he began to suffer, as he always did thereafter, from America's heat. In addition, the work routed out the New Jersey mosquitoes, the pneumatic-drill variety, from their summer homes. They were inclined to resent the intrusion.

His immediate boss on this job was an ignorant loud-talking Italian, who frequently boasted that he could outswear anybody in the Greater New York area. There were times when the men working under him were sure that this was true. The time arrived all too swiftly when the 114th National Guard Regiment, which Peter had joined, was ordered to Sea Girt for two weeks' encampment. The Italian, with properly garnished language, said that was just too blankety-blank bad for Peter! Then, after Peter pleaded his case, he said, "Well, maybe it's nice for an immigrant to be in the National Guard. I'll try to hold your job for you."

But when the 114th returned from training, Peter's job was gone.

He therefore involuntarily graduated from building a golf course to assisting a molder in a Paterson foundry under a glass roof in July and August. "I thought surely," he always said in reminiscing about it, "that I had located the exact site of Dante's Inferno." Working with the big sand molds was not easy. When he returned to his aunt's home on Summer Street at night, his hands would be so swollen and blistered by occasional blasts from the 3000-degree furnaces that he had to have help in unbuttoning his shirt.

This was all very well, but it was not quite clear to Peter how digging in the odoriferous New Jersey clay or firing a blast furnace was getting him nearer his goal. He had long been used to hard work and long hours, to an aching back, to fingers cut with steel turnings, to oil and grease in every pore of his body. It was not that he minded those things, but in five months he had managed no remote connection with any church, and the ministry seemed farther away than ever. Could he have made a mistake in following his cousin Jim's advice? Was *this* the much-vaunted land of opportunity—this land of unbearable heat, of gasoline smells and the stench of dumps burning on the New Jersey flats, of getting up in the middle of the night and working all day, of cities overcrowded with tired and irritable people?

He wondered if somehow he had missed his signals, somehow wandered away from the will of God, been dismally mistaken to leave Scotland at all. God seemed unreal and far away. He was just about to conclude that he should return to Scotland and confess to his family and friends that he had made a mistake, when, at the crucial moment, a special-delivery letter arrived. The letter was from Dave Wood, his boyhood friend, who had come the year before from

Scotland to Birmingham, Alabama. The letter proved to be the clue to the next step in Peter's "sealed orders."

"I've heard through letters from relatives that you are thinking of going back to Scotland," Dave wrote. "Before you do that, why not come on down to Birmingham and talk it all over? You would like the South. Better things might open up for you down here. I feel pretty certain I could get you a job with me on *The Birmingham News*. Think about it seriously and let me know as soon as possible. . . ."

The letter seemed significant. Perhaps it was really revealing the next step in God's plan for him. Eagerly, Peter prayed about it, asking God to make his way plain. Was some open door in the Southland to be his way into the ministry? God had used many different people, sometimes without their knowing they were being used, to help point the way. Was He now using Dave?

A week went by—a week filled with wondering and questioning. Another Sunday came, stifling hot, as if an invisible blanket had been let down over the city of Elizabeth to smother its inhabitants. That Sunday evening Peter went out on the back stoop of his aunt's house, hoping that there he might find a breath of air stirring. A full moon rode high over the grimy roofs and chimney tops.

Suddenly, the answer came—clear as a bell ringing in the still air. It was as definite as if an audible voice had said, "Yes, this is it, what you've been waiting for. You are to go south, and to go immediately."

In order to go immediately, Peter had to borrow forty dollars for the trip. Gratefully, he left Jersey City, Paterson, and Elizabeth behind him. The five months he had spent there had been, in many ways, the most miserable of his life.

As the train traveled south, through the rolling hills of Maryland, on through the pleasant countryside of Virginia, the tobacco country of the Carolinas, and into the cotton fields of the deep South, Peter's spirits began to rise. It *was* a good land. He could see that already. Maybe it was a land of opportunity after all. Suddenly, he had an intimation that God was smiling upon him, and that things would soon be better. He was right. Astonishing things were just around the corner!

His old Coatbridge friends Dave Wood and Bob Hunter met him at the Birmingham station and took him into their room in the house in North Birmingham where they boarded. "The Three Musketeers" were thus together again, after a separation of a year and adventures embracing two continents.

Peter quickly got a job as a "galley slave" correcting galley proofs in the circulation department of *The Birmingham News*. His salary was seventeen dollars a week. This did not leave much room for flexibility in his weekly budget.

$12.00	for room and board
1.00	for streetcar fare
2.50	for lunches downtown
1.00	for laundry
.50	for church, doctors, dentists, clothes, postage, amusements, and incidentals

Total $17.00

Soon he was promoted and began to receive twenty dollars a week, but even that did not leave much toward a possible seminary savings fund.

At that time, the pastor of the old First Presbyterian Church at 4th and 20th Streets, in downtown Birmingham, was Dr. Trevor Mordecai, a Welshman, whose powerful and picturesque preaching was making an impression on the city.

Dave Wood had told Dr. Mordecai, before Peter's arrival in Birmingham, of his friend's ambition to be a minister. When Peter met Dr. Mordecai and told him his story, the minister found himself deeply impressed by the young Scotsman's sincerity and by the faith and sheer determination that had led him so far from home in answer to God's call.

Whenever Peter talked of these years afterward, he was apt to say at this point, in a burr that would suddenly become more pronounced, "And the events of the next few weeks sound just like a fairrrry storrry—just unbelievable. Within several months after my arrival in Alabama, I had joined the old First Presbyterian Church,[1] I had become president of the Young People's Society and had undertaken to be Scoutmaster of their troop. The Men's Bible Class (the Vanguard Class) had asked me to become their regular teacher, and I had accepted. More than once I had assisted Dr. Mordecai in a Sunday service, and

41

had spoken at Prayer Meeting. I had been accepted by the session as a candidate for the ministry. The Presbytery of Birmingham, at its fall meeting, had examined me and had taken me under its care, and it had been decided which seminary I should attend. All that, mind you, in just a few months. Sometimes God seems slow in moving, but when He starts, He really moves!"

About this time, Peter wrote to Barbara Marshall, the widow of his half brother, who had also emigrated to the United States:

> The Birmingham News
> Circulation Dept.
> 10th Oct., 1927

My Dear Barbara,

... It is now two months since I left Elizabeth, and I don't regret it. ... I am very happy. My work in the office is congenial, and I enjoy it. Everybody from the boss right on down is so nice—helpful—and decent. Although I am not earning much, I am hopeful of better things, and I get along fine. Now that cooler weather has come, I feel physically perfect. ... My digs are very nice, and being beside Dave is just lovely. ...

My greatest joy has been getting into church work again. I have joined the First Presbyterian Church, and I see here a big field of work and service. The minister is a Welshman, a very fine man, and the finest preacher I have ever heard.

Already I have addressed the Young People's Guild, and the Christian Endeavour, and I have taken over the post of praise leader. ... Gradually I will become absorbed in Sunday School, Scouts, Choirs, and Church just as I was at home, and I'm going to be very happy indeed.

Gone are the blues. My faith is returning. New hopes are being born, and a "new song is in my mouth." I have passed my time of travail when my soul was troubled, and I don't worry about my small salary, 'cause I am getting a happiness and a joy in service that money couldn't buy. ...

Give everybody my love. God bless you and keep you.

> Affectionately,
> Peter

In the fall, Peter moved into a room at the home of the Matthews— friends who were very active in the old First Church. Everywhere he turned, he found understanding, encouragement, and help.

By that October, Columbia Seminary, the one which he and his new-found friends had decided upon, had already been in session for several weeks. So it was decided that Peter would begin his training the following fall and spend that year in Birmingham.

The reporters on the *News* enjoyed quizzing him about his plans. "How are you going to finance your way to seminary, Peter? You've acquired the unfortunate habit of eating. You can't save anything on twenty dollars a week."

They were quite right. The brown wallet was still always flat. A ticket from Birmingham to Decatur, Georgia, where Columbia Seminary was located, cost six dollars, and at no time that winter did Peter have six extra dollars.

"Well," he would say with a grin, "that's the Lord's business. He sent me to this country to enter the ministry, and it's His affair how He's going to get me there. All I have to do is to obey. He'll tend to the rest."

The boys would look at him in amazement and shake their heads at each other. They were not sure whether that was faith or sheer stubborn Scottish credulity.

On a warm April night in 1928, the Men's Bible Class held a social. Toward the close of the evening, Mr. John Porter signaled for silence and said that he wanted to make an announcement. He called Peter to come forward. At the close of a little speech, full of complimentary things that merely embarrassed their young teacher, he handed him a sealed envelope.

"After you get home, Peter, read it," he said, chuckling. "You'll find it mighty interesting reading, even if I did write it myself."

All the men laughed, and there was an awkward pause.

"Mr. Porter," Peter said, "I can't wait. May I open it now?" As he tore open the envelope, and began to read the letter, all of the men watched his face. On it was written astonishment, then delight, and then tears welled into his eyes. The letter read:

April 16, 1928

Dear Mr. Marshall:

The members of the Men's Bible Class have delegated to us the pleasant task of acquainting you with the action taken by them Sunday morning.

43

Knowing that you have dedicated your life to your Master and have chosen His ministry as your life's work, and learning of the expense involved in the realization of this worthy ambition, we have been asked to say to you that the Men's Class, which you have been teaching so acceptably, intends to stand behind you for the first year of your seminary work to whatever extent you may call upon them up to fifty dollars per month, for the seven months' school term.

We know you will find much to worry and harass you, and that you may sometimes grow discouraged, but let it hearten and cheer you to know that the men you have worked with are anxious to see you realize your dreams, and will follow you—not only with their money, but with their prayers and best wishes.

We understand it will be several months before you leave; so you will have ample time to acquaint the class with your plans and together work out a program.

With assurance of our high regard, we are,

Yours sincerely,

> *The Men's Bible Class of*
> *First Presbyterian Church*
> *J. W. Porter*
> *A. L. Fairley*
> *Sam C. Smith*
> *Committee*

For a time Peter couldn't speak, and when he finally found his voice, his words of gratitude were incoherent. But the look on his face had been enough thanks for those men.

The door into the ministry was opening at last! In later years, Peter always considered himself in the ministry as the special representative of the Vanguard Class.

"To them," he said on many occasions, "I owe a debt I can never repay. That letter they gave me that April night is as precious to me as any of the documents in American history. . . ."

The intervening weeks saw other examples of God's ability to deal with pocketbook problems. The petitions that had wafted heavenward for a better relationship in the family were answered, and it was Mr. Findlay, Peter's stepfather, who provided the money for desperately needed dental work.

On another day, Peter received a telephone call at *The News.*

"Mr. Marshall," the voice at the other end of the wire said, "I'm a clerk in Odum's Clothing Company. You have been presented with a new suit by someone who doesn't wish his name revealed. If you'll come down and pick it out, I'll be glad to help you."

Peter lost no time. During lunch hour that day he got the first specially tailored clothes that he had ever had. He never found out who gave them to him.

Can God provide a suit when you need one? Yes, He can—and Peter never forgot it.

September 1928 saw Peter off to seminary. The problem of the six-dollar train fare that had once loomed so large had been easily solved. Peter was invited to drive to Decatur with the Reverend James A. Bryan, who was to deliver the opening lectures at the seminary. This friend, Birmingham's beloved "Brother Bryan," was to have a profound influence on Peter's life and ministry.

At the close of his first year, the men who stood proudly behind him in Birmingham voted to send him fifty dollars a month for the next year too. By the end of that year, other means of provision began to appear. A letter written to his mother at that time is most revealing:

> *Columbia Theological Seminary*
> *Decatur, Ga.*
> *May 13, 1929*

> *My dear Mother,*
> *I received your last letter. . . .*
> *The weather you have in Scotland is terrible, and in my opinion, is the only disadvantage Scotland has. If you were only living here, for example, how much better would you enjoy the climate.*
> *I am glad that you liked the bulletin of the Seminary. . . . I am enclosing a copy of the programme we submitted last Friday night. It was a great success, and we had a great time. When I sang my songs, I was dressed in the kilt, with a blazer from Oxford.*
> *The members of the quartette, especially Harry Bryan and I, have ever so many friends in Marietta, and I, particularly, have some good folks who are very much interested in me. They all think it marvellous that I should be entering the ministry, having my family in Scotland, and being in a sense, alone in the South.*

They little know that I am never alone, for I feel that my every action is guided by Him who ordains all things for His servants, and supplies all their needs.

It seems as if there is no limit to the good things that are showered on me. I was having an interview with Dr. Huck, who is Superintendent of Home Missions in the Presbytery of Atlanta, and is in fact my "boss." He asked me to take another little church in addition to Barnett for the summer, and to preach in it twice each month in the morning. I agreed, with pleasure, and for that he promises to give me $25 per month, making my monthly salary for the summer months up to $125 or more. Then he asked me if I had ever led congregational singing, and could conduct a choir. It brought back memories of the little choir in the church at home, and when I told him that, he offered me the position of Director of Music at the Young People's Conference at Camp Smyrna this summer. So I accepted with pleasure, and thus will be a member of the Faculty among those young people from all over the state of Georgia.

Isn't it great how things work out! My church work proceeds apace, and the services are growing in numbers and interest. The folks are making me preach, with their encouragements. . . . I couldn't do otherwise than my best, for they are so interested, so loyal, and so devoted.

We are having a fine time, and I am preaching with more confidence, and perhaps better material than I have ever done. I am looking forward to the opportunity of preaching in Buchanan Street when I come home. . . .

Last Sunday was Mother's Day in America. This day is observed all over the country as the day on which tributes are paid to mothers and gifts made, all eloquent of mother's place in human affections. The custom is a beautiful one, but is in danger from the American evil of commercializing even the sacred festivals.

Thoughts naturally are stirred on that day, and although the phlegmatic Scots are not prone to sending cards and all the excesses of Americanism, still the same feeling burns deep. Perhaps we ought to be more demonstrative, but somehow the most tender feelings of the Scottish heart are not easily spoken or written. They must be taken for granted—expressed in living rather than in talking.

But I felt during the day how much I owed MY mother, and although I was 5,000 miles away from you, your influence, your faith in me, and your hopes in me were and are always near and real to me. You have planted well, and the seed which you have planted is bearing fruit.

I esteem your pride in me more precious than all the honours I have received since coming here. When I come home, and you hear me preach, your "well done" will be sweeter music than the platitudes I hear continuously.

I am not in the position to send you gifts. I have no money. It seems that I never shall have enough money even for the ordinary things of luxury. I yet have enough to live and to want for nothing. But I do not have the financial means, for instance, to have an extra suit, nor even to buy myself a new pair of shoes which I need rather badly. But I have what money cannot buy—namely, a great faith in the fact that seeking first the Kingdom of Heaven, all these things will be added unto me.

So I send you not gifts, but appreciations that must be taken for granted, until I can show you by my presence and my life that I mean what I say. You have given me memories that are precious. You have furnished me with the background upon which I am trying to paint the picture you have dreamed of. Anything accomplished by me is not the results of my own efforts, but the result of your prayers and your dreams for my success—not in material things, but in the things that count, that are eternal.

The values I have of life and eternity are mostly the heritages of some mysterious influence you have exerted in my early life. I must be faithful and exemplify the ideals you have always cherished in your heart. May you be satisfied some day when you see the fruits. Your grey hairs and your wrinkled brow are mute but eloquent tokens of your ministrations of patient and loving sacrifice, and I revere them as such.

I must close now, for I have to study. I send my love and tenderest solicitations. May God bless and keep you, Mother Mine. Give Father and Chris my kindest regards and best love. Hope all are well.

Your affectionate son,
Peter

In the seminary quartette, to which Peter referred in this letter, he sang second tenor. Along with Harry Bryan, Sam Cartledge, and Henry L'Heureux, he went on many a combination preaching-singing tour. The boys loved to sing songs like Martin Luther's "Play the Man," or "The Riches of Love," or "I Have My Life to Tell." They thought nothing of filling five engagements, in as many different churches, on one Sunday morning, by the simple process of slipping into a church, singing, slipping out again, and rushing on to the next engagement. Peter was the one of the four most often elected to do the preaching. Already his ability to grip and hold the interest of a congregation was apparent.

Often he went with Harry Bryan to Marietta, Georgia, where Harry was supplying The First Presbyterian Church. One Sunday the two boys were invited to dinner by Mrs. Arthur Davenport. She was then a woman in her sixties, a very lonely widow with no children, not even any near relatives.

She lived in a little white frame house filled with *post-bellum* antiques, all the fading glory of another era. As a little girl, she had witnessed the ravages of Sherman's march through Georgia and the agonies of the Reconstruction period. She always called herself an "unreconstructed rebel."

That Sunday began a rich friendship with Harry and Peter, which was to transform her lonely life. "Miss Mary" became a second mother to Peter Marshall.

During his senior year at Columbia, he began serving the church in Covington, along with the Barnett church. This work enabled him to pay his own way the last year, and to leave seminary entirely free of debt.

On October 21, 1929, the faculty of Columbia Seminary had voted:

Item 4. On motion, Mr. Peter Marshall's educational work in Scotland was accepted as equivalent to our A.B. requirement.

This action, though it seemed routine, actually broke all Columbia Seminary precedent up to that time. Another twenty years was to pass before the seminary repeated this action and gave a Korean student his B.D. without the B.A.

In the spring of 1931, just before his graduation, Peter was offered both the Covington Church and Westminster Presbyterian Church in Atlanta.

Letters which he wrote at that time to friends in Covington reveal clearly what a difficult decision this was for him. It was a foretaste of the fact that, throughout his ministry, he was to be tempted by flattering calls to churches in many parts of the United States.

In the end, Peter felt that "the Chief" wanted him to have the initial experience of a small-town charge. So he accepted the Newton County charge, starting in this little cotton-mill town of three thousand people.

Peter was graduated—*magna cum laude*—and was ordained a Minister of the Gospel on May 15th, 1931, just before his twenty-seventh birthday.

In 1931 the nation's economy was staggering under the blows of the worst depression in her history. Since he began his ministry at such a time, the folks to whom he preached desperately needed a practical Christianity. He preached his most famous depression sermon "Singing in the Rain" all over the state of Georgia. But long after the depression was over, he was still giving other people the message God had given him during those years:

We ministers have undoubtedly failed to connect and apply Christianity to the practical everyday problems of the average man.

In this, we have failed to follow in Christ's footsteps.
For the religion which He taught and revealed in His own life and ministry was an intensely practical and down-to-earth affair.

Christ preached few sermons, so far as we know.
He wrote no books.
He spent at least two-thirds of His active ministry healing people's bodies and supplying their material as well as their spiritual needs.

A laboring man Himself, He loved the so-called common people passionately.
He was, moreover, intensely aware of their practical needs. . . .

Christ made us a definite promise that if we make the seeking of God and His righteousness our primary aim in life . . .
    and if we trust God for our material needs . . .
He will never let us down, but will supply what we need with "good measure, pressed down, and shaken together, and running over. . . ." (Luke 6:38)

That this method works . . .
    that God always keeps His promises when we fulfill the conditions,

49

I can unhesitatingly testify, for this is the way I have lived ever since
I was forced to begin earning my own way.

Out of my own experience I can testify that through faith in God,
through prayer and trust in the promises written in the Old Book . . .
my every need has been supplied.
That has been true from the start . . . from the time I was receiving
thirty-eight shillings in Scotland and seventeen dollars a week in
Alabama.

Of all God's promises in the Bible, I think this is the least believed:
"Seek ye first the kingdom of God and his righteousness; and
all these things [food and clothing, money and material comforts]
will be added unto you." (Matthew 6:33)

In this sophisticated twentieth century, we simply don't believe it!

We are inclined to say, "Well, that was all right for simple peas-
ants living in Palestine in the days when life was not nearly as complex as it is today.
That's all right for Galilee, Lord, but you simply don't understand
Birmingham
or Atlanta
or St. Louis
or Washington!
After all, the disciples never had to work for the government."

Ah, but He *does understand!*

From 1931 on, the little brown wallet was never completely empty
again. In fact, Peter went on from blessing to blessing.
Three joyous years in Covington followed. The church there thrived
under his leadership. In addition, mission work was undertaken at
Gum Creek, Pine Grove, and Hayston. Peter saw certain men's lives
in Newton County utterly transformed by the Nazarene. He never
forgot the thrill of witnessing those first conversions of his ministry.
Soon after going to Covington, he acquired his first car—a Ford.
That Ford symbolized Peter's initial step toward real economic
independence.

As he steadily tithed his small salary, God never failed to fulfill the promise that Peter had claimed. From then on, throughout his ministry, there was a slow but steady rise in income.

His unshakable belief in God's ability to provide real material needs, hammered out during these years of hardship and discipline, was one of the foundation stones of his ministry.

four

THE PERILS OF A YOUNG PREACHER

. . . . to keep himself unspotted from the world.
James 1:27

If ever we saw the elements of greatness in a man, they are in him. Yet, there's an odd boyish shyness about him. . . ." So the Milledgeville, Georgia, paper commented about Peter Marshall soon after he left Covington to go to Atlanta.

He had received his second call to the pulpit of Westminster Presbyterian Church in Atlanta on May 7, 1933. Westminster had gone through a series of reverses that had threatened to close its doors and force a merger with another congregation. The seeming hopelessness of the church's situation was a challenge to Peter. He felt that God wanted him to accept the call. So Peter preached his first sermon as pastor of Westminster on May 28, 1933.

Not many months passed before things began to happen at the church out on Ponce de Leon Avenue. Georgia editorial comment was enthusiastic about the young Scottish minister. He was called that "charming young Scot with the silver tongue." Peter Marshall has "the canny wisdom, searching wit, and rugged character for which his native land is famous. . . ." "I had the honor of interviewing him," said Morgan Blake in *The Atlanta Journal.* "He was gay, and brilliant, and witty, and there was a song in my heart for many days thereafter."

Wrote Dr. Thornwell Jacobs, the president of Oglethorpe University, in his regular column in *The Atlanta Georgian:* "Peter Marshall has everything. . . . He was called to an empty Presbyterian Church on Ponce de Leon Avenue, and shortly thereafter, had it overcrowded. . . . If you would like to see a heartening and amazing sight . . . go . . . and listen to this boy preach . . . but go early. . . ."

Dr. Jacobs was quite right. It *was* necessary to go early, if one wanted to get a seat. The church was often so crowded that the deacons had to stand outside on the sidewalk and listen to the sermon through the open windows. It was soon necessary to build a balcony, but that became crowded too. I can never think of that church without seeing it in my mind's eye as one young deacon described it, "with bulging walls and sagging balconies."

There were many young people in those congregations. They flocked into Westminster from Atlanta's five large educational institutions—Georgia Tech, Emory University, Oglethorpe University, Agnes Scott College, and Columbia Seminary.

It would have been as difficult for the very young to analyze why they were willing to go to so much trouble to hear Peter Marshall preach as it would have been for the older people, who regularly left their own churches to hear him.

A reporter from *The Charlotte Observer* was in Atlanta one Sunday night and went to hear that "young Scotch preacher with his native jargon and his impressive, dramatic personality." "While other Atlanta churches were nearly vacant that particular night," he said, "Mr. Marshall's roomy building was crowded to the hilt and people were standing—and most of them were young people!"

A few cynics tried to account for Peter Marshall's growing popularity on the basis of his Scottish accent. While it was true that the accent gave added beauty to the King's English, that was little more than a garnish to the real spiritual meat he served up. It was also true that his unusual background added a certain degree of glamour for American congregations. As Peter stood in the pulpit, people always seemed to be seeing him against a backdrop comprised of Edinburgh Castle, John Knox, the bagpipes, the Fifty-first Division, with a touch of heather thrown in.

Peter Marshall was a tall, well-built young man with the broad shoulders of a football player, camouflaged by his Geneva gown.

His hair, which had been very blond, was turning darker. It was curly, never slicked down, inclined to be a little unruly.

His face was handsome in a rugged sort of way. There was in it a combination of gentleness and humor along with forcefulness and strength.

He seemed thoroughly at home in a pulpit. While he preached, he frequently used gestures, but they were never strained or artificial. Most of his emphasis was made with his voice—an extraordinarily resonant speaking voice, flexible, dramatic, with a clear, precise diction.

But more than these superficialities was the indisputable fact that, under the impact of this man's praying and preaching, God became real to those who listened. While Peter led them in worship, God was no longer a remote, theological abstraction, but a loving Father, who was interested in each individual, who stooped to man's smallest need. So men and women, who were hungry for the love of God, came back again and again.

The Christian Observer commented:

> A striking example of Peter Marshall's power over an audience . . . was the meeting he held for a week each year in the Central Presbyterian Church, Atlanta, Georgia. It is doubtful if there are more than two or three of the younger ministers of the country who could, year after year, as he did, pack the large auditorium of Central Church each day at a noontime service, with a congregation that seemed almost breathless in their attention. Especially noticeable were the large numbers of young people in attendance. The writer of these lines asked several of these young people what it was that brought them back again and again. Without exception, their replies may be summed up in the words of one young clerk in a dry-goods store, who went without lunch each day to be present: "He seems to know God, and he helps me to know Him better."[1]

Dr. Thornwell Jacobs, the president of Oglethorpe University, asked Peter, about that time, to conduct a two weeks' series of services on the campus for the students. "Something happened at Oglethorpe that spring," Dr. Jacobs reported, "that I have never seen happen at any college. Attendance was voluntary, and those boys and girls left the tennis courts, golf courses, athletic fields, libraries, etc., to hear Peter preach. Beginning with a small audience on the first day or two, it ended with a chapel full of enthusiastic disciples. That was the first of his annual series of services at Oglethorpe."

One might wonder about the effect of such crowds so early in the career of a young and immature minister. Could such popularity not have ruined his future usefulness? It might have, except for the fact that Peter recognized the dangers that go along with popularity, and turned to God for help.

A fellow minister, who had known Peter well at Columbia Seminary, commented, "One of Peter's great qualities, in the midst of all the acclaim and adulation which he received, was that he never lost his deep sense of humility." That evaluation was accurate. Basically, Peter did not "think of himself more highly than he ought to think."

Once, when he was considering a very tempting call—from every human standpoint—away from Atlanta, he wrote to a friend, "I do not yet feel that I am ready for such a position as that would be. I lack so much of scholarship, of experience, of everything. . . ." He had a real sense of inferiority about his formal education, all of which stemmed from the fact that he did not have a college degree. It was a source of great gratification to him that Columbia Seminary had broken all precedent in granting him a B.D. without the basic A.B., but in spite of that, his feeling of educational inferiority always haunted him.

It was true that Peter was stimulated, just as any minister would be, by the crowds that came to hear him. He was constantly encouraged by them and pushed onward and upward to his best work. Yet, he felt the weight of a great responsibility to God for those congregations. He was fearful that his own personality might stand between the people and Christ. He grew so troubled about this that one Sunday he put this paragraph in the church bulletin:

This minister thinks of the assembled people who face him on the Sabbath as a congregation who are to be led to the throne of grace— not as an audience who have gathered to hear him speak, but as a congregation to hear the still small voice of God whispering peace and pardon for weary troubled souls. Let the congregation remember that they should come to church to worship God—not to hear a weak, unskilled mortal man orate. This is a house of Prayer in which we are privileged to keep our tryst with the Chief.

Sometimes when he was out of town preaching and his pulpit was filled by a guest preacher, someone would think to flatter him by speaking of the number of people who had come to Westminster and, upon finding that Peter would not be preaching, had gotten up and gone home. This hurt him almost to the point of anger. A stern look would cross his face, and he would explode, "God was still there! Did those people come to church to worship, or to hear me?"

One day a church member said to Peter, "You know, I'm going to have to work on my next-door neighbor. She's not a Peter Marshall fan."

Peter immediately made it painfully clear to the well-meaning lady that his business was to recruit "fans" for the Lord—not Peter Marshall.

Many years after Peter's Atlanta pastorate, he stood at his study window one Sunday morning looking at a line of people, almost a block long, waiting to get into the sanctuary. There was a cold rain falling; the long double line was a sea of umbrellas. A young girl came to the study on some errand. "He stood there perfectly amazed at the sight of all those people," she said later.

"To think that so many people would stand out there so patiently in weather like this!" he marveled. "When I see *that*, that's when I do my praying."

One well-known religious publishing house wanted him to compile a book of his children's sermonettes for them. Another publisher asked several times to be allowed to publish some of his sermons. Following the publication of a sermon excerpt in the *Reader's Digest*, the editors of the *Digest* wrote asking him to send them some articles. His answer to such requests was always the same.

"My sermons are not good enough for publishing," he would object. "Ask me again twenty years from now. *Perhaps*, by then, I'll have written something worth putting in print."

Peter hated publicity; he avoided it whenever possible. At one time, he incurred the severe displeasure of *The Atlanta Constitution* by refusing four consecutive requests to permit that paper to print his picture and excerpts from sermons. Experience had taught him that usually newspapers picked out only sensational bits, ignoring the real point of the sermon. "If you will let me edit the sermon and write the captions, you can have it, otherwise no," became his policy.

Dr. Frank Mead was asked by *The Christian Herald* to interview Mr. Marshall for a feature article. When Peter found out what was wanted, he refused the interview. "Then," said Dr. Mead, putting on real pressure, "I shall be forced to get all my information from other people. The article has to be written." Peter groaned, finally gave in, and ended up by greatly enjoying his talk with the writer.

One of the healthy checks that God used to deal with the subtle temptations that follow in the wake of success was the ballast of ordinary friendly criticism and teasing. There was no chance of Peter's feet getting off the ground so long as he had such friends around him.

The wealth of poetic imagery in his sermons, which later earned him the title of "Twittering-birds Marshall" among some minister friends, sometimes ran away with itself. But whenever he overdid it, he always heard about it afterward.

Peter's favorite thought was that "spiritual reality is a matter of perception, not of proof." He liked this idea so much that he could, and did, weave it into a sermon on almost any subject. Whenever he introduced this thought, those of us who heard him regularly knew that two things would immediately follow—his famous description of a sunset and part of Milton's "L'Allegro."

> There are some things that never can be proved.
> Can you prove—by logic—that something is lovely?
> Could you prove that a sunset is beautiful?

When the sun, like a ball of fire, sinks lower and lower, until it meets in a blistering kiss the western horizon . . . after having set the heavens on fire, until they glow

with scarlet

crimson

cerise

vermilion

pink

rose

blush

and coral

leaving in his wake clouds curling, like nebulous dust, from under the chariot wheels of the sun?

Either we see beauty—or we do not.

Could you prove to someone, who did not appreciate it, that the lilting beauty of Milton's "L'Allegro" is sheer genius:

> Haste thee nymph, and bring with thee
> Jest and youthful Jollity,
> Quips and Cranks, and wanton Wiles,
> Nods, and Becks, and Wreathèd Smiles,
> Such as hang on Hebe's cheek,
> And love to live in dimple sleek;
> Sport that wrincled Care derides,
> And Laughter holding both her sides.
> Come, and trip it as ye go
> On the light fantastick toe,
>
> And if I give thee honour due,
> Mirth, admit me of thy crue
> To live with her, and live with thee,
> In unreprovèd pleasures free;
> To hear the Lark begin his flight,
> And singing, startle the dull night,
> From his watch-towre in the skies.[2]

In all fairness, it should be stated that although at such times the birds really twittered, Peter held an audience spellbound with this sort of thing. So accurately could he capture the spirit in which "L'Allegro" was written, that it must have pleased Milton himself.

At Christmastime, Peter liked to speak about "the pink and dimpled hands" of the infant Jesus . . . "a baby deigned to be . . . And bathed in baby tears, His Deity," and as he did so, would hold up his own big, square, mechanic's hands. His friends teased him about that so mercilessly that he became self-conscious about ever mentioning that the baby Jesus *had* hands.

Other pet expressions were constantly being thrown back in his teeth. The dawn was always "blushing pink behind the blue hills of Moab." The mist on the Scottish hills was always "like a tulle scarf thrown over a lady's shoulders."

These were apprenticeship years in which Peter was trying his wings. He hated hackneyed theological expressions, and sometimes in his efforts to avoid staleness, he hit upon most peculiar metaphors. The discipline and experience that resulted in such masterful use of the metaphor in later years was not always present in the beginning. In a prayer he spoke of "the brown-paper parcel of speech." "The balloon tires of our egoism have at last been punctured," he might say, "and we are down on the rims of a new humility." "The batteries of our souls" were forever being "recharged."

In a very early sermon that delighted Southern audiences, first preached in Marietta, Georgia, there was a detailed and idealized description of a Colonial mansion. "Sailing daintily across the lawn, comes a lacy, fairy figure in a crinoline gown. Her white satin shoes peep in and out from under her gown *like a pair of white mice furtively darting in and out as she walks. . . .*"

Once Peter attended a luncheon following a ministers' meeting, which was served in the basement of a church. The room had casement windows. Peter was asked to say grace. One of the men present declares that his blessing went something like this:

> Oh, Lord, open the casement windows of our souls, so that the fresh winds of Galilee may blow in and recharge the batteries of our souls. AMEN.

As soon as they sat down, the friend said teasingly, "Peter, don't you think that was rather a mixed use of metaphors?"

Peter looked puzzled. "Why? What did I say?" And when it had been repeated to him, "Now look, Oscar. It couldn't have been *that* bad. I'm dumb. But I'm not *that* dumb."

Alliteration was a constant temptation to Peter. There are sermons preached early in his career in which he carried it to astonishing extremes.

> So much of our modern preaching consists of platitudes . . .
>   polite and perfumed philosophies . . .
>   pacifistic palaver . . .
>   puerile palpitations . . .
>   paltry paraphrases . . .
> in which a great deal is spoken and nothing said.

59

An editorial about Peter in *The Charlotte Observer* (December 29, 1939) accurately analyzed his preaching during this period of his life:

> The chief of my impressions about Peter Marshall was that he was an artist in phrase-making.
>
> The late JOHN TEMPLE GRAVES, who could make the language sing more musically than any man in our memory, was clumsy and a sorry weaver of words in comparison.
>
> This young fellow could transport you whether you especially care about fancifully going places or not.
>
> He could sit you in the lofty atmospheres of mountain peaks, make a bed for you in the silken enfoldments of the clouds, chaperon you among the ethereal stars, and make you feel entirely at home afloat in the stratosphere of the unrealities.
>
> He could make the lexicon yield words one never knew existed, mesmerize you with magnificent participles that had no end of dangling, and by the mere magic of his rhetoric and eloquent tongue, lift you totally out of the spheres of time and space.
>
> Fact is that his language was so enchanting that, so far as our dull self was concerned, his thought and theme were submerged, and the truth he would have his listeners learn was drowned in the magnificent and mellifluous melody of his words.

Perhaps it was necessary for him to go through this stage in order to achieve the real mastery of words, which characterized his later work.

Certain things that happened at Westminster Peter never managed to live down. One of these was a Boudeleon play called *The Key Note* in which he played the leading role of an Arab sheik. "Would you like to see Mr. Marshall as an Arab prince?" the church bulletin asked coyly. "Then come to the Boudeleon Club play on Wednesday, Thursday, and Friday nights, May 22, 23, and 24, in the lecture room."

Westminsterites not only wanted to see their minister as an Arab prince, they would not have missed it for the world. The lecture room was crowded. When the minister emerged from the wings wearing a flowing robe and an Oriental turban, so far as the audience was concerned, at that moment the play became a comedy. Actually, it was supposed to be quite serious.

"Are you a genie?" asked one of the characters.

"No, Madame. I am an Arab," cried Scotland with every syllable. "I am Ali, Prince of the House of Hashim, descendant of Ali, the son of Fatima, the daughter of Kadijah, the first and beloved wife of the Prophet Mohammed."

"All of that?" laughed Mignon, hardly able to contain herself.[3] The effect of an Arab sheik with a Scottish accent was so incongruous as to have the audience bent double with laughter.

It was always very difficult for the other actors and actresses to be on the stage with the preacher. He had a hopelessly disconcerting way of ad-libbing at odd moments, as if he thought he would improve the lines a little as he went, and this confused and befuddled the other players.

In notes made for a sermon to ministers which Peter called "The Perils of a Preacher," to the dangers of popularity, praise, and flattery, he had added that of "designing women."

> Here is very real danger [he wrote], which certainly ought to be stressed in seminary more than it is. The minister seems to have an attraction for certain types of women. They will not only weary you with their problems—real and imaginary—but will often sorely try your patience and your Christian grace.
>
> You are caught in a dilemma. If you are short and abrupt with them, they can accuse you of being unsympathetic. If you are courteous, they will be encouraged and make life miserable for you in many feminine ways. Moreover, young ministers—especially if they are bachelors—have a hard time in their social contacts. Many a ministry has been ruined because of the jealousies engendered among the women members of the congregation. . . .

As a bachelor, Peter had a very hard time indeed with his social contacts. There was a period when the mothers of Atlanta debutantes, no less than the daughters, considered him very eligible husband material and were on his trail. Usually the mother's opening gun of a matchmaking campaign was a family dinner party "to meet Mary." Often, this was followed up by a series of telephone calls, suggesting that the mother had tickets to a play and thought he might like "to take Mary," or asking why he had not seen the girl lately, even sometimes asking bluntly, "What's wrong with Mary?" All of this was painfully embarrassing to Peter.

Peter was a man's man. Yet he was the target for much feminine admiration. It did not seem to matter whether the ladies were nine years or ninety. The effect was the same. In restaurants, if there happened to be a beauty of three or four years sitting at an adjoining table, it was only a matter of one course and a few flashing smiles until the maiden's heart was captured.

Over and over, Peter kept threatening to adopt a little girl. It was not quite clear to his friends what he thought he would do with her between preaching engagements.

One of the fan letters that he kept was written in pencil in a little girl's round handwriting:

> Dear Mr. Peter Marshall,
>   During the past week while you have been preaching at my church, I have enjoyed you very much. I hope that you will come back very soon.
>   My girl friend liked you very much too.
>   Would you please write me a letter telling me about your church?
>
> Your friend,
> Marjorie McMahan

Often anonymous poetry was sent to Peter. There was a sonnet which began, with unusual veracity:

"Before your presence I am bereft of art. . . ." Another poetess complained:

> Reflections tip-toe and wonder
> At the fallacy of Circumstance,
> Its power to purge or plunder.
> Eagerly I offer for its appease
> The hope of dormant dreams.
> In response, only a wary half-smile . . .
> With shifting foot, still heavier it leans.
> Time vainly attempts to console.
> But there is no reconciling the fate
> That permitted a lifetime of searching
> To end in finding you too late! . . .

A third was entitled "Ode to Peter":

> What will you do with all of the hearts
> That you have pierced or broken?
> Will you wear them around your neck
> on a string
> As an ornamental token? . . .
>
> Blame you? No, not much, Peter dear.
> I mostly blame the fools
> The women make of themselves about you.
> Overriding the rules.
>
> But please don't let them smother you,
> (It is you I am thinking of)
> And kill the sense of the need of
> your heart
> Before you find true love.

Every congregation contains women whose hearts cry out for something life has denied them. Inevitably, they see the minister through a romantic haze. They long to do personal things for him. His robes must be mended, flowers must be put in his buttonhole and on his desk, fresh water must be kept at his elbow. Cards, notes, and presents—sometimes very elaborate presents—appear mysteriously in the church office. New ties are laid out on his desk. The lady has a problem a week—always something vaguely theological. She is forever finding an excuse for telephoning the church office. These things are scarcely serious, but often it does not stop there.

When women's motives were square and honest, Peter always dealt with them on that level, and enjoyed their friendship. "But," he asked, "why is Satan always depicted as being of the masculine gender? The Devil is no fool. We associate womanhood with all that is pure, lovely, sweet, and wholesome. But Satan is not above using women. . . ." He had arrived at this conclusion after painful experience.

There was the beautiful woman, the wife of a well-known professional man, who was frankly smitten with the preacher and had tried every ruse and trick, without making any headway. One day she did manage to get an interview with him in his study. But it

63

was no use. Her pride was piqued as he thwarted her at every turn. Finally she left, angrily railing at him, "I hate you! I hate you!"

"Well, thank God," he retorted mildly, as he held the door for her exit.

It is necessary for the minister, and for his wife—if he has one— to keep a sense of humor about this sort of thing, or real trouble can result. One must remember that eccentricity may pop up anywhere, but probably no more often in churches than in lodges, PTAs, or women's clubs. Perhaps it only *seems* more conspicuous in religious groups.

Yet, in every church, the persons whom the preacher would most humanly like to avoid are the ones who most need help. If Christ cannot help them, who can? And what are church members for, except to lead them to Him for sanity, and balance, and healing? They are right in coming to the church for help, but how tragically often we fail them.

The minister is presented with several dilemmas. He must find a way of helping these people, while at the same time protecting himself and his ministry from the harm which they can do. Most men are not naturally suspicious, nor do they want to be. When a woman asks a minister for a conference, even when he has good reason to suspect that she only wants an excuse for another contact with him, there is always the outside chance that she really *is* sincere, and really *does* need help.

"Perhaps," he reasons, "it is sheer egotism to suspect her motives, and besides, I can't run the risk of failing anyone in need." In instances where the preacher feels that the woman should be dealt with sternly, he is up against the fact that the man of God is not supposed ever to lose his temper, or even to be harsh. He knows, too, that there is no wrath like that of a frustrated woman. She has insidious ways of retaliating.

There was a certain married woman who called the church so often that Ruby, Peter's secretary, came to know her voice. Ruby felt that the lady's motives were not what they should be, and that it was her job to protect her young minister.

On some days the woman would call time after time, always hoping to find Ruby out, so that Mr. Marshall would answer the phone himself.

One morning it happened just as the lady hoped. A feminine voice said pleadingly to Peter, "I'm sick in bed with a broken collarbone—all alone here in the house. It's my maid's day off, and my husband is in Florida on a law case. There's no fire, and I'm freezing. I hate to ask you, but would it be possible for you to come over and build a fire in the fireplace for me?" Peter made a mental note that the lady knew that Lee, the church's Negro janitor, was around, but she had not asked for Lee. He agreed to go, but decided, under the circumstances, to take Ruby with him. They built the fire for the lady, and left.

Because Peter often seemed to his secretaries and his friends to be so naïve about "designing women," they were forever marveling that he emerged unscathed and unspoiled from this period of his life. "God must have had a special battalion of guardian angels watching over Peter," one Westminster friend commented. "I never saw one man surrounded by so *much* temptation."

"But it's no sin to be tempted," Peter loved to say. "It isn't the fact of having temptations that should cause us shame, but what we do with them. Temptation is an opportunity to conquer. When we eventually reach the goal to which we are all striving, God will look us over, not for diplomas, but for scars. . . ."

five

THE HALLS OF HIGHEST HUMAN HAPPINESS

> And the Lord God said, It is not good that the man should
> be alone. . . .
>
> Genesis 2:18

I was twenty, and allergic to figures. Unfortunately, the required college algebra had figures, lots of them. Dr. Henry Robinson, a brilliant scholar in his own field, and the head of Agnes Scott's mathematics department, undertook personally to escort me through the wilderness. But mathematics was not Dr. Robinson's only talent. He had side lines, such as a romantic interest in matchmaking and a vital concern for the then much-discussed cause of prohibition. I came in for both, because it was he who arranged my first meeting with Peter Marshall. Along with an Emory University freshman, Dr. Robinson had scheduled the Reverend Peter Marshall and me to speak at a prohibition rally at a little town near Atlanta.

For two full years I had longed to know this young Scotsman whom I had frequently heard preach. Who could have heard such sermons as "Agnostics and Azaleas" or "Rosary of Remembrance" and failed to glimpse the poetry in this man's soul or the deep earnestness of his desire to take men and women by the hand and lead them to God? Both attributes appealed to me strongly; for at this stage (I might as well admit) I was in love with love, fancied myself a poet, and, more important, was groping to find my way out of an inherited Christianity into a spiritual experience of my own.

One of my youthful self-indulgences was a journal in which I poured out my hopes and dreams and let my poetic urge have full reign. In it I had written earlier: "I am neither right with myself nor with God. . . . I can never enjoy life until I learn *why* I am here and *where* I am going. . . ." And then a few pages on: "I have never met anyone whom I so want to know as Mr. Marshall."

My letters to my parents in the little town of Keyser, West Virginia, where my father was pastor of the Presbyterian Church, had also been including comments about Peter Marshall for some time. In January 1934, I had written to them:

> Carol (one of my New England friends) and I went to Westminster again yesterday to hear Peter Marshall.
>
> Westminster is a rather small church—but very quiet and worshipful. Mr. Marshall conducts beautiful services, and I like him more each time I go. He's only twenty-eight[1] and has had just four years of experience, but believe me, he's something already.
>
> I have never heard such prayers in my life. It's as if, when he opens his mouth, there is a connected line between you and God. I know this sounds silly, but I've got to meet that man. . . .

There was, however, no apparent way to meet him. To me, a college girl, Peter Marshall, the clergyman, seemed almost as inaccessible as a man from Mars. Since I was very young and quite transparent, it must have been obvious to my parents that all of my idealism, as well as my natural girlish romanticism, was rapidly centering upon this young Scottish minister.

> You see [I explained in another letter], as far as Mr. Marshall is concerned, he doesn't even know I exist. . . . I've never met such a young man with so much real power. You feel it the minute you step inside his church. He's oh, so Scotch, and very dignified, but he has a lovely sense of humor. [Then I added self-consciously,] All this is awfully silly, isn't it? Oh, shucks, I wish I'd stop thinking about the man!

The night of the prohibition rally was, therefore, very important to me. At long last I was going to meet Peter Marshall. My romantic soul said that the event must have the proper setting. I had suggested to Dr. Robinson that he pick me up in the Alumnae garden. In my imagination I could see Mr. Marshall marching down between the rose arbors to get me, while I waited for him, holding in one graceful hand a copy of *Sonnets from the Portuguese* and dreamily trailing the other through the lily pond.

Dr. Robinson picked me up in the garden all right, but merely tooted his horn; so I climbed into the back seat by the boy from Emory. Mr. Marshall was sitting beside Dr. Robinson in front. I expected him to be thinking about his speech. Instead, he immediately turned around to ask, "What's this I hear about my being engaged? Dr. Robinson says that you said—"

I flushed and stammered, "I—I did hear some rumors to that effect."

"Don't believe everything you hear, my dear girl. I certainly am not even about to be married."

He pronounced the word "mar-r-ied" with a very broad "a" and a rolling of the "r's."

I remembered then another story I had heard about him. One night in Prayer Meeting, he had been talking about gossip and had remarked that everyone in the church seemed to know better than he *when* he was going to be "mar-r-ied" and *whom* he was going to "mar-r-y."

"I'd like this clearly understood," he went on, grinning like a small boy, "I'm not going to get mar-r-ied till I'm good and ready. I'm good enough now, but I'm not ready." This remark soon went the rounds.

The village to which we were going was some twenty miles away and seemed to have a general store, six houses, and a schoolhouse set in a grove of trees. A large group of farmers and their wives from the surrounding countryside came, bringing with them numerous assorted wriggling children and some babes in arms. They apparently had some curiosity to know why we thought the county should not go wet. Free schoolbooks had been cannily promised by the local politicians out of the tax from beer.

The night was blustery, with a wind from the south and frequent flashes of lightning. Soon the schoolroom was filled with people packed in around the old potbellied stove.

The choir was solicited from the audience by a gray-haired man who assured all bashful recruits that the choir was not going to sing an anthem. For this mercy we were grateful. He managed to get together an assortment of folks who looked as if they had stepped out of a Dickens novel. After they had self-consciously filed into the rows of cane chairs facing the audience, the meeting began, as it was to end, with the singing of revival hymns strange to us. The gray-haired man kept waving his arms and urging the choir on. The bass, a large red-faced man in the back row, tried harder, and, as a result, looked as if he might have a stroke any minute. The tremolo of the tall, thin woman in the front row became almost turbulent under his heckling.

Peter, standing beside me, managed to read the music, growing more and more lusty, finally entering into the spirit of the evening and enjoying himself immensely. Whenever I stumbled over the unfamiliar music, he would give me a nudge of encouragement to "car-r-y on."

One by one, we were then elaborately introduced, listened to patiently, and given more applause than we deserved. Frankly, I can't remember much about what we said. The county promptly went wet.

On the way home Peter said, "May I see you sometime this week? I've wanted to know you for a long time." And when I clearly showed my great astonishment, he added, "Not even ministers are blind, you know."

Six dates, four chaperones, and a dozen months later we were engaged.

How it came about I still regard as one of God's nicest miracles and the first big evidence of God's hand on my life.

All public speakers develop pet expressions and clichés. Peter had his, and was often teased about them. Usually, during these years, they were alliterative. For example, whenever the announcement of a recent marriage was made in Westminster Church's bulletin, almost invariably it would end with words bearing the Marshall touch: "May He who has admitted these young people into the halls of highest human happiness richly bless them in their new life."

Peter was an increasingly popular speaker in the city of Atlanta and throughout the South. Moreover, he was now in the full swing of all that is involved in a thriving city parish. Indeed, he was so busy baptizing infants, writing sermons, calling, bowling on the church team, teaching the Boudeleon class, holding meetings, and admitting people "into the halls of highest human happiness" that there was little time left for personal dates. Mostly, we saw each other only as he drove me back to the college after some church service.

Even that took the help of Miss Ruby Coleman, his secretary. As I made my way slowly toward the church door through the crush of the crowds that came to hear him, Miss Coleman would appear, seemingly rising out of the floor like a one-woman orchestra.

"Mr. Marshall requested that I ask you please to wait until he is through speaking to people. He would like very much to drive you back to Decatur."

I waited.

On Mother's Day I had heard Peter preach "Keepers of the Springs," and had been profoundly stirred. Other sermons like "Dancing in Tears" and "Youth and the Stranger" made it clear that he was holding up fluttering white banners of premarital chastity for both men and women, and that as far as women were concerned, he was an idealist and a romanticist.

His own words give best his philosophy of marriage:

Marriage is not a federation of two sovereign states. It is a union—
domestic
  social
    spiritual
      physical.

It is a fusion of two hearts—
  the union of two lives—
    the coming together of two tributaries,
which, after being joined in marriage, will flow in the same channel
in the same direction . . .
carrying the same burdens of responsibility and obligation.

Modern girls argue that they have to earn an income in order to establish a home, which would be impossible on their husband's income.

That is sometimes the case, but it must always be viewed as a regrettable necessity, never as the normal or natural thing for a wife to have to do.

The average woman, if she gives her full time to her home
    her husband
        her children. . . .

If she tries to understand her husband's work . . .
    to curb his egotism while, at the same time, building up his self-esteem
    to kill his masculine conceit while encouraging all his hopes
    to establish around the family a circle of true friends. . . .

If she provides in the home a proper atmosphere of culture
    of love of music
        of beautiful furniture
            and of a garden. . . .

If she can do all this, she will be engaged in a life work that will demand every ounce of her strength
    every bit of her patience
        every talent God has given her
            the utmost sacrifice of her love.

It will demand everything she has and more.
And she will find that for which she was created.
She will know that she is carrying out the plan of God.
She will be a partner with the Sovereign Ruler of the universe.

And so, today's daughters need to think twice before they seek to make a place for themselves
    by themselves
in our world today. . . .

"He still places women on such a pedestal," I confided in my journal, "much as my father's generation did, and he seems quite old-fashioned in some ways—especially toward marriage and the home. . . . Yet, yet, I wonder if I shall ever meet anyone whom I

71

admire so much—Peter, with an inheritance of the best of the European tradition, and an acquisition of the best of the American. Peter, who has such an acute appreciation for beauty, such a delightful sense of humor. . . . I don't think he's really a scholar, but except for that, why must the embodiment of all my ideals be twelve years older than I, and still as remote as the South Pole?"

Like the rest of young America, I would never have taken the philosophy of marriage Peter advocated from any of the older generation, but we took it from him, liked it, and came back for more.

Was it possible, I wondered, under the stimulus of his thinking, that women in seeking careers of their own, were seeking emancipation from their own God-given natures, and so were merely reaping inner conflict? Could this be one of the basic reasons for the failures of so many marriages today? Could God have created us so that, ideally, we achieve greatest happiness and greatest character development as our husband's career becomes our own, and as we give ourselves unstintingly to it and to our homes? I was not sure, but it was worth pondering deeply.

"It suddenly occurred to me today," I wrote, "that with all my wondering about what I am supposed to do with my life when I graduate this year, I have scarcely consulted God about *His* plans for me. . . ." I didn't know it then, but His plans were incredibly wonderful.

Meanwhile it had become something of a distinction to have one's wedding ceremony performed by Peter Marshall. If possible, he wanted three conferences before the ceremony with each couple he married—one with the prospective bride, one with the groom, and a final joint conference. Books on marriage were also loaned to them, and the suggestion was made that they see their physicians and exchange health certificates. Health certificates were not required by the state of Georgia at that time.

"People are so funny," Peter would say to the young couple. "They demand certificates for their horses, their dogs, and their cattle, but their sons and daughters are married off with little or no attention to the hereditary strains of their partners. . . ." If folks resented thus being put in a category a little lower than the animals, they dared not show it. The young Scotsman was so obviously in earnest. Then too, he had a point.

72

The three premarital conferences were used to make sure that the couple had a spiritual foundation for marriage. "The perfect marriage must be a perfect blend of the spiritual, the physical, the social, and the intellectual," he would say. "We are souls living in bodies. Therefore, when we *really* fall in love, it isn't just a physical attraction. If it's just that, it won't last. Ideally, it's also a spiritual attraction. God has opened our eyes and let us see into someone's soul. We have fallen in love with the inner person, the person who's going to live forever. That's why God is the greatest asset to romance. He thought it up in the first place. Include Him in every part of your marriage, and He will lift it above the level of the mundane to something rare and beautiful and lasting."

He liked to say to young people: "There are mysteries all around us. . . . Take, for example, this strange phenomenon of falling in love. Have you ever asked the question, 'How will I know when I fall in love?' I have. I've asked it many times. I've asked it of blondes and brunettes, of redheads and bald heads, and people here and there. The strange thing is that I have always received the same answer, namely, 'Don't worry, brother, *you'll know.*' Exactly, that's the point. You can't have any understanding ahead of personal experience. And as that is true of falling in love, so it is true of finding God. . . ."

Peter first *knew* on a Sunday night in May 1936. I had been asked to review a book on prayer for Westminster's Fellowship Hour. After the talk, when Peter spoke to me, there was profound respect in his blue-gray eyes, and there was something else too—a certain glint I had not seen there before and didn't quite know how to interpret. He lost no time in making a dinner date with me for the following Saturday night. Then we went in to the evening service, where I made the mistake of sitting within three pews of the front.

Love promptly went to my stomach. The stone pillars and the Good Shepherd window behind the pulpit began to swim alarmingly. I was too sick to be embarrassed when Peter mentioned my name from the pulpit in connection with the talk I had just given. By the time he began his sermon, I knew it would be disastrous to stay.

As I rose to begin the longest walk in history, the voice from the pulpit trailed off, and there was dead silence, broken only by the staccato clicking of my heels on the stone floor. I could feel Peter's eyes boring into my back every step of the way up the long aisle. Not until I was well out into the foyer and into the sympathetic hands of the deacons, did the voice resume.

The college infirmary received me that night and attempted to diagnose this strange stomach ailment. The head nurse, properly starched, and equipped with a strong nose for sniffing out lovesick maidens, had her suspicions.

The next day, Peter and Miss Coleman, his secretary, were eating lunch at Martha's Tea Room, next door to the church. As a rule, they used that time to talk about church business or sermons or plans for Ruby's approaching marriage to Willard Daughtry. On this particular day, however, Peter was unusually quiet. Ruby noticed that he seemed tense and introspective.

Suddenly, he said, "You know, every time I meet a nice girl, she leaves town."

Ruby knew what he meant. She had been watching the slow unfolding of our friendship. She knew that in less than a month I would be graduating and leaving Atlanta.

"Well, look," she asked in her quiet way, "can't you do something about it?"

For a long moment Peter did not reply. He appeared to be in deep thought. Carefully, he buttered a roll. Then "Maybe I can."

He did do something about it—within the next hour.

In the early afternoon the infirmary telephone at Agnes Scott rang, and the solicitous voice on the other end had a familiar Scottish accent.

"I'm talking from Miss Hopkins' office," the voice said. "I have secured her permission to come over and see you. May I?"

I gasped. No mere man—unless armed with a medical diploma—had ever, in all the college's history, been allowed inside the infirmary. Male visitors were simply taboo. After all, the young ladies were not properly clothed! How Peter had prevailed on Miss Hopkins I couldn't even imagine.

"I—I really don't think you'd better," I said hastily. "I'm well enough to dress and come over. I'll meet you in the colonnade in ten minutes."

It was an awful mistake. Ever afterward Peter accused me of having thwarted his only chance for fame with future generations of Agnes Scotters. If I hadn't interfered, he might even have rated some day a bronze plaque on the infirmary wall in commemoration of the occasion.

The glint that had been in his eyes the night before was still there. Soon it became perfectly apparent what it was. It represented a Scotsman's clear-cut decision and a Scotsman's rock-ribbed determination. He knew what he wanted now, and he went after it with the same vigor and dispatch with which the "Ladies from Hell" had stormed Saint Quentin. All he lacked was the bagpipe accompaniment.

Yet he framed his proposal in gentle words, like the delicate embroidery surrounding the strong, simple words of an old sampler. I did not feel that I could give him an immediate answer. We agreed to pray about it separately. Years before, Peter's life had been solemnly dedicated to his Chief. Both of us felt that the important thing now was to find out what *God* wanted for us. Were our paths to separate at this point, or was it possible that we together would be a greater asset to the Kingdom of God than we could ever be separately? My heart dictated the answer, but I was fearful that my heart might obscure God's mind on the matter.

As unskilled and immature as I was in prayer, God chose this time to teach me a great lesson. I learned that just because God loves us so much, often He guides us by planting His own lovely dream in the barren soil of a human heart. When the dream has matured, and the time for its fulfillment is ripe, to our astonishment and delight, we find that God's will has become our will, and our will, God's. Only God could have thought of a plan like that!

As I took my last college exams and wandered about the campus in something of a daze, it seemed to me that Someone's benediction was resting on my head. What seemed too good to be true was true. I was having my first object lesson in the fact that nothing is impossible within the providence of God, and that the more beautiful the dream, the more chance it has of fulfillment. There remained only the pleasant talk of telling Peter.

I chose a moment when we were driving from Decatur to Atlanta.

"There's something I must tell you . . . " I began.

In the semidarkness, I could see a strained look cross Peter's face.

"Good . . . or bad?" he asked tensely. Then, a moment later, simply, "Thank the Lord!"

For several moments he drove along without saying anything more. When finally he stopped the car beside the road, it was to bow his head and to pray the most beautiful prayer of his life. God was in every part of that life, he was God's, and with God he wanted to share this supreme moment. Only then did he take me in his arms.

Graduation was only two days off. By then, "with some embarr-r-assment," Peter had met my family, had taken them to see Atlanta's famous Stone Mountain, with rare diplomacy had complimented my little sister, Em, on her new patent-leather shoes, and had agreed to exchange duplicate stamps with my brother Bob. Being a very practical son of the heather, he even discussed his finances with my father and described his insurance program in detail, "Because," he said, "you have a right to know that your daughter will be taken care of."

Justice Florence Allen, a woman of simplicity and charm, made the principal address for commencement. Peter was there, sitting with my family.

"I thought you seemed pale," he wrote afterward, "as you knelt before Miss Hopkins to receive your hood. I have never been so moved or impressed with any commencement. Of course, not before had my hopes and my whole life been wrapped up in a member of the class, not before had my heart been invested. I wonder if it was an omen that the girls sang 'Annie Laurie'? . . . I hardly needed that to start the tears. . . ."

Late that night we came back to an almost-deserted campus. I was to leave the next day.

The ancient oaks cast heavy shadows on the driveway, and the moon shone on heavy white magnolia blossoms. Main Hall had seen thousands of girls come and go. The venerable red-brick ivy-covered walls had stood sentinel over many a tender farewell.

"If anybody had told me three months ago," said Peter, "that I would be standing in front of Main Hall telling the girl I love good-by and not caring whether all Decatur was at my back and all Atlanta at my front, I would have thought they were crazy."

The night watchman, standing somewhere in the shadows, discreetly looked the other way.

"Our life together will be a poem, a song, a monument to Love, and a memorial to the Holy Spirit who brought us together. . . . I hope there will never be any real good-bys. . . . God gave you to me, and I'll leave you in His hands. May He keep you always."

As Peter drove away, the night watchman stepped out of the shadows to see me safely into the dormitory. He walked along, his flashlight bobbing, his huge bench of keys jangling, solemnly agreeing that leave-takings *were* sometimes hard.

I thought then that I was going to spend the next year teaching school in the mountains of West Virginia. I didn't know it, but already Peter had quite a different idea.

The halls of highest human happiness were closer than I knew.

six

THE HOME OF YOUR DREAMS

Behold, thou art fair, my love; behold, thou art fair. . . .
The Song of Solomon 4:1

gnes Scott's commencement was on a Tuesday. By Wednesday I was on my way north to spend a few days with my Tennessee grandmother. That night Peter was busy speaking at other commencement exercises in Atlanta. It was his eighth such address that season.

Having shaken the last hand in sight, he beat a hasty retreat and climbed wearily into his car. The exertion of speaking had drenched his shirt with perspiration and completely wilted his collar. Even the back of his white coat was wet. Though it was now eleven at night, there was no sign of relief from the intense heat. The breeze made by the moving car might as well have been fanned from a furnace door.

Peter always reacted violently to the heat. Under its relentless, sinister influence, as he regarded it, he felt completely thwarted, and became sure that life wasn't worth living. In addition, on this particular night, he was lonely and somehow at a loss. Could the events of the last few days have been just a beautiful dream? They seemed so now. Under a sudden compulsion to communicate with me in any way that he could, he turned the car around and headed for the nearest telegraph office.

The girl in the Western Union office was hot too. Seated on her tall stool, she watched the businesslike hands of the wall clock creep toward a merciful midnight. At that moment Peter strode through the side door. He too looked up at the wall clock, frowned slightly, and reached for the nearest yellow pad and chained pencil.

Instantly the girl was wide awake. There was a decisiveness about this man that fascinated her. His face looked strained, she thought, and there were beads of perspiration on his upper lip. Repeatedly he wiped his face, and repeatedly a recalcitrant lock of damp curly hair kept falling back on his forehead. But as his big hand moved across the page, the tense look vanished, and a smile appeared at the corners of his mouth.

Carefully he signed his name, putting beneath it a precise line with two dots. He hesitated a moment before handing it to the girl, then resolutely shoved it across the counter.

"Make it a night letter," he said.

The girl circled the NL and began reading what he had written. Her pencil ran along the first three sentences, then paused.

"M'm . . . oh, I see . . . *unforgettable memories and thrilling hopes . . .*" her voice trailed off.

Peter flushed violently and looked away, trying to hide his obvious embarrassment.

"This is to go to Johnson City, Tennessee, sir? It's exactly . . . exactly forty-five words. That will be forty-eight cents, sir."

As the girl handed Peter the change from a dollar bill, his eyes met hers. Suddenly, he grinned sheepishly, and in spite of herself, the girl almost laughed aloud.

In Johnson City I was awakened the next morning by some member of the family stuffing a yellow envelope into one relaxed, outstretched hand. It was the night letter. I read it and marveled at the goodness of God and the temerity of Peter.

It read:

HOPE YOU HAD A SAFE PLEASANT TRIP STOP TODAY HAS BEEN SO EMPTY AM MISSING YOU TERRIBLY STOP UNFORGETTABLE MEMORIES AND THRILLING HOPES WILL HELP TIME PASS STOP AM THINKING OF YOU CONSTANTLY AND WILL WRITE TOMORROW STOP LIFE IS WONDERFUL REMEMBER I LOVE YOU DARLING GOD BLESS YOU

PETER

Soon the promised letter arrived:

Dearest Catherine,

How last week dragged on leaden feet—while I was waiting to hear from you. I really did not expect to hear until Friday afternoon or Saturday morning, but when no letter or card had arrived on Saturday morning, I explored all the torments of the lovelorn. I thought all kinds of things! I suffered agonies of secret pain. You see, I was waiting for the first expression, the first reassurance.

You will never know with what transports of joy I received your precious letter sent special delivery. It came about 10:30 last night, as I was working on my evening sermon. I read it with a bursting heart. I could have wept, and did—a little—and I thanked the Lord right then and there for giving me such happiness and such a wonderful sweetheart. Never in my life have I known such happiness and joy and peace. I cannot help thinking of the words of the hymn: "Peace, peace, the wonderful gift of God's love." Everything is turning out so much better than I could have planned it, because He is planning it. It was far better to get your wonderful letter at 10:30 last night than in the morning. It meant more to me then, for I had hoped all day and longed!

I had called———on Saturday to see if she had heard from you! And that was silly—and she said so! This morning at Sunday School I told her I had received a Special last night, and she smiled and asked if I was going to let her read it! Darling, I am so happy! I love you so much! . . .

It was so hard leaving you on Tuesday night. I stood gazing after you a long time. . . . I can never be the same again. I am a different person now, praise the Lord, and you have made all the difference. My heart is in your keeping for ever and ever. I live from now on to serve Him and to make you happy. Life can hold nothing more satisfying or more glorious than this—the joy of building with you, a home that will be a temple of God, a haven and a sanctuary, a place of peace and love, of trust and joy. . . .

Thus began a correspondence rare in the annals of love-making. Certainly, there have been plenty of passionate love letters before. Literature has also preserved a few in which there runs a deeply spiritual note. There have been lovers sufficiently detached to write in a humorous vein. But I doubt if many series of letters, before or since, have more uniquely combined all three attributes.

Peter had the happy capacity of sometimes laughing at himself; so his letters were spiced with drawings of small faces wearing over-eloquent expressions. He said that I was responsible for his current cardiac condition, and that I ought to be ashamed of myself; and at the end of the sentence there was a drawing of an imp with his hair over his eyes looking pleased with himself. He complained that he had had no letter from me that day, and none the day before, and the imp wore an expression of infinite sadness. Would the men in our wedding party *really* have to wear spats? He hoped not! That face wore the corners of its mouth turned down almost to its boot tops.

The letters never failed to include a weather report. This was characteristic of Peter, since the weather was of utmost importance to him. From May till October he suffered with America's heat, and he saw no reason why he should suffer in martyred silence.

Rain, rain, rain, sultry weather, close, stuffy, depressing. I can't even think, I'm so hot, much less write sermons. . . .

Or he would say:

It is still hot here—terribly humid—and I am almost reduced to homicide. If this keeps up—well—it just can't do that! Something will have to burst, the weather or myself.

Sometimes a note on the weather even crept into his frequent telegrams:

LET THIS BE FORGETMENOTS AND SWEETHEART ROSES FOR SUNDAY STOP LAST TWO WEEKS WITHOUT YOU HAVE BEEN MONTHS STOP WEATHER NOT TOO HOT STOP I LOVE YOU DARLING

In his eyes there was nothing incongruous about the juxtaposition of the most lyrical expression of his love alongside a detailed analysis of the weather. He simply assumed that I, like him, would be just as much interested in the one as the other.

He was then thirty-four years old. For years he had dreamed of the day when he might have a home of his own. His wistfulness for it had crept into many a sermon, and perhaps all unknown to him, had colored many a public prayer. In one of his early sermons, he had sketched a vivid word picture of a home he knew whose characteristics were now interwoven with this home of his dreams:

I was privileged, in the spring, to visit in a home that was to me—and I am sure to the occupants—a little bit of Heaven.

There was beauty there. There was a keen appreciation of the finer things of life, and an atmosphere in which it was impossible to keep from thinking of God.

The room was bright and white and clean, as well as cozy. There were many windows. Flowers were blooming in pots and vases, adding their fragrance and beauty.

Hyacinths and lilies of the valley had been placed gracefully and lovingly before a little shrine where the family could worship.

Books lined one wall—good books—inspiring and instructive—good books—good friends. Three bird cages hung in the brightness and colour of this beautiful sanctuary, and the songsters voiced their appreciation by singing as if their little throats would burst.

Nature's music, nature's beauty—nature's peace. . . . It seemed to me a kind of Paradise that had wandered down, an enchanted oasis—home. . . .

And now that his home of his dreams was about to materialize, he could not bear the thought of waiting another year. I had been planning to teach school. Why did I want to do that? He delicately pursued this point through several letters, then followed up with a quick trip to Johnson City so that he might personally plead his case.

He did not have to twist my arm to persuade me. I had found my heart's home, and I knew it. So the decision was made. We would be married in early November, in my home church, the First Presbyterian Church of Keyser, West Virginia. Peter went back to Atlanta in the mood of a knight returning victorious from battle. The only catch was that, for a time, he had to be a somewhat restrained knight. There always remained the danger of gossip.

Since getting back [he admitted], *I have been in Atlanta, but not of it. I never knew I'd be so thrilled over anything. My grin becomes more sheepish every day, my preoccupation more pronounced. In short, every indication points to the imminent incarceration of the writer as a dangerous lunatic! I know I must look stupid as I go around, and I want to tell everybody why I feel like this, and all about it.*

It seemed wise to tell the session of the church of our engagement before the news of it leaked out grapevine fashion or was formally announced. From Covington days onward, Peter had always made his elders his confidants. The result was an extraordinary depth of mutual respect, unity, and affection man to man.

At his request, the men gathered in his study immediately following the morning service. It was a gracious room to which they came, clearly reflecting their young minister's taste. There was a fireplace with the inevitable seascape above it, and low bookshelves around two sides of the room filled with the theological books which he was collecting. The walls were palest blue, and the carpeting deep-blue broadloom. Soft June air poured in through the open windows.

As the men came in, Peter stood leaning against the mahogany desk. He knew, at that moment, how much he loved all these men, with that depth of affection known only to those who have shared many things. A procession of pictures flitted across his mind—an all-night vigil in the bare hospital corridor with Mrs. Zoll and her daughters; the awful inadequacy of his comfort for a big man shaken with sobs; the quiet pride in a father's eyes as his only daughter, a vision of loveliness in white lace and tulle, came slowly down the long candlelit aisle; the look of surprise and joy on Dr. Hope's face (the dean of Westminster's session) the night the session meeting turned into a celebration for his fifty-third wedding anniversary.

Something of the emotion of the moment was written on Peter's face, so that the men sensed that this would be an unusual meeting.

"Gentlemen," he began, and his Scottish burr seemed softer than usual, "I have asked you to come here, to share with you something that I feel you should know first, even before your wives. This will be just once you can scoop them on the latest gossip!" He grinned, then quickly grew serious again.

"Most of you are much older than I. During the three years of this present ministry, you have come to be to me, individually and

collectively, what a father would be. I want to tell you this morning, just as I would tell my own father, were he here on earth, of the
happiness that has come to me. I hope to be mar-r-ied in the fall,
perhaps around the first of November. This girl is Miss Catherine
Wood. Some of you have met her." He broke off suddenly, his face
crimson.

Mr. Pomeroy leaped to his feet and gripped Peter's hand. "That's
the best news I've heard in this church. You've waited a long time,
boy. I wish you all the happiness in the world."

Soon all of the men were clustered around him, laughing, shaking hands, slapping him on the back, and offering him their
congratulations.

> *They were genuinely glad, Catherine* [he wrote me afterward]. *You
> ought to have seen their faces. I dared not look myself, for I was quite
> embarrassed—but some of them must have been studies. When you
> know these men as I do, you will love them too. They're the salt of
> the earth.*

About the same time Peter broke the news to his mother in Scotland. Immediately she wrote him:

> *Coatbridge, Scotland*
> *July 3rd, 1936*
> *My dear Peter,*
> *I received your letter of June 17th. We were in Troon for June
> month.*
> *Well, my boy, I did not know you were interested in any special
> girl. But this I do know. I have kept asking the Lord to guide you in
> all your actions and in all your plans, whether in your work or in
> your choice of a life partner. Peter, this is no surprise, and I feel it the
> best of all things to come to you.*
> *I remember how fond you were of that verse, "Seek ye first the
> Kingdom of God and His righteousness, and all these things shall
> be added unto you." Then when I think of you and Miss Wood pray-
> ing about each other at the same time, I am sure it is an answer to
> prayer.*
> *I have the happiest thoughts about it all. She is a daughter of the
> manse, and her training and education will make her just what you
> need in a life partner.*

I wish you every success in all you undertake, and hope that Miss Wood will find in you her heart's desire, and that you will find in her all your happiness. So may the Lord's blessing rest on you both.

The years are flying fast, and we are getting older. I had my 66th birthday. Thank you for your remembrances.

My love and best wishes and congratulations to you both. Perhaps someday I will meet her and you in your new home. Thanks for telling me about your plans. I am happy.

> *All my love,*
> *Mother*

And to me she wrote, with a gentle reserve typical of her:

> *Coatbridge*
> *August 8th, 1936*

My dear Catherine,

This is the letter of a mother who dearly loves her son, to one whom she is soon to welcome as her son's wife.

It is a difficult letter to write, especially since we are so far apart and have not met. Yet why should it be difficult, when all I want to say is how happy I am because my boy is happy—and to insure you a mother's welcome into her own heart.

Peter has told me some of the things he carries in his heart about you, of which a mother loves to learn. I am sure this happy event is in answer to our prayers, and that is enough to put our minds at rest. God only gives to His own dear ones the best—and that is how I feel about you and my Peter coming together.

With much love to you from Peter's mother.

> *Janet Findlay*

Always in Peter there was the practical businessman as well as the poet—a curious combination that Scotland loves to nurture in her sons. So he wrote an ecstatic half-page description of the engagement ring he had bought, and then added that he had been fortunate enough to secure it at the wholesale price. Another day he was sorely tempted by a sale on flat silver at one of Atlanta's department stores. Then he found a salesman friend who offered him furniture at half price.

Of course, people laugh at this trait in Scotsmen, while the Scotsmen condescendingly endure the crude jokes, knowing them to be the best, most continuous free advertising in the world.

Dreams carried around in one's heart for years, if they are dreams that have God's approval, have a way suddenly of materializing. One September afternoon Peter found his dream house standing on the crest of a hill—and, best of all, it was for rent at only sixty dollars a month. Tall pines stood sentinel over a rambling cottage with casement windows. Peeping in, Peter saw that the living room had an open fireplace, in which he could imagine logs crackling. At the bottom of the hill on which the house stood, there was a little ravine through which a clear stream sang its way. One approached the house by a rustic footbridge and many stone steps.

Peter sent me snapshots, a detailed floor plan, and pages of description. In his mind's eye, he could already see rock gardens, azaleas, clumps of daffodils and iris beside the brook, a vegetable garden in back, hammocks under the trees, and the top of the garage a plaza where we could entertain our friends on summer evenings. He even saw himself raising chickens. In his enthusiasm it never occurred to him that innumerable preaching engagements, wedding conferences and ceremonies, calls, church meetings, and sermon writing would inevitably crowd out the gardening and chicken raising, and that there would never be time for lying in hammocks under the pines. It was always to be that way.

Even then, we were forever bumping into already scheduled ecclesiastical duties and trying to detour personal plans around them. *I find I have a wedding scheduled for Friday afternoon. If I could just persuade the bride to move it up one hour. . . . Or, A funeral on Sunday afternoon delayed my departure. I'm sorry, darling. . . .*

In between the epidemic of Atlanta weddings and eight series of preaching engagements all the way from Athens, Georgia, to Eagle River, Wisconsin, we managed to see each other six times that summer. Peter drove seven thousand miles to achieve it.

There was even trouble finding a date for our wedding that wouldn't interfere with something or other. A two weeks' meeting in Chattanooga, scheduled to end four days after our wedding, was moved up so that it concluded four days before the wedding. That gave Peter time to write a Sunday sermon, preach it, pick up his going-away suit, pack his bag, and drive 750 miles. The meeting, he said, would be "his prematrimonial workout." So it proved to be.

In July he had supplied the then-vacant pulpit of the New York Avenue Presbyterian Church in the nation's capital. Dr. Joseph Sizoo had resigned some months previously to go to the Collegiate Church of St. Nicholas in New York. What had seemed routine pulpit supply quickly turned into something more significant. The people of New York Avenue were immediately impressed with the young Scotsman.

The personalities of another group of men who subsequently proved themselves "to be the salt of the earth" now obtruded themselves into our lives. There was Mr. Frank Edgington, New York Avenue's session clerk—tall, slim, Chesterfieldian in manner, his neat gray goatee making him look as if he had stepped out of the mid-nineteenth century. There were Mr. Edward Martin, the manager of the Lee House Hotel, Judge Claude Porter, and Mr. Adam Weir—all fine men.

The negotiations, then begun, were not to be concluded for another fourteen months. Meanwhile, already there was the agony of indecision, the inner conflict, the prayer and quiet waiting that were always to attend the search for God's will in this matter of calls to other churches.

Our periods of separation during that time were marked with long letters in which we tried to appraise the decision before us. Peter cheerfully admitted how he pined for these letters and laughed at his own eagerness. He preached at Cedartown, Georgia, each night during a week when the temperature stayed at 95 degrees night and day.

It has been four days since I have heard from you [he chafed], *but I know I'll get a letter in the morning, because I called up Ruby in Atlanta, and she told me she had forwarded a letter from you.*

Said the next letter:

You were very kind to write me twice this week. In fact, you saved my life, that's all. Harry Petersen—the minister here—was sorry for me and would go to the post office twice a day to indulge me. In desperation, I believe he was almost at the point of making up a letter for me—so that the services might proceed—only he could never have imitated your writing. No human being could do that!

Couples whom he counseled had often wondered how this young preacher would act when he finally fell in love. Peter knew he could not escape being watched. Above all else, he despised hypocrisy. Hence, he insisted that he and I had to do everything he had advised others to do. His idealism not only "soared through mother-of-pearl skies on frigates of romance" but also stooped to embrace health examinations, insurance policies, and budgets. I had to read the same books he had lent to others. Dutifully, we each went to our doctors and exchanged health certificates. We discussed relatives and made a budget. He made it clear to me in words that admitted of no duplicity that he had practiced the continence for the unmarried which he had preached.

This idealism of Peter's was no mere sentimentality, for it was rooted and grounded in the love of Christ. Indeed, every sermon Peter preached was a word drama, whose gigantic backdrop was a picture etched in bold strokes of God's age-long courtship of the human race. To the preacher, all human history was but the tale of God's tender wooing of the self-willed, stubborn hearts of men and women—a drama that culminated in the Cross. No romance could ever equal the romance of Calvary. But when, perchance, a little of the love of God spilled over into the hearts of a man and woman—and when that love was blessed and sanctified by Christ—there was true romance, a "marriage made in heaven."

We found time for less serious things that summer, such as long hours spent playing games like Monopoly, Parcheesi, and Yacht. Peter came honestly by his honorary title of G.G.P.—abbreviation for Great Game Player, bestowed on him by my young brother and sister. My family thought it would look impressive on his church bulletin—thus, "Peter Marshall, D.D., G.G.P."

The day of our wedding saw a cold rain falling, "an ideal day for staying home and playing games," Peter said. It was indeed. During the morning, I put the finishing touches to my veil, and wrestled with a new influx of wedding gifts swathed in tons of tissue paper and excelsior. I gathered the impression that Peter was rollicking through successive games of Yacht, Parcheesi, and Rummy with anyone who had sufficient leisure to indulge him. That was all right, but I thought he was carrying it a bit too far when, thirty minutes before the ceremony, he was so busy pushing his initial advantage in a game of Chinese Checkers with my little sister Em, that he still had not dressed.

Shortly before we left for the church, a card and a telegram arrived. The card was addressed to the bridegroom-elect. It was from three of Peter's seminary friends and read:

The great event will probably put scores of girls back into circulation. Our sympathy to Catherine.

> *Cecil Thompson*
> *Bill Stewart*
> *Sam Cartledge*

The telegram was from Westminsterites, who could not resist this golden opportunity to rib their preacher with one of his own favorite expressions. It said:

CONGRATULATIONS ON YOUR ADMISSION TO THE HALLS OF HIGHEST HUMAN HAPPINESS

> THE DEACONS, WESTMINSTER CHURCH

seven

THE PREACHER-BRIDEGROOM

> For this cause shall a man leave his father and mother, and cleave to his wife;
> And they twain shall be one flesh. . . .
>
> Mark 10:7–8

he morning after we were married, I opened my eyes to find Peter lying propped up on one elbow, staring at me intently from the vantage point of the other bed. Apparently he had been staring for some time. His inscrutable expression didn't make it quite clear whether he had been thinking, "Oh, you gorgeous creature!" or "How did this happen to me?"

Upstairs, in the Lee House, seven men and a lone woman, Mrs. C. O. Goodpasture, were waiting for us. They constituted the Pastoral Committee of New York Avenue Church, whose duty it was to find a new minister. There wasn't time to eat breakfast; so Peter left the room hurriedly, calling over his shoulder, "Take your time dressing, Catherine. I'll start the ball rolling, and when the men want to see you, I'll telephone you to come on up."

Considering the effect his words had on me, he might as well have said, "I'll call you when we're ready to throw you to the wolves."

The room was fragrant with flowers sent by Mr. Martin, the manager of the Lee House and the chairman of the Committee on Pastor. I dressed carefully, with unsteady hands, trying to ignore the butterflies in the pit of my stomach.

I was just twenty-two, knew the city of Washington only as a schoolgirl tourist, and had not met any of the members of New York Avenue Church. When the telephone rang, I steeled myself, and said meekly, "Yes, darling, I'll be right up."

Of course, the committee was graciousness itself, and quickly put me at my ease. They were not unmindful of the fact that we had been married only the afternoon before, but they were sure, they said, "that we wouldn't mind combining a little church business with our honeymoon. Wasn't it convenient that we had come through Washington on our way to New York?" To them—these men of the world, skilled in the affairs of government and finance—we must have seemed terribly young and inexperienced. Looking back, I know that it was altogether typical that our married life began with a church committee meeting.

On September 27, Peter had preached for the second time in New York Avenue. He had accepted the invitation because he "felt in the whole situation, a strange destiny." "Besides," he added, "I had such a good time with the people of New York Avenue Presbyterian Church." At that time the church had a membership of 1,206 people. Morning and evening, there had been large crowds to hear the prospective candidate.

During the next few weeks, Peter had gone through an agony of indecision. Much pressure was brought to bear on him from the Washington end—letters, telegrams, and long-distance calls. A telegram from Mr. Adam Weir read:

I WANT YOU TO KNOW OUR PEOPLE ARE UNITED FOR YOU BELIEVE THIS MUST BE THE LORD'S WILL AND PLAN WE PRAY IT WILL BE MADE CLEAR THAT YOU SHOULD ANSWER THIS CALL AND COME TO WASHINGTON

ADAM WEIR

And one from Mr. Edgington said:

CHURCH HERE PRAYING FOR GOD'S GUIDANCE IN YOUR DECISION STOP BELIEVE UNITED DESIRE OF OUR CONGREGATION FOR YOUR LEADERSHIP AN ANSWER TO PRAYERS STOP GOD FORBID WE SHOULD ATTEMPT TO HASTEN YOU EVEN THOUGH WE FIND IT A LITTLE DIFFICULT TO BE PATIENT

F E EDGINGTON

Even greater effort was made by Atlantans to influence Peter to stay there. The congregation of Westminster took very much to heart the possibility of his leaving. Some of them telephoned him and wept over the phone. Letters poured into the church office. Many friends came in person to plead their case. Some of them dared to intimate or to express openly the thought that it must be an increase in salary attracting their minister. That interpretation Peter keenly resented; he did not even know what his salary would be, were he to go.

The terrific pressure exerted on Peter was clearly shown by letters such as this one, received at that time from one of the members of Westminster:

Dear Mr. Marshall:

I realize fully that you are capable of making your own decisions, and it is very presumptuous on my part to think that you would in any way need a suggestion from me in handling your affairs. . . .

We are greatly disturbed over the possibility of your going to Washington, because we personally feel such a tremendous need. When we first heard you at Westminster, we were suddenly convinced that here was a man who was apart from the crowd, who had the Divine touch, whose power of interpretation of the Scriptures was the greatest we had ever known, one who would not be touched by the flatteries and luxuries of the world. We found that you had the enthusiasm and magnetic personality that would impel people to want to do the things you stood for. We were aroused from our middle step of inactivity and made to see spiritual things in a new light.

Why do you suppose people are coming from other churches in flocks to Westminster? Not because of the architecture of the building, certainly. Not on account of the cordiality of the members, although they are nice enough. It is because they recognize in you a leader who is carrying the banner of Christianity in a manner that is not being done by the rank and file. You are enthusing them to have a part in this battle, no matter how small.

In short, we have set you on a pedestal. Please don't let us find that our god has feet of clay. We still need you, Peter. Westminster still needs you. I refuse to believe that you are being flattered into believing that this call is Divine because you have an opportunity to contact Senators and Congressmen who will go back to their respective homes and spread the gospel you have given them. No, no, they are wrapped up in their political bundles and are only look-ing for self-glory. . . . I refuse to believe (forgive me for saying this) that the screaming of the eagle on the American dollar has anything to do with this call sounding "divine." No, no, that is an unworthy thought. I refuse to believe it of you.

When you get to the nation's capital, what will there be for you to look forward to? You will have arrived! You can't have the enthu-siasm to keep striving, when you have already attained the heights. Remember that the Lord Himself was taken up into the high moun-tain and shown all the kingdoms of the earth. . . .

It is not necessary for you to have a "national hookup" to be heard. The world will come to your door. We have put our spiritual hands in yours for guidance. Are you going to let us down? A child is not led by his father for a faltering first step or two and then turned loose to fall. We are still wobbly, Peter. We still need your guiding hand. I refuse to say to myself that it is "just as I expected. . . ."

Because Peter was unusually sensitive to other people and to their feelings, letters like this cost him great spiritual agony. Any intimations of rationalization on his part concerning the call, to mask personal ambition, or for financial reward, hurt and angered him. Yet, he well knew that, in the end, it was God's voice alone to which he would have to listen. Somehow, he must find a way to shut out the clamor of all other voices.

A week away from home on a preaching mission gave him a few days for evaluation. During that week he had written me:

Catherine, my dear,

. . . . About the Washington situation. I am enclosing a copy of a letter I sent to Mr. Edgington. I shall be anxious to know when I get back what you think of the way I have stated my position. I am try-ing to be fair to all concerned, and fair to myself and the urgings within. . . .

Of course, your prayers and mine—that the Lord will make His will so clear that there shall be no doubt about it—are the only solu-tion. Remember that a call of God is a two-sided call—there is a call 'to' a work, and there is a call 'from' the present work. I like to think that the Lord sets both in motion at the same time. . . .

The potent consideration in my mind is the question: "Am I yet ready for such a work as that of New York Avenue?" I do not sin-cerely feel that I am equipped for what they would need. I lack the

poise, the balance, the preparation, the academic standing, the con-
fidence, the discretion, and the grace to be bridled in my pulpit utter-
ances. That is how I feel at the moment—which would seem to indi-
cate that I am swerving to Atlanta, wouldn't it? . . .

Thus, on October 15, Peter had written to Mr. Martin declining the overture to the Washington church. His letter gave his reasons and revealed his own sober estimate of himself and his work:

While realizing that no man's work is ever finished, I am persuaded that there yet remains much work which I am to do at Westminster. I could not conscientiously say that I have done all I could have done here. In fact, the thought of all I have left undone . . . is a painful and humiliating one.

I feel furthermore, that I am not yet ready for the responsibilities and the dignities which would be mine as minister of the New York Avenue Church. I am too young, too immature, too lacking in schol-arship, experience, wisdom, and ability for such a high position. Time alone will reveal whether or not I shall ever possess these qualities of mind and heart that your pulpit demands.

There is a definite feeling in Westminster Church that I am obli-gated to remain here for a time, because of the erection of the bal-cony. They feel that, since it was built on the assumption that I would stay with them, I ought to stay at least until it is paid for. . . . They feel that, were I to leave, I would be breaking faith with them, and with the 219 members added during this present ministry. . . .

Perhaps your invitation comes to me as a test, for, much as I would like to accept it, in the hope that in another place and by a new begin-ning, I could run away from mistakes and shortcomings and fail-ures—it may be that my plain duty is to stay here and wrestle with myself for the victory on this battlefield. Perchance I may gain a new respect for myself by electing to remain and take the hard way. . . .

God has not yet indicated that I am to leave here. I am aware, and keenly conscious of the call to Washington, but not, as yet, of any call away from Atlanta.

I regret that I must write this. . . . May God continue to lead you and guide you to the man of His choosing. . . .

The Grace of our Lord Jesus Christ be with you all.

Most sincerely yours,
Peter Marshall

The members of the Committee on Pastor would not, however, take "no" for an answer. They were sure that they had found their man, and that there must be some way to work it out. Hence, on October 24, Mr. Martin wired:

> HAPPY TO INFORM YOU FULL PASTORAL COMMITTEE OVERWHELMINGLY
> VOTED TO RECOMMEND TO CONGREGATION THAT CALL BE EXTENDED TO
> YOU STOP MEETING OF CONGREGATION CALLED FOR NOVEMBER FIFTH
> REGARDS
>
> EDWARD W. MARTIN

It was now November 5, the day following our wedding. The congregation would be meeting that night. Peter made it clear, as the discussion with the committee in the Lee House proceeded, that even if a call were extended, he would not be able to come for many months. The balcony at Westminster, necessitated by constant overflow congregations, was only then being built. It simply had to be paid for. New York Avenue, on the other hand, already had an antiquated and inadequate building and a crushing debt of $130,000.

As it turned out, the Washington congregation waited another eleven months to get the man they wanted. They were determined to wait for Peter as long as necessary. Strangers might wonder why the people of New York Avenue, highly critical, accustomed to a procession of great preachers, could be so sure that this very young Scotsman was *their* minister. Perhaps they, themselves, could never have analyzed it. They only knew that his preaching was unforgettable, that he made Christ seem real and alive—a commanding Presence among them.

During the seventeen months that New York Avenue's pulpit had been vacant, they had patiently listened to a long procession of ministers from this country and abroad, but having heard Peter Marshall, the majority of the congregation wanted no one else.

There could be only one answer to surety of conviction like that. This was without any doubt the call "to" the new work of which Peter had written me earlier. God was apparently determined to have us in Washington—and nowhere else. The Westminster congregation, then, would have to accept this decision as final.

Actually, so much time had elapsed since the first overture from Washington that, by now, the Atlanta congregation had grown used

95

to the idea. When the decision was finally made to go, they accepted it reluctantly, tearfully—but with Christian grace.[1]

The pattern of events that led to our coming to Washington was a strange repetition of that which had preceded Peter's call to Westminster. In both instances, he had at first rejected the chance for a call, and each time for much the same reason. He had accepted the tiny Covington church rather than the Atlanta one (when both had been offered to him) because he honestly had not felt that he was ready, spiritually or intellectually, for such a charge. He had at first refused New York Avenue for the same reason. Then after a lapse of time, both Westminster and New York Avenue had turned to him again. It was a striking parallel.

Eight months later, on a very hot Thursday in June 1937, we were being entertained in the Mayflower Hotel in Washington. Soon we would be having dinner in a private room with the elders of New York Avenue Church and their wives. The elevator door clicked shut, and we began to descend. Peter's blue-gray eyes looked deeply troubled.

"Catherine, I'm scar-r-ed—scar-r-red to death. Perhaps I should never have accepted this church. Suppose I can't deliver the goods? Suppose they don't like me after all? What if . . . ?"

"Main lobby, suh. Watch yo' step, miss," the elderly Negro said, never realizing that he had just interrupted a fine case of pre-installation jitters. I tried to smile reassuringly, but the smile was a little forced. Each of us took a deep breath and stepped out into the bright palm-studded lobby. We were on our way, and there was no retreat.

The formal acceptance of the pastorate of New York Avenue had finally been made, though there was to be no newspaper announcement until we were on the high seas. Saturday morning we were to sail aboard the T.S.S. *Caledonia* for a vacation in Scotland.

"We're sure you wouldn't mind," the Committee on Pastor had suggested, "stopping off briefly on your way to New York, just to meet more of the officers and to see the Manse." This was so reminiscent of that other stop-off the day after our wedding, that it began to seem like an old family custom.

Too late I learned that the dinner being given in our honor was a formal affair. My two evening dresses were packed in the steamer trunk which had preceded us to New York. There was nothing to do but to apologize to the ladies and wear a short dress. But they didn't mind half as much as I did.

We had good reason to be frightened by the awesome responsibilities being thrust upon us. The pulpit of New York Avenue was considered by many one of the dozen most important pulpits in the nation. Peter was succeeding Dr. Joseph Richard Sizoo, an eminent preacher. Ten years seemed a very short time in which to step from the Battery at Ellis Island to such a post in the nation's capital.

"The whole thing," said Peter, "seems like a fair-r-y stor-r-ry or a dream." No wonder he was frightened.

It was a rather large group at the dinner. The long table was beautifully decorated with bowls of spring flowers and white candles, and the food was the Mayflower's best. I was seated between Mr. Martin and the wife of the session clerk, Mrs. Frank Edgington. I tried desperately hard to remember the names of all these new people, whom I had not met in the Lee House meeting. Some of them were famous names in the city of Washington.

"Did you know, Mr. Marshall," asked Mr. Edgington suddenly, "that the first pastor of New York Avenue was a Scotsman too, and that he was only twenty-two when he came to America and took this church?"

Peter smiled. "That makes me feel much better. And I'm glad a Scotsman got the church started right."

But the rest that the clerk of the session had to tell us about the church's history awed us a little.

It had been founded in 1803, the year of the Louisiana Purchase, when Pennsylvania Avenue was still an impossible morass of red clay, in which cows had the right of way, and along which Thomas Jefferson himself supervised the planting of four rows of poplars. Since the church had no building, the little handful of worshipers met in a hall of the Old Treasury building, later burned by the British in 1812. Coal was then a new and expensive fuel; so Dr. Laurie always arrived early each Sabbath morning to start a fire in the wood stove. There, above the roar of burning logs, the young Scotsman, himself a Covenanter, fed his flock on the strong diet of undiluted Calvinism and the Scottish Psalter.

"New York Avenue is sometimes called the 'Church of the Presidents'; more often 'The Lincoln Church,'" Mr. Edgington continued. He paused and stroked his trim gray goatee. "Eight Presidents have worshiped there. . . . Let's see if I can name them . . . Adams, Jackson, Harrison, Polk, Pierce, Johnson . . . that's six. . . ."

"And Buchanan," chimed in Judge McNinch.

"Yes, and most famous of all, of course, Abraham Lincoln."

Mrs. Edgington, who seemed to know as much about the church's history as did her husband, pointed out that even the minister's wife at New York Avenue had quite a lot to live up to.

"My dear," she said, linking her arm through mine, as we rose to leave the room, "your predecessors, our ministers' wives, have been wonderful women. Let me tell you about Mrs. Radcliffe. . . ."

Mrs. Wallace Radcliffe, it appeared, was no mere person. She was rather a *personage*, in the latter days of the Victorian period, when Washington society was still exclusive, when protocol was almost a matter of life and death. Mrs. Edgington painted such a vivid word picture of this beautiful woman that to this day, whenever I think of her, I see her erect and queenly, always with a hymnbook at the small of her back, in her place each Sunday morning in the low-backed Lincoln pew, at that time the pastor's pew; I see her being driven in her carriage to the White House door, punctiliously leaving her calling cards with their turned-down edges on the silver tray of the doorman; I see her entertaining in the first Manse, 1202 K Street, always gracious and charming, always correct, presiding over her tea table with her background of heavy velvet draperies and portières, massively carved furniture, and silver service and candelabra. What frightened girl could ever hope to emulate Mrs. Radcliffe?

After the dinner was over, we went for a walk before bedtime. The fronts of the fashionable shops along Connecticut Avenue were brilliantly lighted for window-shoppers. Peter and I paused to admire the slender reeded posts of a tester bed in Bigg's window, and fabulous cobalt-blue-and-gold service plates in Martin's.

It seemed impossible that this strange city was to be our home. We were still seeing the Washington of the tourists. For us, there was inescapable glamour in the fact that we would be living next door to "Woodley," the beautiful estate of Henry L. Stimson, soon to be Secretary of War; that the church itself stood only two blocks east of the White House, within three blocks of the State Department building.

On Friday, Colonel Walter Clephane, the president of the board of trustees, took us out to see the Manse. We drove across the Taft Bridge on Connecticut Avenue, with Rock Creek Park, green and refreshing-looking, stretching below us, past the Shoreham and Wardman Park hotels to Cathedral Avenue. The car stopped in front of a squarish red-brick house close to the street. It was as much unlike our little hilltop bungalow on Durand Drive in Atlanta as any house could be.

Colonel Clephane unlocked the door, apologized for the musty smell, and threw up some windows. But the heat inside was almost as bad as the heat outside.

We looked over the three floors, and concluded that it was an immense house for two people—ten rooms in all, six bedrooms. "Three bedrooms apiece," joked Peter, and the Colonel looked at him strangely.

He indicated a pile of wallpaper books in one corner. "As you can see, the house badly needs redecorating, Mrs. Marshall. Are you the kind of woman who takes hours to make up her mind about such things?"

I was—but not in the 98-degree heat of a house that had been closed for months. The wallpapers were chosen in record time.

On Sunday, after we were on the high seas, Dr. Albert Evans, the interim minister in charge at New York Avenue, would officially announce Peter's acceptance. On Monday, headlines in the *Washington Evening Star* read: "REV. PETER MARSHALL COMING HERE FROM ATLANTA: Immigrant of Ten Years Ago Preached in Tartan. Will Arrive Here October 1 to Assume Duties."

eight

THE COUNTRY HE LEFT BEHIND

Hadad said to Pharaoh, Let me depart that I may go to mine own country.

Then Pharaoh said. . . . But what hast thou lacked with me. . . ? And he answered, Nothing: howbeit let me go. . . .

1 Kings 11:21–22

We stood on the New York pier, watching our car, encased in a huge net, being swung aboard the *Caledonia*. In September we would be moving from Atlanta to Washington. In the meantime, we resolved to leave all responsibilities behind us and have a real vacation in the British Isles.

This would be my first trip abroad, and every detail was exciting. Peter was determined to make it so. "With the car," he explained, "we'll *really* see Scotland, all the out-of-the-way places most tourists miss."

There was no one to see us off, but the pipers made up for that. The Anchor Line Company wanted to be sure that no one misunderstood and thought this a French or Italian vessel. Six kilted pipers and two drummers drove the point home as they marched up and down the deck playing "The Campbells Are Coming," "The Road to the Isles," and "Cogadh no Sith."

We sailed at five, waving to people we did not know, through a rain of confetti and paper streamers, to the screech of whistles from the bridge, the skirl of the pipes, and the drone of planes overhead.

As soon as we got to our stateroom, Peter rang for a steward. When the man appeared, my husband acted as if he had just found a long-lost brother. He had probably never seen the man before in his life, but that's the way one Scotsman acts when he finds another Scotsman. Two are quite enough to start a new Presbyterian Church or fight a war.

The steward warmed to Peter. His attitude said, "Noo, here's a mon after my ain hert."

Some folding money was pressed into his hand. "I suppose," Peter remarked casually, "that you still have the same pastry cook aboard."

"Aye, and he's a guid 'un."

"That I know. I well remember. How about bringing us a little tray each night just before bedtime, say, with some samples of the pastry and two pots of tea?"

The man beamed. "You shall have it each nicht, sir. I promise. I'll fix it wi' my ain hands." He left chuckling.

I stood looking at Peter in amazement. "Of all the performances I have ever seen. . . ."

He looked pleased with himself. "That's the way you work it, my girl." He patted my head. "You'll learn. Just stick around."

The pastries and the tea—the latter coal black, pure tannic acid—were delivered each night promptly at ten. It became a ritual. But the food turned out to be more for Peter's benefit than for mine.

We were not halfway to Boston before my stomach began to feel a bit queasy. Peter gave me a long look. "You look slightly green, Catherine." He groaned. "But you *can't* be *sick.* You *just can't!* We haven't gotten out of sight of land yet. See, look, there's the shore."

"Yes, I know," I replied weakly, leaning a little farther over the rail. "But something's happening to the land. It doesn't look level."

"Oh, no . . ." the man with the cast-iron stomach groaned. "It just can't be! Now look, Catherine, be sensible. This ocean is as calm as our bathtub at home. It's all in your imagination. Just think about something else."

But by then I could not answer.

It was a cruel blow to Peter, the sailor, to find out that his wife was not a sailor. Definitely not! Most of the time I lay on my back on my bunk and read, trying to "think about something else," while Peter became the dining salon's star customer.

The 17,046-ton vessel might list, so that all dining chairs would go scooting across the floor and the waiters could hardly stay on their feet; that made no difference to Peter. He went right on reveling in grilled fresh herring with mustard sauce, steak-and-kidney pie, roast quarters of spring lamb, buttered beetroot, boiled Ayrshire potatoes, cold salmon, and on down the menu to "sweets," "ices," "cheese," and "dessert."

It seemed a long way to Glasgow, by the way of Londonderry. That might have been because Peter had deliberately chosen the slowest voyage he could find. Only a rowboat would have seemed more leisurely. The pin on the map showing our progress across the 3,369 miles of ocean moved with irritating slowness.

The Emerald Isle, where a tender took off passengers for Belfast, looked good to me. Any kind of land would have looked good. I said as much.

"That, Catherine, shows just how sick you are," commented Peter.

"What do you mean?"

"You are seeing that land through jaundiced eyes, or it would not look good. *That's Ireland.*"

"How," I wondered loftily, "could any intelligent man be so prejudiced?"

"I know just what you're thinking, Catherine. I can tell by that superior Agnes-Scott look you get in your eyes. My attitude is definitely *not* prejudice. It's based on fact."

"And I suppose your feeling about Scotland's superiority over England is based on fact too."

"Naturally. Englishmen have always outnumbered us by four to one. Yet, who's held the Empire together? Who's contributed most of her great leadership? Scotland—of course."

I remembered then that once when we had been on a fishing trip in the United States, the skipper of the boat had noticed Peter's accent. Turning around and looking at him curiously, he had asked, "Are you an Englishman?"

"Man—*no!*" Peter fairly roared, suddenly becoming very Scottish indeed. "Wud ye insult me richt ta my face?"

We docked in Glasgow, as Peter pointed out, right in the heart of the city. On the pier below us, an inadequate number of officials frantically tried to keep the good-natured crowd who had come to meet the boat corralled inside the customhouse.

As soon as the officials saw heads and arms protruding from one opening, and rushed to close the sliding doors in that gap, more heads and arms invariably appeared in the spot they had just left.

All at once Peter grabbed my arm and shouted excitedly above the din, "There they are—look!" It was his mother, his sister Chris, and Jimmy, the wire-haired terrier whose wriggling form they were holding up for us to see.

Though this was Peter's fourth trip home since he had emigrated in 1927, *this* trip was different! He was bringing his bride home to be introduced to his family and his homeland.

Soon we got ashore, and Peter greeted Chris and enfolded his mother in his big arms. Then came the introductions. There was approval in Mother Janet's understanding blue eyes as she looked at me, and I, for my part, immediately fell in love with her. She had short, white, curly hair, very pink cheeks, and an accent easily twice as thick as Peter's. It was a wonderful homecoming. I knew that my reception into my husband's family was real and warm.

The weather into which we stepped was not so warm. It was a soupy combination of mist, fog, and drizzling rain. The land—oh, joy—was solid beneath my feet. I had forgotten what it felt like not to have that Jello-like feeling in my middle.

As we drove from Glasgow to Peter's home on Torrisdale Street in Coatbridge, I saw that the area between the two cities was almost solidly built up. Although all the marks of an industrial area— smoke, soot, the roar and rattle of traffic and machinery—were by no means attractive, still there was a definite Old World atmosphere. I was interested in the gray sandstone and granite houses, mostly alike, with their notched chimneys striking into the sky, and their pocket-handkerchief gardens in front.

Of course, there were a thousand things to talk about. Chris and Mother Janet asked about "Miss" Mary Davenport.[1]

"How she would love to be here," commented Peter. "She could hardly bear to see Catherine and me come without her!"

The next day we started our sight-seeing with daylong excursions into the surrounding Lowlands; later we planned to take one long trip into the Highlands.

One day we made a circular tour up the Clydeside to Luss, down Glen Ogle to Callander, Doune, and Bridge of Allan. We had several sight-seeing days in Glasgow and Edinburgh, one to Blantyre to see David Livingstone's birthplace, one to Ayr and Alloway, a trip to Balmoral and back home by way of Glen Clunie and the desolate Spittal of Glenshee.

My first impressions of the British Isles were like those of any American tourist. Everything seemed built to miniature scale. There were no skyscrapers; the autos were tiny and driven on the wrong side of the road; the locomotives looked like toys; the railroad cars, like small boxes on wheels.

The temperature was cold in the middle of summer. A three-piece woolen suit, plus a couple of sweaters, and a fire in the grate enabled one to stay tolerably comfortable. The unpredictable weather was composed of samples—anemic sunshine one hour, rain the next, cold fog the next. I noticed that the most optimistic report *The Glasgow Herald* could muster was to predict "bright periods."

Colors were unbelievably vivid—the grass a luscious green, the flowers of a size and intense coloring hitherto seen only in seed-catalog advertisements. Vegetation was never dusty or parched, as it is in the United States in midsummer. Yet the cities were obviously very old, and their buildings tried to wear gracefully the accumulation of centuries of soot.

I was struck by the large numbers of prams on the streets, the apple-red cheeks of the children, the giant policemen, the bowler hats of the men, the bad teeth and poorly fitting dentures, the easy grace with which the women wore their tweeds, and conversely, their clumsy shoes. There were hordes of bicyclists, all with their waterproofs folded in neat squares, strapped on behind—mutely eloquent of the unpredictable weather. There was no ice water. In fact, no water at all was served with meals. Ice cream was a rarity. There were few salads, no pies. But the tea—oh, my—the tea! Whether because of the climate, the type of tea used, the water, or just because the British know how to make tea, it was a heavenly brew.

Usually, we would get home from these daylong sight-seeing trips in time for Mother Janet to serve us high tea. Typically, this might be haddock, oatcakes, cheese, cherry cakes, and, of course, tea. For a special treat, we might have a fresh egg—or as the Scots say, "an egg to our tea."

Then the curtains would be drawn, shutting out the damp chill of the outside world, the fire lit, and the family would gather in the living room to talk or play games. The games were inevitable, of course, with Peter around.

Several evenings I spent taking down Mother Janet's favorite recipes. They were, to say the least, unorthodox. For example, this one for Scotch broth:

> The nicht before, ye tak' a pound o' Scotch barley and a quarter-pound o' dried peas, and soak 'till mor-r-n'. The next day, fir-r-st tak' aboot a half-pound from the flank o' a puir wee sheep, pit it in a graund saucepan, cover wi' water, and boil for an hour.
>
> Then ye tak' three leeks (I have to substitute small spring onions), twa carrots, a wee spring cabbage, and chop 'em up al' together and pit 'em into th' pot, together wi' the barley and peas. Dinna forget—alwa' stir wi' a wooden spoon. That makes a bonny dish. Let it boil one hour.
>
> Durin' the second hour tak' a wee handful o' parsley, an' chop fine—an' a carrot which ye grate. After ye pit these in, let it simmer fifteen minutes more. That's all. It's no' so deeficult an' my, it's awfu' guid—

Scotch broth is really not so complicated as this makes it sound. A Scotch accent would give anything a degree of intricacy. Most Americans find that they like this dish.

On these evenings at home, as Mother Janet and Father Findlay reminisced, or as we looked through old family photographs, I began to wonder to what extent that tiny land—smaller than the state of South Carolina—had itself made Peter the kind of preacher he was. How different would the man have been, if the boy had been transplanted say, at the age of five, to another part of the world?

One of the first things people always noticed about Peter's preaching was his sensitive appreciation of all beauty. His good friends might teasingly call him "Twittering-birds Marshall," but his audiences everywhere warmed to this trait. In almost every sermon and in every pastoral prayer, passages could be found to illustrate his appreciation of all lovely things.

As I saw the beauties of Scotland, the more I realized that Peter had grown up in a land whose physical features had nurtured this appreciation.

It is true that Peter's immediate environment, as a boy, had been the industrial atmosphere of Coatbridge and Glasgow, but so compact is this tiny land that its grandest scenery is never more than a few hours away. Within an area of thirty miles, almost at his back door, there was the greatest variety. As Peter had said in the sermon, "Pardon the Scottish Accent":

We know full well that there is beauty in every land. . . .
There is the grandeur of Switzerland . . .
   There is the majesty of Norway . . .
     There is the charm of pastoral England . . .
Yet somehow, they are all combined in the scenery of Scotland. . . .

The patch of the earth's surface that a man calls "home" can become part of the man, in fair exchange for the day when the man will become part of the earth.

Peter liked and often quoted the way Rudyard Kipling had put that truth:

God gave all men all earth to love,
   But since our hearts are small,
Ordained for each one spot should prove
   Belovèd over all.[2]

After long years in the United States, the old gray city by the Northern Sea, and the rain-blurred, wind-swept hills of home were still "belovèd over all."

In an address made before the Burns Club, in Atlanta, Georgia, on January 25, 1935, Peter had expressed the longing that all Scotsmen feel for home:

We love Scotland in the sunshine.
We love her in the rain.
We love her hills, now and again rearing their heads above the blankets of mist, and pushing the shrouds down, to roll wet among the heather . . . while whitewashed cottages nestle fondly in their protecting shelter, and surround themselves with flower-filled gardens

bright in the mist . . .
colorful even in the rain.

We can see—oh how clearly—Scotland's hills folden one against the
other in every shade of brown and blue . . .
    stone dykes running up and down . . .
        rabbit holes and clumps of fern . . .
        green grass and sheep grazing . . .
    fir trees marching down in their companies
        to the very edges of the brown-tinted lochs, in whose deep shad-
ows are locked the secrets of a romantic and stirring past.

And the wavelets lap the rocks and whisper of "Black Rodericks"
"Rob Roys" and "fair Helens."

We have been in the heart of the Grampians and thought it to be the
frontier of another world . . .
    something like the mountains of the moon . . .
        with range after range fretting the sky with their
        varied lines and heights . . .
        mountain piled upon mountain like frozen thunder.[3]

Then from the grandeur of the backbone of Scotland you slip down
to arched bridges, beneath which dark waters lap and gurgle, to run
on through fields, neat and trim, divided by hedges and stone walls.

Oh, for Scotland's low stone houses lovingly tucked away from the
storms . . .
    gray and cold outside
    warm and cozy inside.
The wind impotently shudders at their doors and throws handfulls
of sleet against the glass.

Oh, for Scotland's drizzles and her mists
        her fogs and her smirs
        her love songs and her poetry
    her firesides and her winterdykes
    her ingles and nooks
her buts and bens. . . .

But Peter's own personal joy in all beautiful things would have been of little use in the art of preaching if there had not also been the ability to make others see what he saw. That ability he had, and that too was, in large measure, Scotland's gift to him.

Though his gift for word pictures was an amazing one, which God used in an extraordinary way, it sprang from soil common to the humblest Scot. Peter had grown up in a country where the past lives side by side with the present. To no Scottish child could history ever be the dull, tasteless thing it so often is to American children. Nor does the Celt ever lack a vivid imagination.

To the most humble Scot, with little education, the past is alive, and the present, in his eyes, is but a continuation of that past. For example, Bonnie Prince Charlie, the Jacobite Pretender to the English and Scottish thrones, left Scottish soil two hundred and five years ago. Yet, when we went to Inverness, during our tour of the Highlands, we found hotel maids, guides, and shopkeepers talking about the Bonnie Prince as if they knew him personally and as if he had landed but yesterday.

An antique dealer showed us the bed in which the young Pretender had slept on the nights immediately preceding Culloden. Warmth was in the storekeeper's voice and light in his eyes. He patted the bed. "It's no' for sale *at any price*," he warned, as if he thought we were about to sling the massive thing over our shoulders and stalk away with it.

He was silent for a moment, and his blue eyes took on a dreamy look. "Aye-he . . . aye, it was a terrible tragedy. They did na' hav' a chance, y'know." Abruptly his mood changed. "Noo, if ye'll step richt over here and look on this map. Noo, y'see Cumberland's men were here, an' his were richt here . . . and. . . ." In three minutes the old man's passion had entered into us, and he had us fighting mad too, ready to espouse that glorious lost cause and start the Jacobite rebellion all over.

We met the Border "Prince," Sir Walter Scott, in exactly the same way in the Lowlands, through the eyes of bobbies, guides, waitresses, and folks of whom we stopped to ask directions. To them he was "The Baronet," "his honor, the sheriff of Selkirkshire," "friend," or "neighbor," a personal acquaintance, "a graund maun." The fact that he died one hundred and nineteen years ago had nothing to do with it.

It was this national characteristic that enabled Scott himself to become the first successful historical novelist. He was the most popular literary figure of his day, because he could make the past live again for his readers.

One of the trips both Peter and I most enjoyed, though for quite different reasons, was our visit to the Scott country and to Sir Walter's home, Abbotsford. It is set among the Eildon Hills, at the top of a gently rising slope, with the River Tweed, flowing broad and bright over a bed of milk-white pebbles, at its feet.

The personality of its first laird still permeates every room of that many-turreted red sandstone mansion—with the one exception of the feminine French-Chinese drawing room.

Certain rooms at Abbotsford are more like a museum than a private home. Glass cases are filled with a most heterogeneous collection of things—Flora McDonald's purse; Prince Charlie's glass-bottomed drinking cup through which he could keep his eyes on the dirk hands of his companions; a miniature, with a bit of the Bonnie Prince's hair, and a gold snuffbox belonging to him; a blotter and some clasps of Napoleon's; Rob Roy's purse; a ring taken from behind the altar at Melrose; a glass on which Burns had scratched his famous lines, "Inscription on a Goblet"; and so on and on.

Abbotsford appealed to Peter because he, like Scott, was a born collector. He could also fully appreciate Scott's veritable passion for this home which he had planned and built. Six years later, when Peter finally acquired his own dream house, that home meant just as much to Peter as Abbotsford had ever meant to Sir Walter. It was significant, too, that we named our home "Waverly," taking the name from Scott's "Waverly Novels."

To me, Scott's collections had a different significance. It was their connection with the creative process in his literary work that fascinated me. I felt that it was not that Scott was a collector as a museum curator is a collector—"I have the finest collection of Ming jades in the world. . . ." Not at all. The objects that Scott collected were the wellspring of the creative process for him, the bridge by which the dead past became the living present.

Scott had only to hold in his hands a bit of the brocade from a gown worn by Mary Queen of Scots, and the very crucifix that she had clutched as she walked steadily to her execution at Fotheringay, and the scene sprang to life for him. What was more, he could begin to feel the same emotions that had gripped the original actors in the drama. A story was then about to be born. There remained only the task of transferring to paper the picture his imagination saw and the emotion he felt.

There came into Scott's possession the fire grate which had belonged to the murdered Archbishop Sharp. It was a strange-enough trinket in which to see the past mirrored, but it sufficed, and *Old Mortality* came into being.

Scott knew that real art is always an emotional thing; for no life is lived without emotion, and art must mirror human life. That's why Scott was an artist. He released Scottish history from the strait jacket of mere facts and revealed it vibrant with the life that had always been there.

One day he acquired the keys that young Willie Douglas had thrown into the loch that dark night he helped Mary escape the castle fortress of Lockleven. I can imagine Scott's joy at such an acquisition. For days he would not let the keys out of his sight. As he mounted his mare Sibyl to inspect his land, often his hand would steal into the pocket of his tweed jacket to make sure they were still there. Big, cumbersome, ancient they were. What romance they had witnessed! The baronet could not keep his mind on the sheep-shearing then in progress, or on his henchman, Tom Purdie, and his vociferous complaints about the foresters.

Instead, he is back in the year 1568. Scotland is seething with unrest. He is standing at a narrow barred window looking out over a loch. By his side there is a beautiful woman. A little breeze ruffles the water, so that it makes gentle lapping noises on the rocks below, and the night air fans their cheeks and plays with the woman's fair hair. There is the faint fragrance of a delicate French perfume. Suddenly, on the distant shore—a light. It is their long-awaited signal. Their pulses quicken. Can they *possibly* escape without arousing the sentry on the rocks below . . . ?

Scott sees it all. He feels it all. Mary's emotions have become his emotions. He must ride swiftly back and get it on paper, at least make a beginning this morning. He will call it *The Abbot*. The keys in his pocket have served their purpose. Henceforth they will be one of his most cherished possessions. Peter and I saw them at Abbotsford.

There were other things that Scotland contributed to Peter, as she does to all her sons—a sturdy independence that scorns hardship, a tenacity of purpose that the world sometimes calls stubbornness, a deep appreciation of religious and political liberty, with the will to defend it at any cost.

That tiny land is the most fanatically democratic of all the democracies. Scotsmen have always been fighters. Even the Romans of Julius Caesar's day recognized that. The Roman wall across Northern England was built to keep the Scots *out*. The plan failed, as anyone can see by studying a list of the Cabinet ministers, admirals, and generals in London. Since the thirteenth century, Scotsmen have been fighting, off and on, to gain or to defend their precious independence. This land was one of the cradles of the Protestant Reformation. No wonder the heather is stained red. It has been enriched again and again by good rich blood. There are valleys and glens still echoing the strains of the psalm tunes beloved by all Scots, and many a burn still tells the brave tales of the Covenanters, when dukes and earls, farmers and drapers, merchants and artisans banded themselves into a democracy of the spirit.

All over Scotland the military tradition is still very strong. The Argyll and Sutherland Highlanders, the Gordons, the Seaforths, the Camerons, the Black Watch, and the Royal Scots are world-renowned. During World War I, the 51st Highland Division was rated by the Germans as the most dangerous of any Allied division on the Western Front. During World War II, Scottish troops were piped over the top to lead the Allies into places like El Alamein and Tripoli. The sad consequence of all this is, however, that in each major conflict, Scottish casualties have been heartbreakingly heavy.

Every town that we visited had its own war memorial in the square—always in good taste, always the very best the villagers could afford, always covered with the names of the dead. Peter pointed out to me tiny villages with not half a dozen cottages, from which twenty or more young men had gone out to make the supreme sacrifice in World War I.

Peter was especially anxious that I should see the National War Memorial in Edinburgh. This is a memorial so beautiful as to be quite beyond any adequate description. There, on the highest point of the Castle rock, in a cross-shaped building, the grief of a nation—indeed, the soul of a people—has been caught in stone and stained glass. Here a nation, with restraint, yet with that eloquence of grief of which the Celt is supremely capable, has laid its dead on the knees of God. There is a separate memorial for each regiment, a list of the battles in which they participated, and their colors. The day we visited the Memorial, Peter began reading some of the inscriptions aloud in a hushed voice:

Erected to the glory of God.

Love's strength standeth in Love's sacrifice.

They shall grow not old as we that are left grow old. Age shall not weary them, nor the years condemn. At the going down of the sun and in the morning, we shall remember them.

To Scotsmen of all ranks, who fell while serving with units of the British Dominions and Colonies, 1914–1918. . . .

His voice broke there, and I looked up to see tears in his eyes.

Perhaps it is because Scotland has had to pay such a dear price for continuing freedom, that she does not take it for granted as we Americans are inclined to do. This was a recurring note in Peter's preaching. As he became an American citizen, he transferred a Scot's passion for true representative democracy to the land of his adoption. It was this passion that soon was to make him a prophetic and impelling voice in the nation's capital and, later, in the Senate of the United States.

Our vacation was over. We had already said good-by to Peter's family. Now the time had come to say good-by to Scotland.

Peter and I stood on the deck of the *Transylvania*, anchored in the Clyde, our elbows on the rail, watching twilight thrusting her lengthening fingers into the lanes and streets of Glasgow-town. But our thoughts were far away—up wild glens to the north, down pleasant countrysides to the south, sorting out a hundred memories, mentally packing them into neat bundles to store in mind and heart.

We were eating lemon sole at Crawford's in Edinburgh; poking around Mr. Hay's shop, below John Knox's house, hunting for four-sided egg cosies; exploring that fabulous, fairy-tale Castle on the rock. Once again, we were watching the Argyll and Sutherland Highlanders swinging down the cobblestone street from the Castle, with pipes screaming, and Peter roaring in my ear, "Did you ever see so graund a sight?"

We were laughing as Mother Janet, mopping her red face and fervently commenting after the slightest brush with faint sunlight, "My, but it's awfu' war-r-m!" Or I was enjoying the spectacle of that man who spent half his life complaining about America's heat, lying in bed, shivering, in the middle of summer, pleading, "Catherine, for the love of heavens, *put down that window.* Do you want me to have to hang onto the bedclothes with my teeth, so they won't be blown away in a screaming hurricane?"

Memories are riches, and we had great riches in store—the memory of Oban, where we ate fish and chips on a red-checked tablecloth, where we lingered long over the woolens for sale, soft as a baby's cheek to the finger tips; Oban, where the sea air was cold, sharp with the pungency of salt spray and the romance of the Western Isles just over the tumbling horizon; Oban, where the lone piper on the Esplande issued an invitation hard to resist:

> . . . by Sheil water the track is to the west,
> By Aillort and by Morar to the sea,
> The cool cresses I am thinkin' o' for pluck,
> And bracken for a wink on Mother knee.
>
> Sure, by Tummel and Loch Rannoch and Loch Aber I will go,
> By heather tracks wi' heaven in their wiles;
> If it's thinkin' in your inner heart braggart's in my step,
> You've never smelt the tangle o' the Isles.
> Oh, the far Coolins are puttin' love on me,
> As step I wi' my cromak to the Isles.[4]

How could we ever forget the magic of "the bonnie, bonnie banks o' Loch Lomond" where I had stooped to pick up a pocketful of smooth milk-white pebbles, in an effort to carry some magic away with me; or the banks of the River Tay and the River Tummel, Inverurie, Pitlochry, Drumlithie—places whose very names were music?

On some distant night on a far-off shore, we would unpack and dust off these memories, and find them untarnished by the years. Once again we would be standing on a swinging bridge in Inverness, watching the sun sinking in a soft glow of Turnerian colors behind the chimney tops, turning the River Ness into a painter's palette. And in the distance we would hear again a woman's deep-throated laughter and the haunting strains of the bagpipes.

Or we would be seeing again the wistful ruin that is Melrose Abbey, with the fragile lacework of its Crown of Thorns window, open to the wind and the rain, its cobwebby traceries silhouetted against a darkening sky.

We would not soon forget the jewel-like setting of Dryburgh Abbey, with its yew trees and hawthorne hedges, or that perfect moment when two wee lassies asked us the time of day and then disappeared like frightened deer toward a cottage among the trees, from which smoke curled lazily upward.

We would see again in our mind's eye the proof that God has a sense of humor, that ridiculous-looking monkey fir tree; or the beautiful copper beeches; the rose trees, pink and yellow and salmon; the delphiniums of an intense, heavenly blue.

I would remember inconsequential things, like hotel corridors lined with a battalion of shoes waiting to be polished, brown shoes and black, masculine shoes and feminine; gigantic bathtubs, big enough even for Edinburgh policemen. . . .

Suddenly, someone took me firmly by the arm, and a familiar voice with a burr to the "r's" said, "Come on, Kate, you've dreamed long enough. Let's go below and unpack. It's too dark to see anything anyway. . . ."

And I knew that already Peter had left Scotland behind and was thinking of the new responsibilities that awaited him in the city of Washington.

nine

$\mathcal{W}$ASHINGTON— OPPORTUNITY UNLIMITED

Jesus answered and said . . . without me ye can do nothing. . . .
. . . with God all things are possible.

John 14:23; 15:5
Mark 10:27

$\int$ n the *Washington Times* for October 4, 1937, there was a picture
of a youthful minister in his Geneva gown, standing behind a
large brass eagle. The eagle's spread wings formed the lectern
at the New York Avenue Church. The caption beneath the picture read:
"New Pastor in Presbyterian Pulpit—Preached First Sermon in Historic
Edifice Yesterday."

This was a picture of Peter. The *Times'* photographer had faithfully captured his youthfulness and his more-than-slight bewilder-
ment at the events that had catapulted him to that spot behind the
eagle. At that time the bird looked somewhat more confident than
the minister.

Peter's Washington ministry began on the third of October 1937.
In the morning, he preached "Salvation's Paradox" to a large congregation; in the evening, "The Failures of Christ." He was installed
as pastor of New York Avenue on October 20, with Dr. Albert Joseph
McCartney, of the Covenant–First Presbyterian Church, preaching
the sermon. The Reverend John A. Wood, my father, gave the charge
to the minister. Dr. Albert Evans, the Associate Pastor of New York
Avenue, gave the charge to the congregation.

A few weeks later, Dr. Oscar Blackwelder, of the Lutheran Church of the Reformation, who was then president of the City Ministers' Association, asked Peter to address the ministers. "We met that day at the National Cathedral," Dr. Blackwelder said later, "and Peter talked about getting lost in the church. Haunting memory!"

Dr. Blackwelder found himself much interested in trying to appraise this thirty-five-year-old man who had been called to New York Avenue. "He seemed to me to be a very sincere, guileless, transparent, naïve boy. His predecessor, Dr. Joseph Richard Sizoo, appeared by comparison, a sophisticated divine. I knew that morning that plenty of difficulties and heartaches were ahead for Peter, but I also knew that he would win out in the end. He had what it took."

"Later, as I got to know Peter well," Dr. Blackwelder continued, "I watched my initial prophecy, made that morning, come true. As the years passed, he spoke often in the church I serve. At a young people's banquet he talked on 'Dancing with Tears in Your Eyes.' He preached his sermon 'The Calling of the Twelve' twice for us and he promised to do it again. On a hot June Sunday night he delivered that sermon to a congregation that overflowed into the parish hall. He had become a fixture with us on Tuesday in Holy Week."[1] Dr. Blackwelder told me later: "At first he was a very conservative preacher, clinging rather too tenaciously and defensively to his conservatism. I watched Peter grow during those difficult years here, until he became one of the most thrilling evangelical preachers I have ever heard."

Peter's reputation as a "thrilling evangelical preacher" soon resulted in long lines of people waiting outside New York Avenue Church on a Sunday morning. Often four abreast, they were patient and cheerful about the wait. They hoped to be able to get into the sanctuary and find a seat. Loud-speakers had to be installed in the Lincoln Chapel and the downstairs lecture room to handle overflow crowds. When these rooms were filled, there was nothing left to do but turn would-be worshipers away.

There came the time when the *New York Ave–News*, the young people's paper, reported: "In recent weeks an average of 500 persons has been turned away from the overflowing sanctuary of New York Avenue Church every Sunday morning." Finally the church officers decided that the only possible way to handle the situation was to hold two identical services Sunday morning—one at nine, one at eleven.

These huge congregations were comprised mainly of government workers, GIs, ordinary citizens, a constant stream of out-of-town visitors, and a sprinkling of Washington's renowned. In our congregation, it was not unusual for a famous judge to worship beside a mail carrier or for a Senator to take the Sacrament of Holy Communion in fellowship with a little government clerk. This was a thrilling thing to watch. One felt that it was the very essence of Christianity.

Peter had himself come up the hard way. He had never lost touch with the so-called common man. The democratic ideal was in his blood. At first, therefore, he was so afraid of paying any servile regard to the capital's notables that he was blinded to their real needs. He soon discovered that the rich and the famous have heartaches just like other folks. They cannot escape sickness, pain, and bereavement. They and their families need succor, consolation, and counsel just as the rest of us do. It soon became apparent that serving any of them, from the President of the United States down, was just an integral part of a ministry in the capital city.

In fact, less than three months after coming to Washington, Peter was asked by the Washington Federation of Churches to preach at the annual Christmas service to be attended by President Franklin D. Roosevelt and his family.

Because it was necessary to build a special ramp into any church the President attended, it was impossible to hold this service in our own church. The sanctuary there was on the second floor, with all stairs leading to it too steep for the necessary ramp. Hence the service was held in the Covenant–First Presbyterian Church on Connecticut Avenue.

An immense crowd filled the poinsettia-and-spruce-trimmed building, and overflowed into the streets. I was allotted a choice seat almost directly behind the President, with one pew between. Most of Mr. Roosevelt's immediate family, including his mother, were there. The Chief Executive entered the church on the arm of James Roosevelt.

Outside of the service itself, I have two lasting impressions of that day. One was the eternal vigilance of the secret-service men. I could watch one of them closely. He stood in the left front section of the church during the entire service. Never once did he allow himself to become interested in any part of the service. His eyes were never still. They searched tirelessly back and forth across the gathering for any unusual or suspicious movement. I have never witnessed such faithful and disciplined attention to duty.

The other impression was my shocked surprise at the extent to which President Roosevelt was crippled. As is customary, the congregation was asked to remain standing at the close of the service, until the President and his party had left the building. It took minutes of violent and torturous effort for the President to wriggle forward on the pew and pull himself to a standing position. Watching his patient struggle at such close range, I realized for the first time the extent to which newsreel cameramen had chivalrously shielded the affliction of this courageous man from the public at large.

Headlines in *The Baltimore Sun* for Sunday, December 26, read:

ROOSEVELT HEARS SERMON ASSAILING MOCKERY OF WAR

Crowd Overflows Church of the Covenant
Attended by President's Party

Christianity Still Holds Cure to World's
Ills, Says the Rev. Mr. Peter Marshall.

A lengthy résumé of the sermon followed.

An editorial in *The Charlotte Observer* was entitled, "A Preacher Makes the Front Pages." An editorial in *The Atlanta Journal* said:

The Rev. Peter Marshall . . . a preacher who was a favorite among Atlantans a short time ago, awoke last Sunday morning to find his name, and excerpts from his sermon, on the front page of practically every newspaper in the nation. . . .

A native of Scotland . . . he combines with deep religious sincerity an arresting pulpit personality and holds his hearers enthralled by the almost dramatic forcefulness of his delivery. . . .

He won more than local popularity during his Atlanta pastorate and now, in Washington, has made his name one of nationwide significance.

The opportunity to serve that has thus come to the Rev. Peter Marshall at an early age is one enjoyed by few men. . . .

The *Journal* was discerning. Peter and I soon saw that God's way of dealing with us was to throw us into situations over our depth, then supply us with the necessary ability to swim.

From the beginning of our Washington adventure, there was opportunity for unlimited service. We felt inadequate and unequipped to meet such a challenge. We *had* to rely on God. Life in Washington was thus a methodical, day-by-day demonstration of the reality that the Apostle Paul had to learn—"I can do *all things* through Christ which strengthens me" (Philippians 4:13).

Peter was telling the simple truth when he had said that on coming to Washington he was "almost scar-r-red to death."

I, in turn, discovered that Mrs. Edgington had not exaggerated when she told me that New York Avenue expected a great deal of its minister's wife. To say that the pastor's helpmate was expected to be gracious, charming, poised, equal to every occasion, would be a gross understatement. She should be able to meet the most undistinguished or the most famous persons with equal equanimity. She should know how to entertain two or two hundred. When called upon unexpectedly at a banquet or other church gathering, she should know how to speak well—entertainingly or inspiringly, as the occasion demanded. She was presumed to be the diplomat supreme. And she needed especially an unfailing sense of humor.

There was need for the Christianity of the minister's wife to be of more virile stuff than the hearsay, garden variety. She, no less than the minister, had to know God as a personal and ever-available Friend. She had to have much firsthand experience in the art of prayer. She had to love other people deeply and genuinely. She had to accept the responsibility for her husband's flock on a coequal basis with him.

No wonder I felt inadequate! I could, by no means, measure up to such a standard. God had to make many painful changes in me before I even began to measure up.

One other superficial though nonetheless important qualification remained. New York Avenue, like most congregations, liked its minister's wife to dress becomingly and to be as attractive as possible. There is a very real sense in which a church feels that its minister and his wife belong to *them*, and they want to be proud of *their* possession. Gone are the days when congregations wanted their first ladies to appear in black or somber colors. Nevertheless, she cannot overdress or appear extravagant or flamboyant. The package a minister's wife comes in is important. Even that can be used by God for His own purposes.

A certain fuchsia-colored hat taught me this much-needed lesson. It was the only new hat I had one winter. It was bought at one of Connecticut Avenue's most expensive shops. It was a lovely American Beauty shade—one of those most becoming, once-in-a-lifetime hats. The fact that the congregation enjoyed that hat even more than I did was a revelation to me. I suppose hundreds of people commented on it during the winter. Thereafter, I began to pay more attention to my clothes.

The two ministers' wives at New York Avenue Church were asked to sit in designated places. The congregation watched for Mrs. Albert Evans and me, in our respective pews, and felt that something was drastically wrong if we were not there. My place was the pew directly in front of the Lincoln pew. It bore a brass plate with the word "Pastor."

The Lincoln pew, although roped off, was given either to distinguished guests or to those who had reserved it. If it had not been reserved, the ushers always filled it with late-comers—after all other available seats in the sanctuary had been filled.

Whenever that spirited unreconstructed rebel "Miss Mary" visited us in Washington and worshiped at New York Avenue Church, as she passed the Lincoln pew she always jocularly stuck out her tongue.

This low-backed uncomfortable pew, with its maroon-velvet cushions, was the actual pew in which the Civil War President had regularly worshiped. New York Avenue's minister at that time was Dr. Phineas D. Gurley. He became a close friend and advisor of the Lincoln family.

When Peter and I came to Washington, Mrs. Emma Gurley Adams, the daughter of Lincoln's pastor, was still alive, still full of anecdotes and reminiscences from this epoch of the church's life.

At first, I was suspicious that New York Avenue's Lincoln tradition, if not unauthentic, had at least been exaggerated and glorified with the passing years. I determined to find out for myself just how accurate it was. Several old safes in the church were filled with musty records. Finally, I found the trustees' book of pew rents covering the

Civil War period. Under the "L's" was one page with the unadorned notation, "A. Lincoln." The President had been a bit behind in his pew-rent payment at the time of his assassination. Other fascinating records and documents completely satisfied me. It was all true—together with more, much more, that has never been published.

All of New York Avenue's Lincoln stories testified to the man's humility, his friendliness, and his innate spirituality—despite all that has been written since then to the contrary.

Because Mr. Lincoln had such long, ungainly legs, he was forced to sit at the end of his pew sidewise, with his legs partly in the aisle. One Sunday, during the days of the Radcliffes, an elderly couple who had spent their honeymoon in Washington told Mrs. Radcliffe of seeing President Lincoln at New York Avenue. Just as the service began, they had seen a forlorn, bedraggled-looking man come wandering down the center aisle looking for a seat. The President noticed him. Instantly, out shot a long arm, and the young couple heard the President whisper, "Come right in beside me, brother, there's *plenty* of room. . . . "

Not all of the church's history was quite so inspiring; some of it was spicy. A case in point was Peggy O'Neale, the "Gorgeous Hussy" of the Andrew Jackson administration. Peggy, once portrayed on the screen by Joan Crawford, was a regular attendant at New York Avenue. She was the cause of the capital's bitterest social and political feud. Because her minister, Dr. John Campbell, who disapproved of her conduct, self-righteously interfered and incurred President Jackson's wrath, he was forced to resign his pastorate. It was said that, after that, New York Avenue's ministers were inclined to leave politics alone.

Two events of our first year in Washington deserve mention here. On January 26, 1938, Peter Marshall became a naturalized American citizen.

This was by choice, rather than by necessity, since he had come to this country under a permanent visa within the immigration quota. Shortly before we were married, he had quietly determined to take this step. Our moving to Washington merely strengthened his decision. Twice previously, he had taken out first citizenship papers but had let them lapse. It was not easy for him to relinquish his British citizenship. Watching Peter at certain moments, one could not fail to glimpse just how much his British citizenship *did* mean to him.

I was with Peter when we heard, over the car radio, King Edward VIII's famous abdication speech. As the poignant words, charged with a king's very human emotion, came over the air, I watched Peter's eyes fill with tears that overflowed and rolled down his cheeks.

> . . . . A few hours ago I discharged my last duty as King and Emperor. . . . I have found it impossible to carry the heavy burden of responsibility and to discharge my duties as King . . . without the help and support of the woman I love.
>
> . . . . I now quit altogether public affairs and I lay down my burden. It may be some time before I return to my native land. . . .
>
> . . . . And now we all have a new King. I wish him and you, his people, happiness and prosperity with all my heart. God bless you all.

Peter drove on steadily, not even bothering to wipe the tears away. He did not often weep. "Women are lucky," he told me once. "They can cry when they want to."

Watching him then, I knew something of what he was thinking and feeling. On this, he had the British rather than the American point of view. Americans had their eyes on the romance of the situation. To the British, there was more to it than that. Their sovereign was not just relinquishing the British throne. He was abdicating his heritage—his own solemn responsibility. He was deserting the post for which he had been trained from birth.

Peter returned to Atlanta to take his oath of allegiance before Judge E. Marvin Underwood, in the Federal District Court. There were thirty-three others taking the same oath, including some Britishers, Austrians, Bolivians, Germans, Russians, Swedes, Turks, and Syrians. It was, for Peter, a solemn moment. For weeks he had studied the government document "The Citizenship Program of the Immigration and Naturalization Service" and Sol Bloom's *Story of the Constitution.*

"I had no selfish motive in becoming *an American,*" he explained to Medora Field Perkerson of *The Atlanta Journal,* who interviewed him at that time. "America could give me no more than it has already given me—opportunity, friendships, my lifework. . . . I felt that I could better express my sincerity in seeking to do my part to make conditions better if I identified myself with my people. I felt that perhaps it would mean more to the church. I, of course, hope to spend my life in this country—to live here and to die here. . . ."

What he could not know was that, had he not become an American citizen, one of the greatest doors to service to open to him in the future could never have been opened. That opportunity was the Senate chaplaincy.

The other noteworthy event of that first year was that on May 30, 1938, Peter was given an honorary doctorate by Presbyterian College in Clinton, South Carolina.

Peter had no illusions about the real value of honorary degrees. Nevertheless, it heartened him to receive this one. All of his life he had been haunted with an inferiority complex about the fact that he did not have a college degree. True, the faculty at Columbia Seminary had recognized his academic work in Scotland as more than the equivalent of a B.A. and had presented him with his B.D. That had helped some. The D.D. was another little lift in the right direction. Yet, to the end of his life, the inferiority complex lingered.

It always revealed itself when he was with other ministers whom he particularly admired. A prominent New York clergyman once heard Peter protest to several of his colleagues, "But I don't even belong in the same room with you boys. I haven't any scholarship or background or degrees."

The ministers present were just amused. "There Peter was," commented the clergyman, "actually able to preach rings around any of us—and we knew it—talking, in all sincerity, like that!"

Though inferiority complexes are certainly not to be desired, perhaps it was just this very sense of inadequacy that enabled God to make Peter so adequate. Paradoxically, in the pulpit, he impressed his listeners as being not only competent but one of the most able preachers they had ever had.

A businessman in Dallas, Texas, who heard Peter preach in the Highland Park Presbyterian Church there, wrote a letter to Peter's mother in Scotland:

> . . . *I have been a member of the Presbyterian Church since I was a little boy . . . and in the course of my life I have heard the greatest preachers in America. . . . I have revered and do revere them all for*

their greatness, but in my opinion, your son—Peter Marshall—just
a young man, is the greatest of them all.

An official in educational circles in Washington commented: "No other person I have ever known has influenced my life so profoundly as has Dr. Marshall. Whatever faith I have found has been lighted from the torch of his magnetic faith. . . ."

Peter's magnetic faith appealed to the very young, as much as it did to the older people. When we came to New York Avenue, a total of about twelve young people comprised the Youth groups. This changed almost immediately. In fact, it changed so much that soon New York Avenue acquired something of a reputation as a young people's church.

Peter's first step was to organize and begin teaching a Sunday School class for senior high-school and college students. The parish hall classroom was soon crowded to the doors, with standing room only.

Within a short time, the Youth groups had increased from twelve to two hundred, and were steadily growing.

The young Scot's influence over young people is illustrated by an incident which took place in 1937, a few months after we came to Washington. It was told to me many years afterward by a girl who was there, who was sixteen at the time.

In a certain city a new high school had just been completed. A wide cross section of local citizenry was represented among its students, from society leaders' to tradesmen's children, from the best residential districts to humble suburban homes. Trouble resulted. There had been several "fighting" wars between the two groups.

Discipline was quite out of hand. An ugly spirit permeated the school. During the attempted talks of several guest speakers in the chapel, peashooters and paper airplanes were all over the auditorium. There were hisses and boos. Humming groups held forth first on one side, then on the other. Once a smoke bomb had blown off one of the doors in the middle of a talk. More than one speaker simply had to give up and walk off the stage. All of this was so embarrassing to the principal that no chapel at all had been attempted for two months.

Then the principal heard of Peter Marshall and invited him to address the students. Whether or not Peter knew of this background when he accepted the invitation, I don't know.

The youngsters heard that a preacher was coming and determined to fix him. Said the girl, "I fully expected Dr. Marshall to be ridiculed and booed off the stage."

At first, the girl was fascinated by the preacher's smile and by his accent. He was talking about gardenias—of all things—her favorite corsage flower.

"You know how a gardenia's petals reveal any telltale fingermarks by turning brown," the preacher said. "Your lives are like that. Purity is like that. . . . Young people, don't give anything to the world to destroy. Don't be ashamed of high ideals, dreams, and beautiful thoughts. . . ."

Suddenly the girl woke up to the fact that there was dead quiet in the auditorium. No peashooters or paper airplanes were in evidence. The eyes of all the teen-agers around her were glued to the speaker.

"I can wish for you nothing better than that God will plant in your hearts a growing yearning to meet the Galilean, to know Him as your Friend. . . ."

As the preacher concluded, the room was swept by a tremendous ovation.

Fourteen years later the girl still remembered the theme of that talk and the gardenia illustration.

"We kids liked to hear Peter Marshall," she said thoughtfully, "because he spoke our language. He didn't talk over our heads. And he put the responsibility for what we made of our lives squarely on us."

It was significant that it was the young people of New York Avenue who put this notice in the church bulletin, at the end of our first year among them:

The members of the Tuxis Group and the Young People's Bible Class present the flowers of the sanctuary on this occasion of the first anniversary of Dr. Marshall's ministry among us, as a tribute of love and gratitude for his leadership in the young people's work of the church.

ten

THE MAN AT HOME

... and the blessing of the Lord was upon all that he had in the house, and in the field.

Genesis 39:5

To step into the living room of our home was like entering a marine museum. Seascapes were everywhere—Peter had seen to that. A huge reproduction of Winslow Homer's "Nor'easter" hung over the fireplace. Three sailing ships listed at various angles on the other walls.

In the dining room, when one looked to the east, there was a calm and beautiful sea; a glance to the west produced an uneasy feeling stomachward, as one rolled inwardly with a large reproduction of "Mighty Waters." Even in the bedrooms there was the same general queasy effect. I had tried to slip in at least one landscape or nice flower print just for variety; Peter would have none of it. As far as he was concerned, landscapes were a dead loss. Why suffer a landscape, when you could have a seascape? We ended up with five of his choice on the walls of our bedroom.

"You either see beauty, or you do not," Peter said in a sermon. "If you do not, no amount of argument can make you see it. When you stand before Homer's 'Nor'easter,' do you not thrill to that rolling, majestic, angry sea, so that you can almost feel the cold spray on your face and lick the brine from your lips? If you do not. . . ."

Most people did.

When they entered our house, they not only felt like licking the brine from their lips but also like hastily drying themselves off.

My husband's tastes knew no half measures. Furthermore, he was at heart a collector. Seascapes were not his only hobby. He accumulated clocks too, with all the avidity of a small boy gathering birds' eggs. There were thirteen clocks in our house, in addition to wrist watches. He was always thinking of buying more. He wanted a grandfather clock for the hall, and a real ship's clock, and a banjo clock, and almost every clock he saw.

It was not that he was a clock watcher or a split-second-schedule man. Far from it. He just enjoyed having plenty of clocks around.

He also collected stamps (British colonials), pot lids (old pomade-jar tops for framing), Summertime china, pressed glass of the Argus pattern, and games.

In this last-mentioned field he was an authority. Our game collection soon attained such proportions that it was necessary to house it in a special game closet. We had everything from tiddly-winks, pick-up-sticks, and checkers, through innumerable board games, to elaborate ivory sets of mah-jongg and chessmen. Every game was well used.

Peter got rare joy out of his home. With a zest characteristic of everything he did, he had entered into every detail of furnishing our first home in Atlanta. Several of his friends in the furniture business had come to our rescue. One of them had offered to let us come to his warehouse and select furniture at a discount. "Miss Mary," our Marietta "mother" and "unreconstructed rebel," had given us many things which Peter had admired, including a needlepoint stool and fireplace screen, and three hand-carved rosewood Victorian chairs.

Peter snatched time off from the office to go shopping with me. Whatever we were selecting, whether rugs or draperies or upholstered furniture, it was hard to keep him from getting everything in blue. Fortunately I liked blue, too.

Another of Peter's requirements was that all furniture had to be sturdy. That meant that it must not wobble when he threw his full one hundred and ninety pounds against it. Many a furniture salesman must have held his breath as his furniture underwent this earthshaking test.

My husband marveled over and over at the change he already saw in himself so soon after marriage. Earlier he had written me:

127

I find it difficult to realize that Peter Marshall, the nomad, the lone wolf, should at last be thinking in terms of china and furniture and rents and houses . . . but I confess to you that I like the new picture much better. It is the real one, the lasting one, the only one to give joy and happiness.

Now wherever he went, he noticed the furnishings of other people's homes. He had a deep appreciation of lovely things. Many a hostess delighted in his enthusiastic appreciation of her silver pattern, her china, her linens, or her eye for color. It astonished Peter that he was now so conscious of these things, whereas he had scarcely noticed them before.

He loved to preach. He would rather preach than eat, and out-of-town preaching engagements were a temptation to him—as they would always be—but now, when he was away, he was eager to get back home. Months after we were married, he wrote me:

My dearest,
   Since getting down here I have longed to get busy in the garden and plant flowers, longed almost poignantly for the things I left behind. I mean apart from my longing for you and to be with you— everything we have seems to mean so much to me now. . . . This is the first time we have been separated for so long since our wedding, except for your trip home. Only three more days. . . . I'll be so glad to get back on Friday night. . . . Expect me about 11 or earlier, if I can get away. . . .

Then his irrepressible humor flashed out:

If you need any money, let me know, and I'll send you my sympathy. . . .

As a new husband, Peter took the greatest pride in showing off his home and his wife to his friends. While my mother was visiting us for a few days, he commented with the utter unself-consciousness of a small boy, "Mother, don't you think our house is tastefully arranged? Isn't it gran-n-d? You may not know it, but both Catherine and I have *quite* good taste!" Later he wrote home to Scotland, after our first Christmas together:

*We had a Christmas tree, decorated with nothing but BLUE lights
and icicles—with some cotton to represent snow and some artificial
snow sprinkled on the top of it. We put it in the bay window, and it
was lovely. . . .*

*Our Christmas dinner was a great success—a tender turkey given
to us by Dr. Hope and cooked by Catherine herself!! Catherine is
managing quite nicely. We are all proud of her. It amazes me the way
she has taken hold and manages like a veteran! It was a proud
moment for me to sit at that table, so tastefully laid out, and look
at Catherine at the other end, and serve turkey, which I carved
myself, believe it or not. . . .*

Part of Peter's pride of possession took the form of coddling our
new furniture with innumerable polishings, of zealously guarding
it against any tiny scratch or misuse. He was always an extremely
neat and methodical person. I was not always so neat.

Faux pas number one was that sometimes I left the top off the
toothpaste or failed to squeeze it from the bottom, rolling the tube
up as it was used. What was even worse, often I failed to close dresser
drawers completely. The man of the house decided to teach his new
wife a nonverbal lesson on drawer closing.

One night I walked into our bedroom. It was quite dark. Suddenly, I bumped into something—something very hard, with sharp
cruel edges. Ruefully rubbing my injured leg, I snapped on the light.
Every drawer in the chest was pulled out. I got the point, but my
pride, as well as my leg, was hurt. It was days later before I was able
to see the funny side of this. Thereafter, I carefully closed drawers
all the way.

My husband liked a room to be well lighted. To him, that meant
lighted like a General Electric showroom. He intensely disliked the
supposedly exotic atmospheres of darkened restaurants and cocktail lounges. Somehow, we could never seem to get enough light in
our living room to suit him. He was always threatening to go around
striking matches, to see his way across the room.

If I dared to have candlelight at the dinner table, I knew that I
could expect ribbing. "I hope, Willard," he might say to a guest,
"that you can grope your way to your mouth in this light. It's right
there—no—a little to the left. There, *you made it.* Catherine, for
the love of heavens, do we *have* to be fashionable?"

We had exactly the same humorous little difficulties that every couple has. Peter was a terribly bad "finder." Something in the closet might be right under his nose, and "it was simply not there at all."

In typical husband fashion, he declared one fall that I had given his best winter topcoat to the Salvation Army, when he could not immediately find it. He was just as irritated as any husband when he pulled a button off his shirt, or a collar button was missing.

One evening he had to wear a tuxedo to address a banquet meeting. He left the house looking very handsome in a spotless dinner jacket, wearing a white silk scarf and a black Homburg hat.

Later that evening, when this impeccable man was in the middle of his speech and reached into his jacket for a handkerchief with which to mop his face, he drew out, not a handkerchief, but a handful of mothballs. No wonder something about him had given the impression all evening that he had just gotten out of storage.

Peter's taste in food was as decided as his other tastes. He was not difficult to please except for a few things like a boiled egg and a cup of tea. Like most Britishers, he still looked upon an egg as something of an occasion—a sort of "blessed event" whose joy he shared with the hen. This precious object had therefore to be boiled just so. I had more difficulty learning to boil an egg properly than I had in learning to make hollandaise sauce or vichyssoise.

"Now look, Kate," Peter would explain patiently, "let's go over this once more. You lay the egg in the pan and—"

"Perish the thought! I'm not in the habit of—"

"All right, all right. So you had an English course once at Agnes Scott. You *place* the egg in the pan. Then you cover it with water until all but about one-fifth of it is covered—"

"Is there any instrument I could buy to measure one-fifth of an egg?" I asked.

"Don't be silly. That sounds farfetched, I know, but it's important, because all eggs are not the same size."

"Thoughtless of the hens, isn't it?"

"Catherine, stop wisecracking. No *wonder* you can't boil an egg. To go on—the water with which you cover the egg must be cold, not hot, not tepid, but cold. Then from the instant it starts to boil, not just a simmer, not a turbulent boil, but a good rolling boil, you time it—two minutes. No more, no less. You see, it's really not hard to do properly."

I sighed. "But there are so many contingencies, so many possible places to slip up in boiling an egg," I objected. "Darling, let's have something simple, like waffles."

It was much the same story with the making of tea. Peter's pet abomination was a tea bag swimming limply in a cup of not-so-hot water.

Most of the time when he ate in restaurants, to be certain that he would circumvent this tragedy, he just gave up and ordered coffee.

Certain ladies in our church had culinary specialties, which their preacher came to regard as works of art, "almost on a par with the reds of Titian or the sunsets of Turner."

One Sunday evening, Peter was preaching on Elijah. He came to the place in the story where an angel provided a baked cake and a cruse of water for the starving prophet.

> The Bible does not tell us the name of the cook [Peter said], we only know that he was an angel of the Lord. Am I too whimsical in suggesting that they are still with us, those "angels of the Lord" who minister to the spirits of men in preparing food . . . even a cup of tea, or angel-food cake, or boiled custard, Scotch shortbread or Virginia ham? I can think of times when a cup of tea and a tasty bite to eat would perform miracles with the heart of a man, and he would be willing to say it was the work of an angel of the Lord.

The angel-food cake, inches high, feathery light, came to the Manse several times a year from Mrs. Schoenhals; the boiled custard, smooth as a baby's cheek, was always "Mom" Stokes' contribution; the Scotch shortbread, "the best he ever ate, bar none," was the triumph of Mrs. McCarty, a gracious lady who hailed from Edinburgh; the Virginia ham was the specialty of our friend Anita Ritter. Undoubtedly it was Peter's intense articulate appreciation of these dishes that kept them flowing Manseward.

One of Peter's idiosyncrasies, well known among our friends, was that he was a night owl. Many of his habits, like this one, were set in concrete. I found that I lacked the physical stamina to stand his hours. Few people did. He had to take his friends in shifts, because a few evenings with him left them limp.

Peter was actually being quite serious when he once wrote me:

Went out to some friends for a little while after the evening service, but got to bed quite early. About 1:30 A.M.

His doctor, about this time, seemed to have a premonition of trouble ahead for Peter. My husband was born with a sturdy constitution, he was naturally the robust, athletic type of man. Yet, the doctor's report said:

Pursuant to your examination at the office this morning, I wish to emphasize again the importance of your reducing the outside demands upon your time and talents. Flattering though they are, you are not in condition to accept them. You must get some relaxation. You must also save time for proper exercise. It is essential that you have the normal eight hours sleep. As it is now, you are burning the candle at both ends.

But the habit was deeply ingrained. About midnight he was at his brightest and best, with his mind working on all cylinders. It was at such times that his great barrier of Scottish reserve went almost entirely down. During a midnight conversation, he could let his friends see into his heart more completely than at any other time. It was also the time when the depths of his convictions about the reality, the love, and the availability of God were expressed in homely, unforgettable ways, very reminiscent of the homespun philosophy of Will Rogers.

"Where on earth are we going to get the money for our next income-tax payment?" I asked one night.

"The Lord only knows, and He hasn't told me yet," Peter replied.

He was not being facetious. Often he spoke of "a God who knows folks' names." There was no doubt in his mind that God was interested in our income-tax payment and would help us with it.

One night a friend questioned him about whether he really thought we shall ever have to stand before God on a Judgment Day and hear the roll call of our sins.

"Yes, the Bible makes it quite clear," Peter answered promptly. "Some day, somewhere, somehow, there will be an accounting for each of us."

He paused and seemed lost in thought as he stirred his third cup of tea. "I think I may have to go through the agony of hearing all my sins recited in the presence of God.

"But I believe it will be like this—Jesus will come over and lay His hand across my shoulders and say to God, 'Yes, all these things are true, but I'm here to cover up for Peter. He is sorry for all his sins, and by a transaction made between us, I am now solely responsible for them.'"

Suddenly Peter smiled, "And, sister, if I'm wrong about that, *I'm sunk.*"

A feature article by Genevieve Reynolds, appearing in *The Washington Post,* carried the following headlines:

MARRIAGE A FULL-TIME JOB FOR ANY WOMAN,
ASSERTS PASTOR

Dr. Marshall Sees Menace in Career Wives. Believes Their Ambitions Threaten Home Life. Grants Exceptions for Economic Necessity.

A girl who is not willing to give up her name, her career, her own selfish ambitions, for her husband's sake had better stay out of marriage, for she will not create a successful, happy home. This is the theory of Dr. Peter Marshall, pastor of New York Avenue Presbyterian Church, who bases his opinion on his wide experience in helping young people solve their problems.

"Many girls today are unwilling to make marriage a full-time job," said Dr. Marshall. "They prefer a career to a home or try to mix both. The idea of a woman's taking time out from business to start a family is not only absurd, but it is breaking down the fundamental ideals of family life.

"Of course, there are many exceptions, and I am not referring to those married women who are forced by economic necessity to continue working. . . ."

Ambition, desire for luxuries, and boredom with domestic life are many married women's incentives for jobs or careers, Dr. Marshall believes. Such an attitude, plus economic independence, accounts for many unhappy homes and eventually leads to divorce, he maintains. . . .

Woman's greatest chance for making marriage a success depends upon her willingness to lose her life in that of her husband, Dr. Marshall holds. He means that the wife's interests must be those of her husband, she must be willing to make little sacrifices to help him along the way. . . .

"Despite the fact that one marriage in every six in this country ends in divorce, young people want to make their marriages succeed, and they want it desperately. I can testify to the deep sincerity of purpose in the hearts of the young men and women who speak to me about being married. Yet, aware of the pitfalls and dangers that lie ahead in modern marriages and armed with sincerity of purpose, still many of them fail. From this, one must conclude that the average modern view of marriage must be wrong, and that the old-fashioned idea of marriage must be the soundest after all."[1]

By and large, the reaction of modern young sophisticates toward such an apparently old-fashioned viewpoint was not at all what one would have expected. They liked it. This may have been due, in part, to the great charm which Peter undeniably had. Yet, there was more to it than that.

"Keepers of the Springs" was probably the most popular sermon Peter ever preached. He repeated it many times by special request. Thousands of copies of it were sold in pamphlet form by the Sermon Committee of New York Avenue—mostly to women.

Apparently even the most modern young women found something refreshing and appealing in this sermon. It was perfectly apparent to them that Dr. Marshall was not an antifeminist, but rather an idealist and a romanticist.

They recognized clear common sense in his assertion that women become progressively less attractive as they desert their essential femininity, and seek either to copy or to compete with men. Conversely, he felt that a woman rises to her maximum attractiveness, usefulness, and maturity as she accepts her God-given prerogatives and glories in her femininity.

I had realized that if I married Peter, I would certainly have to accept these ideas wholeheartedly. The matter of making my husband's career my own would involve no great sacrifice on my part.

I was only a schoolgirl and had no career unless the chance to teach school in the mountains of West Virginia could be dignified by such a title. I was very much in love, and the word "sacrifice"

never once occurred to me. I believed supremely in the career that
Peter had chosen. I counted it a great privilege to share his life.

Inevitably, however, Peter's philosophy of marriage came up for
discussion in our correspondence during the engagement period.
Did he mean, I asked him, that a woman should submerge herself,
all that she is, and feels, and does, in her husband's life? Peter replied
promptly, gently chiding and correcting that interpretation:

> *It does look as if the Lord's will for my life was definitely magnifi-*
> *cent, if it includes the gift of your love and your life. But darling, it is*
> *not that your life and love and gifts will be poured into my coffer . . .*
> *but that we both shall be poured into that new vehicle—and our joint*
> *lives—our blended hearts and fused souls—now one in the sight of*
> *God. You see, "For this cause shall a man leave his father and mother,*
> *and shall cleave to his wife; and they twain shall be one flesh. . . ."*[2]

This Peter sincerely meant, but early in our married life, certain
practical difficulties of achieving the real oneness that was our ideal
presented themselves.

Peter was thirty-four when we were married. His tastes and habits
were already solidly formed. He had lived a bachelor existence for
many years. In my husband's case, there was no question about
whether his home life or his ministry had priority. He loved me;
there was no doubt about that—but, he had been "tapped on the
shoulder" by the Chief. Therefore he was first, last, and always God's
man and His servant, at the beck and call of thousands of people. I,
his wife, would simply have to accept that fact completely.

Though I enjoyed homemaking, this in itself was not enough to
satisfy me. If I was to make Peter's career my career, he would have
to share it with me. In all areas of our life there would have to be a
real partnership.

That was difficult for both of us. It seemed to me that Peter was
altogether capable of carrying the responsibility of his ministry with
no help from me. He had already been doing it for some time.

Shortly before Peter and I became engaged, I had written in my
journal:

I think Peter is trying to make me believe that he is serious about me
. . . but I really think it would probably be best for him to be a bachelor all his life. He seems to be altogether self-sufficient, independent, and perfectly happy that way. . . .

His circumstances had forced him to be independent. Having had
no home of his own, he had fallen into the habit of keeping all-day
office hours in his study at the church. Neither did he take a day
off each week. Therefore, after we were married, I did not see him
all day long. At night he usually had a meeting or speaking engagement. In addition, he was frequently out of town for a series of services a week at a time.

Immediately there was some conflict between us on the subject
of so many out-of-town engagements. I felt that he accepted too
many of these invitations. It seemed to me fair neither to the church
he served, nor to his health, nor to his home life.

Peter the preacher could never understand why I believed he was
accepting too many engagements.

Of the constant stream of invitations to preach that crossed his
desk, he would accept only a few. That usually meant an average
of five separate weeks of services out of town each year, as well as
innumerable "one-night stands."

His point of view was, "See how many invitations I've turned
down." I was all too inclined to note the number he had accepted.

Peter the husband thought that my objection to these engagements must rise from some sort of jealousy of his work and a certain degree of self-centeredness. Some day, he felt, I would grow up.

It is perfectly true that jealousy, whether of one person or a whole
churchful, is still jealousy. Many a parson's wife has harbored resentment and nursed bitter thoughts as she sat alone by the parsonage
fire. Peter was partly right; I was by no means free of such selfishness. After having indulged in it, I would be eaten by remorse and
almost dissolved in tears of penitence. I had to gain years of maturity and of understanding before I saw this for the despicable thing
it was. Moreover, I did not understand, at that time, the full force
of the inner compulsion that drove Peter to preach and preach, even
at the risk of his health.

Always in our marriage, we were striving to push through new
frontiers in understanding each other and in our sharing of life. Peter

did not easily open his heart and mind to anyone—even to me. The Scot always has difficulty in expressing his deepest feelings. There was in Peter a real shyness and a hampering reserve that seldom admitted anyone to the innermost sanctities of his spirit. This minister, popular, beloved, and revered by thousands, was nonetheless sometimes alone behind that wall of reserve. Many a man in his church longed to know him better but could not seem to push beyond the barrier. It was not that Peter wanted to withdraw himself. He could not seem to help it.

It was really Peter's incessant desire to hurdle this barrier of reserve that drove him to be with a few choice friends socially as often as possible. Playing games with friends relaxed him mentally and physically, but did not satisfy that inner hunger.

Strangely enough, the one place above all others where he could open his heart was in his pastoral prayers. It was an inexplicable paradox that this man, who could not share in private his deepest longings, under the stimulus of leading a vast congregation in public worship could literally pour himself out. He could there, as in no other circumstance, articulate his thirst for God, the reality that is God, his contrition for not measuring up to the highest he knew, the haunting regret that he felt. And so, his congregations, unlike many worshipers who secretly sigh over the prospect of a long prayer, looked forward to Dr. Marshall's prayers. In voicing his own deepest needs, he seemed to know intimately every heart in those great congregations. That was why he looked forward himself to those services and why they released tension in him.

In the pulpit or out of the pulpit, in the church or at home, in his office or at play, there was this same utter transparent sincerity about Peter's Christianity. It admitted of no duplicity, no sham or pretense. He could not have persuaded himself to make any assertions from the pulpit of which he personally had the slightest doubt. This was one of the appealing qualities about his preaching.

One Sunday, I referred to a statement he had made in his morning sermon in such a way as to make him feel that I questioned his sincerity. He turned on me sharply, and spoke with such sternness as I had never heard him employ. "Catherine, don't *ever again* question anything I say in the pulpit in that cynical tone of voice. You can tease me about my preaching all you like, *but not like that.*"

This same sincerity was evident in even the smallest spiritual exercise in our home, from the blessing at meals to the family prayers which we endeavored to have after dinner in the evening. Peter would not tolerate any pretense about these things.

Sometimes this led to very funny situations. He was extremely fond of turkey, but disliked any dishes in which the ingredients had been cut into small pieces and mixed together. He hated the time when the Thanksgiving or Christmas turkey was reduced to hash.

One night when we came to the dinner table, Peter lifted the top of the tureen before him and saw that it was filled with turkey hash. A look of undisguised disgust crossed his face as he sat down and unfolded his napkin. "Catherine," he said, "I guess you'll have to ask the blessing tonight. God knows I'm not grateful for turkey hash, and I can't fool Him."

Though like every normal couple, Peter and I were sometimes in disagreement, we found that these differences could never become serious or bitter so long as we could pray together. So thoroughly did we learn this lesson that it was one of the chief bits of advice Peter always gave to couples whose marriages were almost bankrupt. "If you will get down on your knees together," he would tell them, "your difficulties will soon be solved. You just can't pray together and stay mad at each other."

After our household grew in numbers, we discovered, too, that family prayers did not take the place of more intimate husband-and-wife prayers. Moreover, such prayers together were needed for our routine everyday lives, rather than just at the time when difficulties or disagreements arose. Peter always spoke of these prayers as "lubricants for the machinery of life."

That was a supremely accurate description. Thus we tried to have a few quiet moments together in our bedroom before breakfast. On these mornings when we gave our day into God's hands and asked Him to bless it, we found that for each of us the whole day went more smoothly. There was a reassuring feeling of accomplishment at the end of it. When we omitted this brief prayer time together, things became snarled. We felt that we were battling uphill against terrific odds for meager accomplishment.

The same shrinking from all hypocrisy that had made Peter refuse to pretend to God that he was grateful for turkey hash when he wasn't, made him insist on our leaving off this morning prayer for a while if he felt that it was becoming routine. Peter's fear was that unreality in any religious exercise would soon end in hypocrisy.

We early discovered in our marriage that the important thing, however, was not the differences between us, but the will, the determination, to work them out. After all, every couple has difficulties. No two lives are fused into perfect oneness without a certain amount of painful adjustment.

Some marriages are still made in heaven. All marriages have to be lived out on earth. Heaven comes to earth only as we work for it. This is as true for a minister and his wife as it is for any other couple.

eleven

CHRISTIANITY CAN BE FUN

> These things have I spoken unto you . . . that your joy might
> be full.
>
> John 15:11

"The fellow who doesn't like dogs or little children," Peter had said in a sermon called "Youth and the Grail," "must be regarded with suspicion. There is something wrong with the man who cannot make friends with a dog or a baby, or who will not try, who cannot gain their affection. The chances are that he is not worthy of the respect or affection of men either."

The fact that all babies and dogs seemed to have a penchant for Peter Marshall, and that he was intensely proud of this, was well known in his church. In fact, it was one of the things about which he was constantly being teased.

For example, the young people staged a broadcast in which they predicted:

> Prediction Number One: Peter Marshall . . . , a well-known minister boasts, "Thus far no baby I've baptized has cried in my arms" . . . so here is my prediction. . . . To him will come a great blow! At 11:15 A.M., Sunday, the 23d of May, 1938, a baby will lift the rafters with a tremendous wail, while in the arms of Peter Marshall, who will find on that day, defeat in a tiny open safety pin!

On a pleasant Sunday in November, an infant about to acquire the name Charles Parkes Reardon 3d was wearing an heirloom christening gown once worn by his great-grandmother. But Charles Parkes was completely unimpressed. A sudden, urgent pain had appeared in his middle, and he thought the world should be informed immediately. As his parents got about halfway down the long church aisle, he gave a lurch in his father's arms, opened his mouth wide, and let go—with complete abandon. His mother flushed, and reached over a small gray-gloved hand to administer a reassuring pat. Charles kept right on. He seemed actually to be enjoying the impressively loud sounds that rent the sacred air.

The organist moved uneasily on his bench. His soft interlude was being quite drowned out. Dr. Marshall was smiling as he stood behind the pulpit waiting. Secretly, he was thinking that this situation might prove quite a test for his record. At the moment, Charles Parkes Reardon 3d looked anything but docile or inhibited. By the time the little procession, led by two elders, got to the front of the church, the sounds issuing from the baby's rosebud mouth resembled those of a steam calliope in full swing. Mr. and Mrs. Reardon were red with embarrassment.

The minister's voice could scarcely be heard as he said, "He shall feed his flock like a shepherd: he shall gather the lambs with his arm, and carry them in his bosom . . ." (Isaiah 40:11).

"Beloved in Christ: Baptism is a sacrament given by our Lord to His church, as a sign and seal of the remission of sins and our union with Christ. . . ."

Mr. Reardon jiggled Charles in his arms, and the crying subsided somewhat.

"It is to be administered not only to believers, but also to their children, to signify their membership in the household of faith. . . ."

People were always glad when there was to be a baptism during the morning service. Now, as Dr. Marshall came down from the pulpit to stand beside the baptismal font, they were craning their necks, half rising out of their seats, standing in the balcony, to be sure they didn't miss anything. They enjoyed watching the preacher's face as he laid down his Book of Common Worship, gently took Charles Parkes from his father's arms, and stood for a moment talking softly to the weeping baby. Surprisingly, the crying stopped almost immediately, as if a faucet had been turned off, and one chubby hand reached for Dr. Marshall's black silk robe, while the other grabbed the front lock of curly ministerial hair.

The young mother sighed softly, and smiled with relief. She had not wanted *her* baby to be the one to spoil the minister's record.

The congregation was laughing now, and whispering, but no one cared. For, at such a time, it was as if the Spirit of God filled the church in a special way. Invariably, there stole over the congregation a feeling of warmth and tenderness, much the same feeling that creeps into human hearts at Christmastime. People needed no pulpit oratory then to assure them that "God is love." They knew it; they felt it; the building was filled with it.

The Reardon baby was not the only one who cried in his father's arms and stopped crying the second he hit Scottish territory. It frequently happened.

One Sunday, Gayle Whitney, the infant daughter of one of the elders, whimpered and fussed until Peter took her. Then she began smiling and cooing. Nothing could have given Peter's ego quite such a boost. As he handed her back to Mr. Whitney, he whispered, with an appreciable degree of triumph in his voice, "See me after the service, Maynard, and I'll tell you how it's done."

Perhaps it should be stated that Peter's record was not broken until the seventeenth year of his ministry.

Strangely enough, on that day, Peter seemed to have a premonition that something was going to go wrong. Just before he left the rostrum to administer the sacrament, he confided to the congregation, "Most of you know that out of the hundreds of babies I have had the joy and the privilege of baptizing during a ministry of seventeen years, so far, no baby has ever cried for me. I cheerfully admit that I am very proud of that record. But now, after all this time, I never take a baby in my arms without thinking, as does the Army football team just before game time, 'This *may* be the day!'"

The thirteenth of April turned out to be *the day*—a black Sunday indeed in Peter's life. David Hampton Davis cried for him, and that would have been bad enough. But what was worse, it was a Sunday that he was on the air, and Peter's fall from grace was broadcast far and wide. In addition, when Peter got back to his study at the close of the service, he found that one of the deacons had rushed up and put crepe over the study door and on the back of his desk chair, with a sign that read, "Cheer up, Peter. It had to happen sometime." But that consoled him not one whit.

These baptisms were not the only part of the services which taught us that humor and whimsy and humanity are as much a part of worship as any of the starchier emotions. Reverence and the innate dignity that springs from simple good taste were never lacking, but neither was the common touch.

Throughout his ministry at Westminster and for the first years in Washington, Peter used a sermonette, which the grown-ups enjoyed as much as the children. Usually, it lasted five to eight minutes. Peter loved to use Scottish stories for these, quote something from A. A. Milne's *Christopher Robin* (almost his favorite poetry), or derive a moral from a baseball game, a fishing trip, or a movie cartoon.

There was the story about the delightfully naughty little boy who squeezed toothpaste in neat, zebralike stripes across the back of the dozing cat, then added insult to injury by shaking all the apples off the trees in the orchard, and whacking off a sleeping barber's hair.

In the movie cartoon, from which Peter derived this little gem, the boy was required to go back and put everything right—and did.

"But," said Peter, "in real life, boys and girls, you can't do that. Life has certain finalities. You know, you can't fasten apples back on a tree and make them grow. There is nothing quite so final as the barber's scissors. And say, have you ever tried to push toothpaste back into a tube? It just can't be done. I'm a Scotsman, and I ought to know!

"It's just the same with the unkind things we say about each other. You can't take them back. All we can do is to ask Jesus to forgive us. Then ask the person to whom we said the unkind things to forgive us, and try never to say them again. But the best thing is not to squeeze the tube in the first place!"

One successful businessman, who had been reared in another denomination in which he had acted as an altar boy, was one of those who claimed he had received an overdose of religion, and so had ignored the church for many years. His wife started hearing Dr. Marshall preach, and became an enthusiastic regular worshiper. Finally, after about a year, she prevailed on her husband to "try it just once." He came, and made the most astonishing discovery of his life—*that Christianity can be fun.* He never missed another service, if it was possible to get there.

143

For a host of people, it was a new thing to look forward to Sunday, to anticipate eagerly every part of the service, to enjoy the sermon. There was never any problem about pulling back wandering thoughts or keeping one's mind on what the preacher was saying. It would have been hard *not* to listen.

This was true even of Communion services. An eminent judge attended a Communion service, went home, and wrote Peter in longhand:

> *I never attended a communion service that I enjoyed so much as this one this morning. Christ and His life must be very real to you; otherwise, you could not make Him so real to others. . . .*
>
> *Your invitation to the congregation to participate in the observance of the Lord's Supper was without flaw. It was warm, cordial, most appealing; indeed, I thought it irresistible. . . .*
>
> *Sir, "Almost thou persuadest me to be a Christian. . . ."*

Said one young man, "I hitchhiked many a mile to hear that man preach. . . . After my first visit I could not stay away."

Peter was grateful that folks enjoyed hearing him preach, but he strenuously objected when anyone referred to the rest of a service as "the preliminaries." To him, every word spoken in a service—the Invocation, the Offertory invitation, the hymns, the Scripture reading—was terribly important. He tried never to use hackneyed phrases, but to make each part meaningful.

"The whole service," he once told a group of theological students, "should be carefully planned as a progression toward an emotional and spiritual climax, in which the sermon is the hammer blow that drives the nail completely home. . . . An atmosphere can be created in which we feel spiritual presences, have that glow of the heart, that confirmation to the soul of the reality of what it worships, that sense of God's nearness, that charges the very air, and makes us aware—however we vary in our spiritual sensitivities—that 'The King Is in the Audience.'"

"The King Is in the Audience" was one of Peter's best-known sermons in his early ministry. It had been preached on his first Sunday as pastor of Westminster Church. Thereafter he had preached it every year, so long as he was there, on the anniversary of his coming.

Because the presence of the King was so real to Peter, he could make Him real to his congregations. Often he would say, "The King is in the audience—walking these aisles or sitting beside you. You may whisper your own prayer to the King—now," and heart-searching silence would follow.

Said one woman in reminiscing about this, "And then we seemed actually to *feel* Christ beside us, to hear the rustling of His robes."

People often commented that this minister would have made a first-rate showman. Whatever particular ability it is that an expert master of ceremonies has—that instinctive rapport with an audience, Peter had it to a marked degree. In his case, however, this gift had been consecrated, and was used for the glory of God.

He never "conducted" a service. Instead, he worshiped along with us. This was apparent when he read Scripture. As he read, we, his listeners, were first of all impressed all over again with the timeless beauty of the Biblical narratives. Peter's fine voice, his feeling for the rhythm of the King James version, his almost perfect diction threw that beauty of language into sharp perspective.

To many moderns, the Bible is a closed book; it seems dry and unintelligible. But when Peter read it for us, somehow it lived and breathed—and throbbed with life. Part of the effectiveness of it was due to a proper word and phrase emphasis and inflection of the voice. Peter had never studied speech as such. These things seemed to be instinctive with him.

Speech teachers were often amazed at that and sometimes referred their pupils to Peter Marshall as a model. One such teacher remarked to her pupils, "For my money, the two persons with the best diction I've ever heard are Orson Welles and Peter Marshall."

Peter also had a feeling for the beauty, and rhythm, as well as the meaning of Scripture. This he had acquired as a boy, when he used to read aloud from the Bible to his blind grandmother for hours at one sitting. Even the words of the King James version, often rendered almost meaningless by their very familiarity, sprang to life as he read them. He *liked* to read Scripture, and when he read a passage like that of the fourteenth chapter of John: "In my Father's house are many mansions: if it were *not* so, I would have told you . . ." not only did we like to listen, but the beauty of its message lingered in our hearts.

A young businesswoman wrote to Dr. Marshall:

I suddenly realize with what degree of anticipation I have come to await my Sunday morning worship in your church. . . . That full and overflowing church is like an oasis in a barren desert. . . . P.S. Sometimes I suspect that your greatest sermons are given in your morning prayer.

Many people felt the same way about the pastoral prayers. "As we wait in His house to keep this rendezvous with Jesus Christ," Peter might say, just before his prayer, "our Lord, through the Holy Spirit, is waiting now to hear, to forgive, to strengthen, to cleanse, to bless. Whatever your burden of care, of anxiety, whatever your sorrow or worry, or whatever the joy that bubbles within you and makes you feel it is a joy to be alive . . . whatever impulse brought you here, you may use these moments of silent prayer to make your own prayer, and to seek your own peace with God—for He is here."

Then, after a minute or so of silence, he would pray:

. . . O God, our Father in Heaven, make this experience real. May it not be a theoretical ritual. Help us to feel that we are in communion with God, and that in this sacred moment, God Himself may commune with us; and enter into our hearts, that we may feel the surge and thrill of Thy power and know that Thou art here. We dare to pray that something may happen in this service; that as we go out from here and return to familiar places and familiar things, it may be with a new light in our faces, and a new song in our hearts. . . .

Our Father, wilt Thou take away from us now all that does harass and annoy, all that lays upon our hearts burdens of anxiety and care. Wilt Thou help us now to relax before Thee, to lay our burdens down, to forget for one hour all the anxieties of the week, to open our hearts to receive Thy blessing, that the furrows may be smoothed from our brows, the lines from our faces, the loads from our hearts, the doubts from our minds, and the fears from our souls.

Deal with us, we pray, as Thou dost deal with children. Calm our fears, soothe our distress and our sorrow, and help us to lean back on the everlasting arms. For Thou hast never failed us in the past, and we have good assurance Thou wilt not fail us in the future.

Wilt Thou have mercy upon us all. Extend Thy patience, we pray Thee. Cast us not away from Thy presence, but in Thine infinite pity, renew right spirits within us and cleanse our hearts. Wilt Thou pluck out the briars, and wilt Thou soothe the wounds? Let us begin again. Even as the sun did rise to rule the day, to banish the darkness of another night, and to wipe out every shadow, so may Thy love and mercy dawn upon our hearts and give us new life, new light and new hope.

All these things, Our Father, we ask in the strong lovely name of Jesus Christ, our Lord. AMEN.

One man articulated what most people felt about these prayers when he said: "You know when you are physically tired and you go to a comfortable chair, sit down in your weariness, and are relaxed, rest comes. When Peter offered prayer, my soul had just that feeling. I leaned back on that prayer, and my soul rested, and was refreshed."

Even the hymn singing demonstrated that Christianity can be fun. Peter obviously enjoyed singing, and sang with relish and gusto. One watched his face and drew the inescapable conclusion that here was a preacher who actually enjoyed life, and one to whom worship was just as much fun as baseball games, bowling, Chinese checkers, or Monopoly—and that was saying a lot.

In the early years of his ministry, Peter was often asked to sing. He had been known to preach a sermon on the love of God, close his book of sermon notes, go to the choir loft and sing, "His eye is on the sparrow, and I know He watches me. . . ." Sometimes, especially in the more informal evening services at Westminster, he had sung a duet with one of the choir members, Hazel Harrison. When one of the elders died, the daughter's one special request was that Peter not only conduct the service, but sing at the funeral. This he did, though it was difficult because of his own emotion.

Outside church, Peter loved to sing sea songs, of course—John Masefield's "Roadways" and "Sea Fever," and the vigorous "Drake Goes West." Then there were always the Scottish songs dear to his heart, like "Hail, Caledonia!" "Roamin' in the Gloamin'," the rollicking "Road to the Isles," or "My Ain Folk." He could sing something like "Lassie O' Mine," and feminine hearts would really flutter.

Gaelic, said to be the best of all languages for love-making, contains at least fifty words for "darling." It was easy to believe this when Peter sang any of the songs in Gaelic, arranged by Kennedy-Fraser. The favorite among some of the women who knew Peter was "An Eriskay Love Lilt." One, who was frankly smitten, would listen to this song:

> When I'm lonely, dear white heart,
> Black the night or wild the sea
> Vair me o—ro van ee
> Sad am I without thee. . . .[1]

and as soon as the last note had died away, would look at him with her heart in her eyes and plead, "Oh, Dr. Marshall, sing it again. . . ." Among his intimate friends, with whom he could not get by with a thing, this became a password, "Oh, Dr. Marshall, ple-e-ase sing it again!"

The *New York Ave–News* reported gleefully some of this ministerial singing:

Doctor Marshall in Kilts Wows Canteen Crowd
Sings Bonnie Songs of Old Scotland

Direct from the land o' the mist and the heather was the feature attraction of the December 9 Saturday Night Canteen.

By overwhelming popular request, our incomparable PETER (the great) Marshall, Scotland's gift to New York Avenue, stepped out in full Highland dress replete with kilt and knee socks of green and yellow tartan (plaid to you) and silver-buckled shoes. In his own inimitable style, Dr. Marshall explained the military significance of each part of his regalia which was typical of the uniforms worn by Scottish regiments. Even the blanket-size safety pin which "keeps the kilt neat" is GI in Scotland. . . .

The crowd was generous in its applause and frankly delighted when Dr. Marshall consented to recite poetry in Gaelic and sing several Scotch ballads, notably "I'm Tickled to Death I'm Single."

The familiar caricature of a parson—a long-faced, dour-looking individual, dressed in black broadcloth, carrying a long-handled umbrella—may be a bit exaggerated. The fact remains however, that most people are still surprised when they find that preachers are human. A young girl actually once expressed amazement when she found out that Peter went to picture shows and enjoyed a good movie as much as anyone else.

A woman wrote:

> *I remember when I first heard Dr. Marshall preach in Atlanta, I had him up on so high a pedestal that no human being of flesh and blood could ever climb down from such dizzy heights. It was good to see him at play and to realize how deeply human he was. . . . We, who knew him personally, were greatly blessed by that contact. . . .*

No one could have known Peter well without seeing him at play. It had not taken him long to become an avid fan of both American baseball and football. He went to every baseball game for which he could find the time. In Atlanta he had become a regular booster for Atlanta Boys' Hi Football team, and had loved to warm the bench sitting beside their coach. Several times, he had simultaneously received two invitations to Georgia Tech games—one from Dr. Brittain to sit in the president's box, and one from Professor Armstrong, to sit on the roof beside the radio booth. He had chosen to sit on the roof.

In Washington he was always presented each year with a season pass. Probably no minister in Washington followed the fortunes of "The Washington Senators" with greater interest.

His love for competitive games of all kinds was as much a part of him as the color of his eyes. Any game from baseball to bowling, from tiddlywinks to chess, from rummy to contract bridge, was in order. Everything he played, he took very seriously. He could outsit and outplay almost anybody. Whatever the game was, he maintained that if it was worth playing, it was worth playing to win. Usually he did win.

One might wonder how a busy minister could find so much time for game playing. The answer was that Peter stole the time from sleep. Ever since he had worked in the Tube Mill, where often he had had the graveyard shift, he had been a night owl. By about midnight, he was just getting warmed up and seemed to be widest awake. It was then he got his most inspired ideas for sermons. Long after everyone else was openly yawning and ready to call it a day, Peter was fresh and ready for more. Finally, when he could persuade no one to "play just one more," he would say, resignedly, "Well, then, I guess I might as well give up and go to bed," as if he could think of nothing so awful.

Somehow, he succeeded in taking God into his recreation. He knew perfectly well that there are plenty of good, sincere Christians who do not approve of any card games, and while he respected their views, he could not see it that way. Being somewhat of a game connoisseur, he thought of contract bridge as a fine game, exactly as he considered chess a fine game. His viewpoint on this matter was expressed in one sermon he called "Do Whatever He Tells You":

God is a God of laughter, as well as prayer . . . a God of singing, as well as of tears.
God is at home in the play of His children.
He loves to hear us laugh.

We do not honor God by our long faces . . . our austerity.
God wants us to be good—not "goody-goody."
There is quite a distinction.

We must try to make the distinction between worship
        and work
    and play
less sharp. . . .

If God is not in your typewriter as well as your hymnbook,
    there is something wrong with your religion.

If your God does not enter your kitchen
    there is something the matter with your kitchen.
If you can't take God into your recreation
    there is something wrong with the way you play.
If God, for you, does not smile,
    there is something wrong with your idea of God.

We all believe in the God of the heroic.
What we need most these days is the God
        of the humdrum . . .
        the commonplace . . .
    the everyday.

The proof that Peter succeeded in taking God into his recreation is that often people's lives were literally redeemed by the contact they had with him at such times. This might be a revelation to those who feel that certain games are wrong, *per se*.

A friend asked Peter if he would be willing to play bridge some evening with a couple whose marriage was on the rocks. The bridge, of course, was only a camouflage. The real point of the evening was to bring Peter and the couple together.

In this case, the husband and wife had been separated for two years, but were still on friendly terms. The real trouble was materialism. The husband had a $3,000-a-year job in the Department of Agriculture; the wife, being a very clever woman, was earning several times that much elsewhere. Money had become the woman's first love. The husband, feeling unable to cope with such a rival, had left her.

Sometimes God has so prepared a human heart for His help that even one or two sentences spoken at the right moment work the needed transformation. It turned out to be so in this case.

During that evening, Peter privately asked the wife two questions:

"What good is a beautiful house," he asked, "filled with expensive furniture, if there isn't any love between those who live inside the house? What good are expensive clothes and beautiful adornment if there aren't love, contentment, and happiness in the hearts of the people wearing the clothes?"

Those simple questions suddenly stabbed the woman's consciousness with a shaft of inner illumination. For the first time she saw clearly just how foolish she had been. Her attitude toward money and the things money could buy changed completely. The marriage was saved and has lasted.

At another time, a bridge game was also the initial contact Peter used to help a prominent Washington attorney who was rapidly drifting into alcoholism. I shall call the lawyer "Bill."

Bill was rapidly losing both his health and his law practice. His wife appealed to Dr. Marshall for help. "But, Dr. Marshall," she said, "you'll have to slip up on Bill's blind side. My husband is wary of preachers. He's been to church about three times in ten years. He would never agree to come to your study to talk about this."

The bridge game was arranged, and Bill decided that Dr. Marshall was a regular guy after all. After that the lawyer started coming to church. It took a year's work and several conferences and a specially arranged luncheon date on Bill's birthday before God and Peter won the battle. The point is, it is doubtful that this man could have been reached through the usual channels.

A soldier who was stationed at Camp Ritchie, Maryland, hitchhiked to Washington while on a three-day pass. On a rainy Sunday he wandered into New York Avenue Church.

"It was, for me, a period of particular spiritual darkness," the soldier said later. "That Sunday morning God wakened me through Peter Marshall. . . . There was in him a serenity and Christian charm that gripped me and strangely blessed me. . . . He was a man of men. . . .

"I thanked Dr. Marshall after the service. He invited me to come to see him in his study the next day, and I did. It ended up by my going home with him to spend the night. We rifled the icebox and talked earnestly into the early morning hours."

This boy later decided to enter the ministry. "That decision," he said later, "dated back to the terrific spiritual impact Peter Marshall had on me that never-to-be-forgotten night. . . ."

There were many teen-agers to whom Peter Marshall was a real hero. I know of three of them, and undoubtedly there were many more, who had framed pictures of him hanging over their beds. Peter was perfectly aware of the fact that such hero worship carries a great responsibility to God with it. The temptation to the minister, however subtle or strong, is to accept adulation for himself. Often, when men, as well as women of all ages, were personally attracted to Peter, he would say, "The only reason they feel that way about me is because they have a deep hunger for God, but Christ, as a Person, is still not real to them. Now, I have to find the way to transfer their admiration from me to Christ."

On one occasion when Peter preached for a minister in another city, the preacher's teen-age daughter was in the congregation. Later, he wrote Peter to tell him what had happened:

. . . . One thing which touched me very personally last night was when I went out of the small room, after saying good-by to you, and found my senior high-school daughter wanting to speak with Mr.

Marshall. I think she wanted to have a more personal word with you, but the crowd prevented it. Her mother said she came of her own choice. As I walked away with her, her head was bowed, tears were in her eyes, and not a word was said. Christ only knows what was there!

For your ministry I am deeply grateful. . . .

Even to those who worked most closely with Peter through the years, and who helped him solve many serious problems—the members of his church staffs—this faculty of being a joyous Christian always seemed one of his outstanding characteristics.

The Reverend James Bryden, director of religious education at New York Avenue, said, "I received so much from Peter that will go on always in my life—his enthusiasms, convictions, and gaiety in meeting life. Even his low moments, when we talked and talked in his upstairs study, gave color and warmth to the rest. . . . There was more joy in Peter's religion than in that of anyone I've ever known. . . ."

Incidents and comments like this prove what Jesus Himself demonstrated to us at times like the wedding feast in Cana—that Christianity can be fun, that fun can be Christian, and that it is the King's joy to share our good times. If our hearts and our motives are pure, the secular becomes sacred, the commonplace is suffused with the eternal.

twelve

THE SECOND YEAR IS THE HARDEST

Whither shall we go up? our brethren have discouraged our heart. . . .

Deuteronomy 1:28

uring our second year at New York Avenue, all was not sweetness and light. Peter was constantly reaching for the soda box in the kitchen cupboard.

The doctor's report said: "There is the suspicion of an ulcer in the stomach or duodenum. . . . An insight into your own nervous make-up and your own tendencies to pressure in your work will help you. . . ."

The pain in the duodenum was merely symptomatic of pain in the mind and heart. A group of people at New York Avenue, including a few of the officers, were intent upon resisting any changes, and Peter felt that the old church would have to change, or eventually die. Their attitude was: We called you to preach, not to turn the church upside down.

For some time, prior to 1938, the church had shown a deficit at the end of each fiscal year. That very first year of Peter's ministry pulled the budget out of the red, and each succeeding year showed a steady increase in receipts, as well as in expansion and expenditures. The $131,050 debt, most of which was for two small pieces of property adjacent to the church, was rapidly dwindling. In five years it was paid in full.

In spite of this happy return to solvency, the trustees had been through such a grim time financially that they were understandably cautious. They liked Peter's preaching. In fact, most of them rarely missed a single Sunday morning service. They were gracious and generous with him personally. He was given steady increases in salary. But they fervently wished the new preacher would keep his fingers out of their province.

They were conservative businessmen, and they wanted to run the business affairs of the church by sight rather than by faith. To each forward step advocated by the session, the policy-making body, the trustees' battle cry was, "But where is the money coming from?" Again and again, there was conflict between the two boards.

Peter, on the other hand, felt that money would be forthcoming for whatever expansion God wanted. During his eight years in the ministry, he had never seen it fail. He lived by the verse, "Seek ye first the kingdom of God, and his righteousness; and all these things shall be added unto you" (Matthew 6:33). And that applied to the church as well as to the individual. He also felt that the improvement in New York Avenue's financial status spoke for itself, and that, by now, these men should trust his leadership more than they did. It was no wonder he haunted the soda box after meetings of the trustees, the session, or the congregation.

In addition to these difficulties, the four women's groups did not always pull together; there was a certain amount of conflict between the older people and the young people, who were now coming into the church in large numbers.

Some of Peter's troubles stemmed from the fact that certain church members just couldn't understand some of their new minister's habits and idiosyncrasies. For example, when Washington's temperature mounted into the nineties, Peter was sometimes seen in a silk polo shirt at the office. He soon found that that just wouldn't do! He might get away with not wearing a clerical collar, but a sports shirt, no!

Then there was the matter of the report buzzing around the church that sometimes when Dr. Marshall went into the church's empty lecture room to pick out hymns for Prayer Meeting, he ended up having a wonderful time banging out unhymnlike melodies such as "Old Soldiers Never Die" or "O You Beautiful Doll."

Peter—for his part—was, at first, slightly bewildered by the pseudo-sophistication which criticism of such trivial matters revealed.

"If there's anything I can't stand," he fumed one day, after receiving a four-page, single-spaced letter full of vindictive advice, "it's being told things in *love*, for my own good!" He hated any unpleasantness, and was inclined to crumple temporarily under such criticism.

One morning Dr. McCartney, then pastor of the Church of the Covenant, telephoned Peter. At this point the young Scot's troubles were piling up. Several persons were currently estranged because the Westminster Plan of Choirs had been instituted to replace the church quartet. Others were disgruntled because the new minister advocated union of the four women's groups. Later that morning the older minister wrote Peter a gracious, helpful note which he always cherished:

> *My dear Brother Peter:*
>
> *I think I caught a note of discouragement in your voice on the phone this morning, and I hasten to buck you up with this word before Sunday.*
>
> *I was just your age when I took on a big job in Chicago. Along in my second year—and second years are testing ones—I chanced to meet a minister friend in an art gallery, and we fell into conversation. He asked me about my work. "Don't get discouraged," he said, "the second year is always the hardest. Stick to it, and in the course of time, you will build up your own following."*
>
> *I also recall a saying of old Dr. Riddle of Western Seminary: "Young gentlemen, when you feel like resigning, don't!"*
>
> *Let's get together soon and have a heart-to-heart talk.*
>
> *Affectionately,*
> *Albert Joseph McCartney*

Peter often felt like resigning. He was not fooled either by flattery or by crowds. So long as there was any dissension within the church family, any lack of Christian love, he was certain his ministry was a failure. "What good does preaching do," he would ask, "if church members can't even like, much less love, each other?" About once every quarter he warned me he was about to resign. In response to my wifely answer that he ought to be ashamed of himself, and that "All discouragement was of the Devil," he would merely sigh and walk away muttering to himself "O for the wings of a dove."

One look at him of an evening as he came in the front door was enough to indicate whether the day had been a difficult one, perhaps with derogatory letters in the mail.

These letters were usually by-products of personality conflicts within the church, or from heresy hunters, or from someone who bitterly resented any criticism of the United States from a "foreigner."

Now with the help of immigrants, like yourself [the printable part of one tirade went] *you cannot stand a small measure of success and are unwilling to remain as meek as you were when you came under the quota. . . . Now, you with your drooling oral slime, tell us Americans how to run the country. You talk rabble rousing with a touch of God thrown in and a bit of flag waving at the end, for applause. We do not need or want your cowardice. Be born again, or move out!*

Said Peter from the pulpit one Sunday morning:

Sometimes we receive biting letters that cut to the quick.
We should promptly search ourselves in the light of these letters and see how we may profit by them.
Then we should just as promptly burn the letters and forget them.

"But," you may ask, "how can we forget the unkind things that are said . . .
the cruel and unfair treatment one has received?
How can we simply forget these things?
It is not as simple as that!"

There is just one sure way.
Never talk about them, and never think about them.
If you want to forget something, never speak even to your dearest friend about it.
When it bobs into your mind, banish it at once.

It will surprise you how quickly you can forget anything by that treatment.

The minister did not, however, always follow his own good advice. Through the years, he kept a few of the worst letters, perhaps thinking they would help to keep him humble.

Peter wanted an efficiently organized church, but even more, he wanted happy Christians and peace within his own church. He suffered—suffered acutely—even when no harsh words had been spoken, if an atmosphere of disunity prevailed. Conversely, like most of us, he rose to his highest self in the midst of harmony and understanding. During the first few years at New York Avenue, this atmosphere of unity was lacking, especially in the Sunday morning services. That was because there were still a few people who were not in sympathy with their new minister or his program. Those few were usually in their places on Sunday morning, rarely of a Sunday night.

"I'm still not at home in my own pulpit," Peter would fume. "I feel hampered and restricted. I just can't be natural. I'm not preaching as well as I do when I'm in other cities."

The same keen spiritual sensitivity that enabled him to sense a congregation's mood and needs, and to lead them in worship to the very feet of the Master, also made him aware of this lack of sympathy every time he mounted the pulpit.

Once he was asked to preach in a church whose minister had resigned during a bitter church controversy. People had been left full of bitterness, with two sharply divided antagonistic factions. Peter reported later that he found it almost impossible to conduct a service there, much less preach. The spiritual temperature, practically at zero, affected Peter like contrary waves on a heavy sea. Getting through the service was like running an obstacle course in worship. Experiences like this revealed to me what a concrete reality the world of the spirit was to Peter.

In vain, those of us close to him pointed out that this rebellious faction at New York Avenue represented only a handful, and that he should forget them and concentrate on the big majority who *were with* him. Somehow, he just could not forget them. One stray sheep, recalcitrant and unhappy, sulking outside the fold, seemed even more important than all the rest. He took Jesus' words literally and seriously:

> Therefore if thou bring thy gift to the altar, and there rememberest that thy brother hath ought against thee; Leave there thy gift before the altar, and go thy way; first be reconciled to thy brother, and then come and offer thy gift (Matthew 5:23, 24).

It must have been situations like this that prompted Peter to pray:

Lord, where we are wrong, make us willing to change,
and where we are right, make us easy to live with. . . .

But there was always the practical question of *how* to be reconciled to the disgruntled ones, when the cause of their unhappiness had been a policy in which Peter had felt led of God, and which he felt was best for the good of the whole church. How much program and organizational efficiency should be sacrificed for church harmony? How far could one conscientiously go with appeasement? Christ had considered the individual all-important, but should the welfare of many church members be jeopardized because of the individual?

Peter tried just about everything in an effort to find God's answer to this dilemma. In the case of the women's work, he decided not to try to push through what he wanted, but to let the women go their own way. He hoped that time and a keener insight into their own needs would eventually bring about a united work. This was an example of the fact that it is one thing to organize a church on paper, and quite another thing to get the organization off paper and into practice. Even in churches, one has to deal with quite lovable, but ordinary human beings—sinners struggling to be saints. On paper the organization looked fine. Off paper, it produced or revealed personal conflicts and animosities. Peter was always envious of Dr. John Rustin of Mt. Vernon Place Methodist Church, who had a great gift for church organization. John had the knack of cultivating in rows and masses. Peter always seemed to be tripping up over the individual.

Once Peter read a critical paper to the three boards which comprised the Church Council, summarizing some of the things about the church's life and work of which he did not approve. Somehow, his approach seemed to contribute to further dissension, rather than to the peace he wanted so much. He decided to do the hard thing and apologize. The soda box figured prominently in the making of that decision. At the next council meeting he said:

The members of the Council who were present at the last meeting will recall that I read a paper. I regret very much having done so. I consulted no one about it. Had I done so, the paper might never have been presented. No one read the paper before the meeting. No one has seen it since. There exists only one copy of it, and that I propose to destroy. I wish now to retract the statements made in the paper, and to delete all references to it that might appear in the minutes of the last meeting. I wish to express to the Council my sincere regrets.

Saying this cost Peter exactly what it costs any of us to say, "I was wrong and I'm sorry; please forgive me." But I'm sure he grew a full inch in Christian stature in the process.

With some not-to-be-reconciled individuals, he went ninety per cent of the way. With one individual, he made overture after overture, effort after effort.

One summer day on Cape Cod, where we spent our summers, he was busy working in the garden, snipping dead blossoms off the rambler roses and retying them to the little white picket fence. I went into the yard to call him to lunch. Obviously, he was deep in thought as he tugged at an especially stubborn and thorny branch. His voice was wistful.

"Catherine, I've been thinking about————. I believe God's telling me to try once more. I think I'll try to compose a letter this afternoon and get it off right away."

But he got busy with other things, and the letter was not written that day. The next morning, he slipped out of the bedroom very early and, when the rest of us got up, was sitting at the maple table in the living-room bay window, typing. Since he was anything but an early riser, I was curious to know what had gotten him up at such an unprecedented hour.

"Funny thing, Catherine," he greeted me, "I wakened up suddenly, thinking I heard church bells. They were loud and clear. I got so wide awake there was no chance of going back to sleep. I think it was God's way of waking me up and telling me to get that letter off without any more stalling."

The letter he wrote was so full of tenderness and the love of God that one would think no mere human being could have resisted it. It did not, however, bring the immediate reconciliation for which he hoped. Even so, it may well have been God's prompting, and it may have helped, because years later he had the joy of seeing the person to whom it was addressed climb the narrow winding stairs to his study and shake his hand. That was one of the happiest moments of his ministry.

Once, probably because he had been ill for a few days, Peter neglected to send a message of sympathy to a good friend in the church whose mother had died. Soon afterward, at the close of a church meeting, the friend cornered Peter and administered a prolonged verbal spanking. When, finally, we climbed into the car and started home, Peter was obviously in a blue funk. I could see that he was mentally kicking himself around blocks and blocks because of his lapse.

"Oh me!" he mourned. "When will I ever learn? Catherine, I just stumble from blunder to blunder!"

Any preacher who had such depth of convictions and preached those convictions as fearlessly as did Peter was destined to tread on a few toes. He recognized this, as he related in the sermon he called "The Perils of Preaching," but he suffered under it nonetheless.

The same zealous young man who in Atlanta had incurred the wrath of the debutantes, the League of Women Voters, even some of the local politicians, by openly flaying laxity and whitewashing in the police department, did not hesitate to speak out against certain evils that he saw in the nation's capital. He preached the Gospel, and he preached it straight, but he believed that Christianity had to produce fruit in everyday life, and that where it did not, the pulpit was cowardly to hold its peace.

Commented Dr. Cranford, our good friend, and pastor of Washington's Calvary Baptist Church: "There was in Peter the rare combination of poet and prophet. His sermons were poetic prose. His phrases were arresting. His word pictures were unforgettably vivid. When he spoke, men listened. Yet there was something of the Amos in him, crying out against the sins of a pagan world. . . ."

It was the Amos in Peter that sometimes got him into trouble. Folks enjoy hearing poetic prose; they don't relish hearing about their sins. Many times he was painfully specific, such as the night he criticized an official of the fire department who was reported as directing fire-fighting while intoxicated. There was the matter of the District slums against which he spoke:

> The fact that many of these slum dwellings are owned by church people and that they are making money off them does not make the church feel any better.

This we do know ...
We have no doubt as to the wickedness of that sort of thing.
We have no doubt as to what Christ thinks of it.
What is the church—and that's you and me—going to do about it?

On many a Sunday he lashed out against the rising consumption of alcoholic beverages in Washington during wartime:

The city of Washington has but one reason for being.
It is exclusively devoted to the business of governing the nation.
If clear heads are needed anywhere on earth, it is here—

Yet, it is shocking to discover that the per capita consumption of alcohol in the District of Columbia is more than twice that in the next wettest state in the union—
And the consumption figures are still rising.

The war can be lost just as easily in the cocktail bars of the nation's capital as in the waters of the South Pacific
    or the factories of Detroit.

What are our men fighting for anyway?
Are they fighting so that the brewers and distillers may stay in business?
    so that business may go on as usual ...
    so that official Washington may attend its cocktails parties and have a good time?

Morale is very important.
But it is a matter of soul and conscience.
One thing we do know—
    The morale that comes out of a bottle is not the morale to put into a battle.

Peter grimaced the next morning when he saw his picture in the morning papers under headlines that read: PASTOR ASSAILS "STRATEGY" OF DRINKING WAY TO VICTORY. He strenuously objected to these condensations of sermons, because almost always the reporters were content with quoting a few sensational sentences. Lifted thus out of their context, with no effort made to give the real point of the sermon, they left quite a wrong impression. Often he clashed with reporters over this point. As he came increasingly into the public eye, the whole matter of the press became difficult. Far from seeking publicity, he dodged it however and whenever possible.

The Washington press had a field day with him over the much-publicized case of *Esquire* versus the Post Office Department. The issue was the sending of obscene matter through United States mails. Dr. Marshall was called as a witness for the post office. Reporters played up the story. Headlines in the *Washington Evening Star* for November 4, 1943, said:

PURITY OF WOMANHOOD BECOMES INVOLVED IN ESQUIRE HEARINGS.

Part of the testimony was printed. In cross-examining Peter, Mr. Bromley, *Esquire's* counsel, asked:

"You deplore the trend of modern times as detrimental to our morals, don't you?"

"Yes," Dr. Marshall replied.

"You have advocated that women return to the standards of purity of 1900, have you not?"

DR. MARSHALL: "Did I specify a year? I don't remember specifying a year. I don't know what standards prevailed in 1900. I wasn't born then."

"Will you please answer the question asked you?"

"I can't say I see what the question asked has to do with the matter at hand."

MR. BROMLEY, sternly: "Answer the question, please."

"Well," Dr. Marshall said, "I believe that womanhood has been definitely lowered by equality with men. For nineteen centuries woman was revered and respected and on a higher plane than man. To achieve equality, she had to step down from that high plane and take over men's vices."

MR. BROMLEY: "Father Flanagan, of Boys Town, George Jean Nathan, drama critic, the late William Lyon Phelps have all been regular contributors to *Esquire*. Do you really think they would have been associated with the magazine, if *Esquire* carried 'obscene' matter, as the Post Office charges? *Do you?*"

DR. MARSHALL: "The act that these men were contributors may have been an error in judgment on their part. . . ."

When Peter saw all this in the paper, he put his head in his hands and assumed a cocker-spaniel look of complete dejection.

"Catherine," he groaned. "I made a fool of myself. *Why* do I have to suffer so . . . !" But there was the hint of a twinkle in his eyes.

He dreaded the next Friday when he would lunch, as usual, with a group of minister friends. Nothing that any one of them said or did ever escaped the others. That Friday, as they ate lunch at the Annapolis Hotel, Peter got the ribbing of his life.

The "gang" was made up of five ministers, from a variety of denominations, each pastor of one of Washington's large downtown churches. Dr. Anderson, of First Congregational, was a sort of ecclesiastical Bob Hope to the group. It was impossible to be overly serious when Howard was around, and any ministerial stuffiness was immediately punctured. There was Dr. John Rustin, nicknamed by the group "pack-'em-in-Rustin," because John always dealt in large numbers. There was Oscar (Dr. Blackwelder), of the Lutheran Church of the Reformation, whom they called "Sun-crowned Oscar" because of a favorite sermon he preached called "Sun-crowned Men"; and "Cranny"—Dr. Clarence W. Cranford—of Calvary Baptist. Dr. Edward Pruden, of First Baptist, later President Truman's pastor, was another charter member. Ed, they called "Peace-at-any-price-Pruden," and Ed grinned and bore it. Peter was known as "Twittering-birds Marshall" because of the poetic imagery for which his sermons were famous.

The fellowship between these men was rare and wonderful. They had all come to Washington at about the same time. There was complete frankness, much letting down of the hair, and much levity. But underneath all the fun, they had the greatest respect and affection for one another and the prodigious job that each man was doing. There was deep and lasting bonds between them. To this day, each man cherishes the memories of their group friendship as one of the richest and most unforgettable experiences of his life.

One day John Rustin was complaining about his troubles with Methodists. As he talked, Peter was relieved to hear that Presbyterians didn't have a monopoly on unredeemed human nature.

"You mean," he asked teasingly, "that over there at Mt. Vernon, some of your people have fallen from grace?"

John vigorously cut his chicken, as if he were dismembering a few stewards.

"Peter," he said, "we've got more backsliders over there than a dog has fleas."

Peter stirred his tea. "That's a good term, John—'backsliding.' You Methodists preach a lot about that. The Presbyterians never mention it. They just go ahead and do it!"

Howard could not bear to be left out of the conversation for long.

"Have you heard this bit of doggerel? One of my trustees who happens to have a sense of humor told it to me the other day:

> Tell my trustees when I am dead,
> > That they should shed no tears,
> For I shall be no deader then
> > Than they have been for years."

One year, on April 1st, a union service was to be held at noon in the First Congregational Church. Several of the ministers had parts in the service; Peter had been delegated to preach. At five minutes to twelve, while the men waited in Dr. Anderson's study, a Western Union messenger knocked on the door and delivered a telegram to Peter. He read it, and his mouth dropped open.

"Is anything the matter?" asked Cranny.

Peter sat there, turning the yellow sheet over and over, as if hunting for some clue. Then he handed it to Dr. Cranford. "Read it. Read it out loud, so the others can hear."

Cranny started laughing. The telegram said:

ALL IS DISCOVERED FLEE

A FRIEND

The "gang" promptly accused Howard of being the culprit, but he vigorously denied it. The identity of the April-fool prankster was never discovered.

Stories about Dr. Anderson could be multiplied *ad infinitum*. He was irrepressible. One day he was presiding at an interdenominational ministers' meeting held in the Cleveland Park Congregational Church. Dr. Anderson was in the midst of delivering a quite serious talk. Peter came in late, and finding the church well filled, was forced to take a seat in the front row. Just as he got seated—unobtrusively, he hoped—Howard interrupted himself suddenly, leaned far over the pulpit, and stared at Peter. There was a long, awkward silence broken by Howard's saying in a resounding voice, "And who is this sinner come to justice?" The laughter that followed almost broke up the meeting.

Eight years later, at the service commemorating our tenth anniversary at New York Avenue, each member of this group of ministers was asked to have a part in the celebration. Across the front of the sanctuary all our officers sat very straight, in rows, prepared to pay us tribute in a dignified and serious manner. But they reckoned without the spirited leadership of the "gang."

Dr. Anderson was out of the city, but sent a telegram that was read from the pulpit:

PLEASE CONVEY MY CONGRATULATIONS TO CHURCH AND PASTOR AS PETER MARSHALL COMPLETES 10 YEARS OF LUMINOUS LEADERSHIP PROPHETIC PREACHING AND PERIPATETIC PASTORAL WORK AT NEW YORK AVENUE HE HAS THE LANGUAGE TO GILD THE LILY AND PIN RUFFLES ON THE STARS WHEN HE SPEAKS HEAVEN AND EARTH HUSH THEIR CLAMOR AND LISTEN HE IS A FUGITIVE FROM THE CONGREGATIONAL FOLD AND DAILY I PRAY THAT THE RASCAL WHOM I LOVE LIKE A PRODIGAL BROTHER SHALL RETURN TO THE TRUE FAITH HE IS DOING A GREAT WORK

HOWARD STONE ANDERSON

The confusions and difficulties of our early years in Washington were clearly reflected in the congregational meetings at New York Avenue. Peter always dreaded those meetings; there was always the outside chance of real clashes.

Presbyterianism, of course, is truly and basically democratic. Despite the careful plans laid for conducting congregational meetings, that unpredictable element, the democratic procedure, could and usually did throw a monkey wrench into the works. There was no question about these meetings being democratic.

There was the meeting, for example, when the matter of the use of the parking lot owned by the church was brought to our attention. One of the women present got to her feet, and was promptly recognized by the chairman.

"I move," she said, "that we do something to prevent those sight-seeing buses right behind the church from using our property as their headquarters for taking people to the race track. After all, we're responsible for that property. I've even heard spielers shouting their sales talk for the race-track buses while the Sunday morning crowds were coming into the church."

There was a general murmur of approval.

A lawyer promptly objected. "I sympathize with the motion. But unfortunately the bus company's contract is perfectly legal. If the church puts them off the property, we could be sued for breach of contract."

"But," interrupted the lady, "it's a disgrace. We've simply *got* to do something about it—and immediately."

There followed a series of amendments. Then several amendments to the amendments.

Several motions later, the chairman asked, "Would the persons who made and seconded the second amendment care to withdraw it?"

Dead silence.

"Would those who made and seconded the original motion care to withdraw it, so that we can start over?" he persisted.

They *would not*—and didn't.

Soon five top-ranking government lawyers and several judges were involved in a heated debate, trying to straighten out the morass of parliamentary procedure.

The mess was even too much for Judge Sam Whitaker of the United States Court of Claims, who had had a lifetime of experience in complicated court procedure.

At this lucid moment, another woman got to her feet. She had in mind someone she wanted to nominate for the Board of Deacons, but couldn't quite recall his name.

"I want to nominate Mr.————uh . . . uh, oh dear, I can't think of his name. You know . . . his wife is in the Missionary Society.

He works for the government and drives a gray Buick. He has sort of straight gray hair and a little boy in the Junior Department. . . . You know who I mean. . . ."

But nobody did.

The chairman, thoroughly baffled, said gently, "I don't think the congregation can have any clear idea how to vote, when not even the sponsor is sure of the nominee's name. . . . "

During all of this, Peter sat on the front pew, with that cocker-spaniel look on his face, sinking lower and lower into his seat.

One young couple, the Folgers, who left Washington for Indianapolis, wrote back saying that they were positively nostalgic, remembering those congregational meetings. In other churches, such meetings were stodgy by comparison.

Eventually, of course, that unbeatable combination of specific prayer, patient work, love, and time won the battle. Most of the tensions in New York Avenue and in Peter disappeared. No longer did he reach for the soda box. There came the time when even Washington cab drivers referred to the old church on the triangle as "Peter Marshall's church."

But Peter never forgot this second year—this period of "trouble in the duodenum." Years later he broke all precedent for prayer in the United States Senate by praying:

. . . . Help us to do our very best this day and be content with today's troubles, so that we shall not borrow the troubles of tomorrow. Save us from the sin of worrying, lest stomach ulcers be the badge of our lack of faith. AMEN.

He was speaking from experience!

thirteen

Man wi' His Laddie

For I was my father's son, tender and only beloved. . . .
                                                    Proverbs 4:3

It was a warm Sunday afternoon in May. The Marshall family was enjoying a bit of relaxation after a strenuous Sunday morning. My husband, whose shirt was always wet and wilted after preaching, had put on a silk polo shirt. His carefully polished black shoes were parked beside his easy chair. The ministerial feet were luxuriously encased in tartan bedroom slippers. Our small son's toys, together with the Sunday papers, were strewn from one end of the living room to the other.

I had just finished saying, "Look at this room! You'd think a cyclone had hit it. Wouldn't it be *awful* if we had callers?"—when, out of the corner of my eye, I saw two people coming up the front walk. I took one look and moaned. It was the Secretary of War and Mrs. Stimson!

There was no time to do any tidying-up. Our distinguished guests were even then on the porch, about to ring the bell.

The Stimsons entered, sat down unconcernedly in the midst of the litter, and visited with us like the next-door neighbors they were. They talked with Peter about their many trips to Scotland, played with our child, and appeared to enjoy themselves thoroughly.

Our small, blond son was already an old friend of the Secretary of War. One day, Mr. Stimson had sent word by his Scottish overseer, Kenneth Gray, that Peter John was to play in the sandbox anytime he wished. The sandbox, in a shady wooded spot on the rolling acres at the back of the house, had been placed there for occasional visits of children of Stimson's friends. The stables, the curving driveways, the ancient elms and magnolia trees made a delightful place for children to play. "Woodley," one of Washington's historic mansions, had been built in 1806 by Philip Barton Key, a Georgetown lawyer, the uncle of the famous Francis Scott Key. Four Presidents had used the mansion as a summer home. Colonel House had lived there during the Wilson administration.

Mr. Stimson was in the habit of taking a daily constitutional around the grounds of the estate. On many a day he would encounter our son riding his tricycle or building a sand castle. Invariably, the tall erect man, with his trim mustache and his graying hair, would pause for a few minutes of grave conversation with the little boy.

One day, I remember, the topic of conversation was Capital Transit buses. "Is that a bus you're playing with, Peter?" the Secretary of War inquired.

"Yes. . . . My daddy gave it to me. See, it has a driver too."

"Looks like a Washington bus to me. Is it packed to the doors with people, as all the buses are these days?"

Peter rescued the shoulder strap of his sunsuit which had slipped off, and brushed a damp curl out of his eyes. "It has *lots* of peoples in it. They're holding on to straps."

"Yes, and they simply *will not* move to the rear." Mr. Stimson chuckled.

Listening in on this amusing conversation it was obvious that neither Peter nor Secretary Stimson had more than a nodding acquaintance with public transportation. The Capital Transit buses didn't even *have* straps.

This kind of informal contact with famous Washingtonians is, of course, typical of the life to which many a Washington child is born.

Peter John Marshall, or "Wee" Peter as his father loved to call him, had arrived at 8:53 on a snowy January morning in 1940. His arrival had interrupted a sermon. Thereafter, he managed to inject himself into many a sermon.

On the Saturday night before his birth, my mother had arrived to take over the household during my stay in the hospital. Later some friends had dropped in for an evening of game playing. There were

Ruby and Willard Daughtry, Dr. Marshall's secretary and her husband who had come to Washington soon after we had, and Charles and Mildred Beaschler, our minister of music and his wife. This sort of impromptu fun in his own home with a few close friends made the kind of evening that Peter enjoyed most, and that seemed to refresh him best in preparation for his heavy Sunday schedule. He always tried to reserve Saturday nights for some kind of relaxation.

During the evening my physician telephoned me, and seemed quite surprised to hear what sounded like a party going on in the background. "You're sure to have to come to the hospital soon. Why not come on down now, so that you will not have to get up in the middle of the night?"

But I assured him that I felt fine and was certain that going to the hospital now would be premature. Our friends left about eleven o'clock.

Part of our regular Saturday night schedule was for Peter to read his Sunday morning sermon aloud to me. He was always apologetic about this, thinking that it would surely spoil the sermon for me on Sunday. Somehow it never did. On this particular night he read the sermon the last thing before turning in—or so we thought.

In the very middle of it, strange things began happening to me. Remembering the doctor's briefing, I watched the clock on the night stand and counted the intervals between pains, while listening, with half a mind, to the sermon.

Suddenly, the situation seemed urgent. "I'm sorry, Peter, to have to interrupt you. I hate to do this to you on a Saturday night, but you'd better get me to the hospital right away." The reading of the sermon was never finished.

At eight o'clock the next morning, the doctor telephoned Peter, "I suggest that you come to the hospital immediately, if you want to be here when the baby is born."

At nine o'clock at the hospital the doctor said, "Congratulations, Dr. Marshall. It's a boy—a fine son."

Mother was watching Peter's face. A look of amazement and incredulity, then undisguised delight crossed his face. "A boy? We have a *son*. . . . How wonderful!"

It was typical of Peter, however, that he went on down to the church, taught the Young People's Class, and even went through the eleven o'clock service, without telling a single soul his big news. Several people commented on the fact that he looked very tired, almost as if he had been up all night, as indeed he had. It was not until one of the women in the church came up to him at the close of the service and inquired about me, that finally he broke his self-imposed silence. He had simply been afraid that if he told the news to a single person before the service, he would get too excited to preach.

The entire congregation enjoyed this event, and considered Peter John their baby, too. "Re-Pete" was immediately voted in as Mascot of Choirs, was officially enrolled in the Cradle Roll of the Sunday School, and was flooded with such a supply of silver spoons, bootees, sacques, blankets, and carriage robes as few babies ever have.

"The flowers in the sanctuary," said the church bulletin, "are presented by friends of Dr. and Mrs. Marshall, who shared their joy over the birth of their son, a week ago today."

Even Dodson, our incomparable Negro janitor, came through with a laboriously composed "poem" which he dedicated to the baby and sent to the hospital. It was written as if the baby were speaking:

Two weeks old, and not a bit cold,
They are going to keep me, so I'm told.

I am rolling with lots of fat.
I think I will stay here just for that.
Signed, Dodson

As our small son followed Dodson's advice and "stayed here," he made many a change in our lives. "I knew a baby would change things," commented Peter one day. "After all, babies insist on being old-fashioned."

Peter adored his old-fashioned son. He could handle him skillfully. Yet he was not one of those fathers who mixed the formula or bathed the baby. Peter considered such things my province.

I turned out to be one of those disgustingly conscientious modern mothers who sterilizes every article in sight, boiling everything but the baby. After Peter John's advent, not only were the days of easy housework gone, but also all easygoing vacation trips. I thought that this lone child had to have a ton of equipment even for a brief holiday. It always took us at least three hours of hard work to load the car for any trip.

First came innumerable suitcases, then a collapsible baby buggy, a folding play pen, a bathinette, a baby seat for the car, and a sterilizer for bottles. At first quite patient, Peter would grow more and more exasperated as I continued to trot out load after load. "Catherine, where in th' thunder do you think I'm going to put all this stuff? One baby couldn't possibly use *all that*. This car is *not* a truck." But he would roll up his sleeves, shove and heave, carry and figure and shift, with beads of perspiration standing out on his forehead, until finally, somehow, everything was in the car.

Peter always had a box of books he hoped to read, a bulging briefcase filled with work he had not been able to finish, and a big stack of games neatly tied together. A holiday would be a poor thing indeed without a great deal of game playing!

Finally, I would come out, with a toidy-seat in a laundry bag flung over one shoulder, a Sterno stove with cans of baby food—assorted spinach, peas, and prunes—in one hand, juggling with the other Peter John Marshall himself. Then wedged in between boxes, bundles, and suitcases, Peter would drive off, muttering that he really did not think a few days away from the office was worth all this, and that this car might not be a truck, but it surely drove like one today. The trunk of the car would be so loaded it was scarcely off the ground. By the time we reached the outskirts of town, I had already begun to wonder whether I had remembered to leave a note for the milkman, to stop the evening paper, and to put down the bedroom windows.

Inevitably our child reached that painful period every to-be-civilized child reaches, when he had to be "trained." The parents get training of a different sort—in patience.

I had read too many books on child care and sanitation; I was germ-conscious. Hence the aforementioned laundry bag also contained a bottle of Lysol solution and clean rags. Wherever we were going for a holiday, our path across the United States was marked by a string of filling-station rest rooms which I had sanitized for the benefit of our baby.

A MAN CALLED PETER

Peter, a man of about average patience, had to learn to wait and wait—and wait. He would stand outside, chaperoning the car, always hopeful that surely the baby and I couldn't take *much* longer. He hoped that I would emerge from the mysterious depths of the ladies' room with the gleam of triumph in my eyes. If the gleam were missing, he knew we would have to stop at another filling station thirty miles down the road. Those poor creatures who have not gone through this period with a child really have no chance to learn patience.

Our baby also made a change of another kind in Peter. From the beginning of our marriage, he had been extremely reticent about mentioning his wife or home life from the pulpit. That, he felt, would be parading his family, and he had no right to impose his personal life on his congregation. His shyness about this made him carry it to scarcely credible extremes.

In January 1937, at the time my church membership was transferred from the Keyser Presbyterian Church to Westminster, I wrote home:

> My church letter was presented to the elders just before the morning service on Sunday. Two other people were also received. Peter preferred not to call out my name to the whole congregation, so he didn't.

There was more to this simple statement than met the eye. Peter had never before received anyone into the church without receiving him publicly, but his wife—that was different.

By the time my membership was transferred to New York Avenue, he had gotten over a little of this shyness. He did call out my name and ask me to stand for a moment. Even so, it was still something of an occasion when he mentioned his family publicly. There were people who came to hear him regularly who actually did not know that he was married.

It took Peter John to challenge this reticence. After all, babies tell us much about God. The business of being a parent is really a series of object lessons in how God deals with His children.

Babies, therefore, are an irresistible source of good sermon illustrations. One day Peter slipped up, and Peter John crept into a sermon. The delighted response expressed by the congregation was a

174

revelation to the minister. As the fact that people liked and profited from personal illustrations was proved to Peter, the congregation at New York Avenue began to get many intimate backstage glimpses of life in the Manse.

In an evening sermon (always more informal than the morning ones), Peter was once trying to describe the color of the beach-plum jelly made on Cape Cod. He had a spur-of-the-moment inspiration. "It's a lovely cranberry shade," he explained, "you know, sort of a spanked-baby pink!" Peter, the bachelor, would never have thought of that description.

In a Christmas sermon, "Stars in Their Eyes," Peter suggested that to very young children the most commonplace things are as fresh and interesting "as the first tiny green leaves on a birch tree in April." He had only to observe our son to make that specific:

The child wakes each morning with anticipation of a day to be filled with exploration and adventure. He lives in the same world with adults; he sees the same things, but he sees them through different eyes.

He chuckles because the sash of his bathrobe trails behind him down the stairs, quite like a train! He laughs with glee at the fireworks of a thunderstorm and says the lightning looks like string beans dancing. He is delighted because a squirrel dares to stick his nose right against the windowpane; and the snow which has fallen unexpectedly during the night, has put a funny little white cap on each fence post and even on the fireplug.

The typical Scotsman, no matter how stern his Calvinistic background, can never be a completely dour individual. The same Scotland that produced John Knox also produced Robert Burns and Robert Louis Stevenson. In Scotland's true sons, rigor and realism are always colored by poetry and humor. Peter was no exception to this. Actually, the type of illustration which he used most tellingly was, in essence, the whimsical humor of the heart of the child, suggestive of much of Stevenson's poetry.

Peter could never remember jokes—except one. That one was his favorite story of all stories. He included it in a lighthearted talk, addressed to young people, called "The Sermon of the Water Beetle":

The tragic loss of a sense of awe is illustrated in what I regard as a delightful story.

A little boy in Aberdeen, Scotland, was disciplined by his mother, who used to say to him when he was naughty, "Now God won't like that." And when he was particularly unruly or disobedient, she would say, "God will be angry."

Usually these admonitions were sufficient, but one night when she had prunes for his dessert at supper, he rebelled.

He refused to finish the prunes in his plate.

She pled.

She coaxed.

Finally, she said, "Now God won't like this.

God doesn't like little boys to refuse to finish all their prunes."

But the little fellow was quite unmoved.

She went further to say, "God will be angry."

But for some reason or other, the little boy stubbornly refused to take the last two prunes which lay in his plate—dark blue, wrinkled tokens of his rebellion.

"Well," said his mother, "you must now go to bed.

You have been a very naughty boy, and God is angry."

So she packed him upstairs and put him to bed.

No sooner had she come down, than a violent thunderstorm broke out.

The lightning was more vivid than usual.

The thunder clumped up and down the sky with shattering reverberations.

The suddenly angry wind threw handfuls of rain against the windows.

It was a most violent storm, and she thought her little son would be terrified, and that she should go up and comfort him.

Quietly she opened his bedroom door, expecting to find him whimpering in fear, perhaps with the covers pulled over his head.

But to her surprise, he was not in bed at all, but had gone over to the window.

With his face pressed against the windowpane, she heard him mutter,
"My, my, sic a fuss to mak' ower twa prunes."

If Peter wanted to preach about the almost universal sin of covetousness, Peter John provided a good illustration.

We have all been infected with the virus of covetousness.
Even our children are not immune to it.
As soon as they are able to read, they begin to scan the catalogs and make a list of the things they want.

Our little boy, for example, pores over the Lionel catalogs and has neatly typed up a list of the stuff he wants—hundreds of dollars' worth of electric-train equipment.
It begins early, and it tarries late.

Did Peter want to show how needless and futile the sin of worry is? That very week his son had demonstrated it. Having advanced from kindergarten to the first grade, Peter John was stunned to discover that something new had been added. The first grade was no longer all play. He was expected to learn to read and write.

He questioned us sharply about this none-too-welcome change.

"You might as well get used to it, Peter," his father said bluntly; "you'll have to go to school for a long time—eleven years, then four more years of college, and maybe more."

Peter looked crushed, and went away disconsolate. It took him several weeks to get used to this new and awful revelation. He would be sitting on the floor playing with his wooden trains and blocks, apparently quite content, when suddenly his lower lip would begin to tremble, and tears would overflow.

"Peter, what on earth is the matter?" we would question.

Between sobs he would say, "I'm worryin' about when I'll have to go to college. . . ."

The next time you start fretting about something, rather than trusting God to take care of it, remember that an all-wise God knows your worrying to be just as futile—just as silly—as our six-year-old worrying about when he will go to college. . . .

Our child was not always an angel. Ministers' children never are. People would be disappointed if such children did not kick over the confining traces now and then.

There was the Sunday morning an over-demonstrative lady at the church persisted in ohing and ahing and hugging our small son. Finally he could stand it no longer. He looked her straight in the eye and blurted out with embarrassing frankness, "I'm tired of spoke to people."

Most congregations feel that such episodes merely confirm their worst suspicions about preachers' children. I should know; I was one myself.

Undoubtedly I was worse than most—far worse than Peter John ever was. My exploits were well known in the little town of Canton, Mississippi, where we lived until I was nine years old.

Peter John merits no wild tales, though he hurled his share of balls through the neighbors' windows, and he did go through a stage of fire building. His passion for setting occasional fires in odd places reached a climax when Peter and a playmate laid one under the front porch of the Manse right by the oil tank. Fortunately, the attempted fire didn't get going.

Peter often unconsciously mimicked his father in typical preacher's-child fashion. "Excuse me," he would say, rising abruptly from the lunch table. "My friend Kathleen and I have to conduct a service." Or, "Mommy, I'm in an awfu' rush. I have a wedding ceremony."

Our son's particular interests were clearly revealed by the pictures on his bedroom walls. There was a picture of Jesus, a picture of his father, a picture of the Capitol Limited, and a picture of the Lone Ranger.

Whenever Peter John did do anything naughty, and corporal punishment was necessary, his father usually administered it.

One day when Wee Peter was about four, he initiated a one-man revolution against cod-liver oil. "I will *not* take it," he announced, shutting his mouth, stamping his foot, and fleeing to the yard.

His father heard the ultimatum. "I'll take over, Catherine," he said, appearing in the doorway.

I watched out the window to see how the man of the house would handle this one.

Our obstreperous son was standing by the hedge at the side of the house looking pleased with himself. Peter walked up to him and took him by the hand. There was not a trace of anger in him. "Peter, you're just a *glaikit lump*," he said very quietly. "You're coming into the house with me."

A door shut downstairs. There was a period of dead silence. Then the resounding smack of a firm hand making contact with a little boy's seat. Then violent crying. The door opened—father and son emerged, still hand in hand. Wee Peter never again refused cod-liver oil.

In spite of such times, if anyone had listened in on dinner-table conversations at the Manse, they would not have noticed our son standing in any awe of his father.

Peter wanted all meals to be jolly, entertaining family sessions. He contributed more than his share toward making them so. He liked to relate interesting anecdotes from the day's experience, if he could do so without betraying any confidences. Another favorite mealtime pastime was playing a game of nonsense conversation with our son.

In a sense, Peter John had really started this. Almost from his first word, we discovered in our son a mind of his own. He had his own way of expressing himself.

One humid summer day, when he was about three, I was complaining about the heat.

"Mercy—I'm hot," I sighed.

"Sepawate yo'self, and you be cooler," advised Wee Peter.

Even our son's first words were his own. We tried to teach him to say "mummy" and "daddy," but he refused to parrot us. His first words were "snookum-dookum," and "dockum-budgums." We were never quite sure what they meant; the two words had become a family tradition nonetheless. The nonsense game merely went on from that point. On any given night, it might go like this:

"Peter, now I've talked about my day at the office. What happened to you today?"

"Oh, nothin' much."

"Well, tell me, did the radiator get fixed, so that ballawags could get warmed up with the fuminas, when it bit the elephant?"

A broad grin appeared on our little boy's freckled face. He knew that his father had not suddenly gone crazy, but that this was an invitation to play their favorite game.

Young Peter laid down his fork, and against all rules, planted his elbows firmly on the table, as if getting ready for action. He knew he could carry his half of this game.

179

"No, Daddy, but the rug scooted under the budgums, and the scheezechs ran into the big fat man."

"Oh, really!"

"Yes, that was the big red fire truck that run over the booky, and the boy went running down the street yelling 'blankybats.'"

His father made an elaborate pretense of drawing back in horror. "Peter, that just can't be! Why would a little boy yell 'blankybats'? It's a good job you didn't yell such a silly thing. Do you mean to tell me that the pretzel, the marzipan, the football, and the apple dumpling didn't try to stop the radiator when it sizzled the big fat man smack in the dockum-budgums?"

"No, Daddy, it was in the snookum-dookums he got sizzled," corrected Peter, "and it didn't stop the radiator."

"Look, boys," I dared to interpose, "I want to know just one thing. Why does a certain radiator always feature so largely in these conversations?"

"Because," the man at the table explained with mock solemnity, "that's Peter's favorite radiator. And besides, radiators go well with dockum-budgums."

"No, with snookum-dookums," a small voice insisted. So it would go, getting more and more hilarious.

Often we would hear muffled giggles coming from the kitchen, where the Negro maid had an ear close to the door, listening to every word.

It was nothing unusual for Peter to lay down his napkin between courses, stroll over to the piano, and play and sing a Scottish ditty. This might be "The Laird o' Cockpen," or "Hail Caledonia," ending with an American football song. Peter never had a piano lesson in his life, but he could pick out any tune by ear. The only trouble was that the accompanying bass was not so good. We noticed that he had a way of playing on the *black* keys.

There was only one shadow on the happy times we had together. There were not enough of them. I was often troubled, and Peter was often conscience-stricken that he could not find a way to spend more time with our son.

In the Zimmerman lectures, which he gave to budding theologs at the Gettysburg Theological Seminary, Peter spoke of this:

In your zeal for your parish work and your willingness to be of service to all that need you, do not neglect your own family.
They need you, too!

Remember when you marry, you are a husband and a father, as well as a pastor.

I shall not soon forget the indictment I heard in our little boy's prayer one night.
"Thank you, God," he prayed, "that You let my daddy stay home this one evening!"

fourteen

OD STILL ANSWERS PRAYER

"... then I will restore her ... and make the dale of Trouble a door of hope."

Hosea 2:15 (Moffatt's translation)[1]

The March meeting of the Washington City Presbyterial was in progress in the basement lecture room of our church. I sat near the windows looking out on New York Avenue's heavy, rumbling traffic, waiting for the talk I was to make. The room, with its deep-silled windows, slim columns, and little altar at the front hung with maroon velvet draperies, was almost filled with women representing sister Presbyterian churches in the Washington area. The Presbyterial president was intent upon obtaining a series of quick votes on business details.

The early spring sun, streaming in on my back, was pleasantly warm, and I felt drowsy. But suddenly, there was a different sensation. The bottom seemed to be dropping out of everything. Though I had never fainted in my life, I knew only too well what this strange sensation of all blood suddenly leaving my head must mean. Taking deep draughts of air, I began praying inwardly, desperately, "Lord, You know I have to make this talk. I'll never get through it without Your help. Please, just keep me from keeling over."

In a few minutes the dizziness cleared. Somehow I got through the talk. I have no idea what I said. From that morning, I knew that I was a sick woman.

At the completion of three days of examinations and laboratory tests in Baltimore, my doctor was ready to give me his verdict. He toyed with reports on his desk, twisted his pen in his long slim fingers, and cleared his throat, feeling for words. His voice was gentle, as if he were speaking to a child. "Nine months ago, as you know, your examinations revealed several indications of some kind of a chronic infection. We were not quite sure, at that time, what it was. There was an increase in the white blood count, and X rays of your chest showed some markings radiating out from the hilus, though the lobes were clear." He paused and looked at me, again feeling for words.

"New pictures now show definite intrapulmonary markings and heavy linear shadows radiating out into both lungs. There are evidences of a light, soft spotting over both lungs. You are probably running some temperature in the afternoons. We recommend a period of absolute rest, perhaps in a sanatorium. You should not have the temptation to do any housework, or in fact, work of any kind."

In spite of the diagnostician's studied effort to soften the blow he was forced to give me, I felt my heart pounding, and the walls of the room and the doctor's voice seemed to be receding. Tuberculosis! It had always seemed to me the most loathsome of all diseases. I could not even bear to speak the despised word.

"Is . . . is there danger of giving the germs to my husband and child?" I stammered. I could think of nothing but germs.

The doctor smiled, trying to force a little levity. "I don't think you are a very dangerous woman. We were unable to locate the bacilli. However, your doctor in Washington will undoubtedly want to try again."

"How long do you think it will take me to get well?"

He hesitated a long moment. "Oh—possibly three or four months." Then seeing my stricken face, "Mrs. Marshall, don't feel so badly about it. People *do* recover from tuberculosis. There are worse diseases, you know—much, much worse."

On the train going back to Washington, a very talkative woman shared my seat. Perhaps it was just as well. I listened to her chatter about the war overseas and the price of meat, and watched the blurred landscape slipping past, thinking ruefully of Peter's oft-repeated comment that trouble sends us no night-letter warnings. It seems to have a way of lurking in ambush and pouncing on us unawares, shattering the peace of our quiet lives. Up to this time my life had been smooth and happy, without real difficulty. I sensed that now I was embarking on a new era. Yet, what had happened to me an hour before in the doctor's quiet office seemed fantastically unreal, like a bad dream from which I would awaken any minute. I wondered if the numbed feeling one has at such a time, as if one's spirit were anesthetized, is not God's loving way of cushioning us from the immediate impact of sudden calamity, so that we are able to bear it.

The tears which were just below the surface did not overflow until I had reached home and told Peter my bad news. He seemed stunned and said little. I remember throwing myself into his arms, sobbing, "I can't take it. *I just can't take it.*"

But I was about to learn that with God's help, with God standing beside us in the midst of trouble, we can bear anything and come out victorious. I already knew that God is with us in our happiness. Now, I was to find Him in a new and deeper way, in the midst of heartache and disappointment, leading the way out.

I went to bed at the end of March 1943, staying at home because I had a "closed case" of tuberculosis, with no cough, and the bacilli never found. For the first four months I had a nurse. After that we had a Negro maid and a housekeeper. I tried to supervise the running of the household from my bed. However, eighteen months later, by September 1944, I was still in bed all the time, and there had been no change in the X rays. Five doctors, including the best lung specialists we could find, seemed unable to help me. Their only advice was to "Wait, and rest."

This was a time of great soul-searching. I began reading the New Testament, pondering Christ's healing miracles with my own great need in view. Up to this time I had given no particular thought to the question of whether or not Christ still performs miracles on peoples' bodies today. The advances made in medicine and surgery had seemed to me quite sufficient.

I was a child of the Scientific Age. I knew that God set up this universe to be governed by unwavering scientific and mathematical laws. My generation believed in things we could "prove." But the strides made by the great god Science had already shown that all around us, everyday, were things real enough, yet quite beyond the perception of our five senses. What if the only real boundary between the physical and the spiritual world was just those five senses? If that were true, then that boundary too could be progressively pushed back by research.

If that were true, then the spiritual world was governed by laws, laws just as immutable as the law of gravity. That would explain why some prayers were answered, and some were not. Surely, it was not just the caprice of God. The New Testament reveals that Jesus actually expected ordinary men and women in all ages to be able to do the same miracles He did.[2] Wouldn't that point to the fact that those miracles worked for Jesus because He knew the inexorable spiritual laws of the universe, whereas we did not?

As I pondered these things and read my Bible, I found that Jesus never refused anyone who came to Him asking help. There was no record of His ever having said, "No, I won't heal you. This illness is good for your soul." Instead, He was surprisingly concerned with the welfare of men's bodies, and the Bible assures us that not only is this same Jesus alive today, in the twentieth century, but that He is always the "same, yesterday, today, and forever."

Why, then, could I not ask this same Jesus to cure me? I felt, however, unworthy to ask such a thing.

The practical ramifications of the fact that "God is Love" began to dawn on me. I knew that anything unloving in me, any resentment, unforgiveness, or impurity shut out God, just as a muddy windowpane obscures the sunlight. Painfully, in an agony of mind and spirit, I began thinking back over my life, recalling all too vividly all my transgressions and omissions. True, I had been busy in church organizational work all my life, but I wondered now how much of it had counted for anything.

Through many days I put down on paper all of the things of which I was ashamed. Some of it I shared with my mother, some with Peter. To some people far away, I wrote letters asking their forgiveness for things they had long since forgotten, or never known about. It took me days to muster the courage to mail those letters. Then I claimed God's promise of forgiveness and cleansing.

Peter bore all this patiently, almost silently. He already knew what I still had to learn, that we human beings can never deserve any of God's good gifts, that when we have done the best we can, our best is still not good enough to merit anything from the Lord of all the earth. Peter knew that we can get nothing from God except, as he loved to say, "on the same old terms," always simply "by grace (the unmerited favor of God) through faith." But he was also wise enough to know that there was a definite therapy in confession, and that I was traveling a spiritual road, which I must needs travel alone, in my own way.

When this methodical task of confession was completed, I asked God to make me well. Confidently, with what I believed to be real faith, I awaited the verdict of the next X rays. But, they were just the same. The shadows were still there, all the soft spotting, the same intrapulmonary markings.

I was puzzled and hurt. The barometer of my faith fell sharply. It appeared that God had failed me. I was desperate, at rope's end.

Peter thought that a few weeks on the eastern shore of Virginia with my mother and father might break the dreadful monotony of life in bed. I could stay up just long enough to get dressed, then could take the steamer to Norfolk, lying down on the back seat of a car to and from the docks. I had to be carried up all steps.

As he told me good-by, Peter casually slipped a pamphlet into my hand. "I found this the other day in the church office, while straightening my desk drawers. It seems to be about spiritual healing. I haven't had a chance to read it myself. Just thought you might like to see it."

That pamphlet turned out to be momentous. God had not failed me after all. He was just leisurely, as He usually is. My prayers had been heard and were about to be answered.

On the morning of September 14th, I could think of nothing but a nugget of a story imbedded in that pamphlet on healing. It was about a former missionary who had been bedridden for eight years. During those long years, she had steadily and persistently asked God "Why?" She could not understand why she should be laid on the shelf, when she was doing the Lord's work. There was rebellion in her heart, and the drums of mutiny rolled every now and then. The burden of her prayers was that God should make her well, in order that she might return to the mission field. But nothing happened. Finally, worn out with failure of these prayers and with a desperate sort of resignation within her, she prayed, "All right, Lord, I give in. If I am to be sick for the rest of my life, I bow to Thy will. I want Thee even more than I want health. It is for Thee to decide." Thus leaving herself entirely in God's hands, she began to feel a peace she had known at no time during her illness. In two weeks, she was out of bed, completely well.[3]

The first part of this true story seemed strikingly like my experience. Suddenly, an inner illumination, playing on that missionary's experience, revealed to me my mistakes in prayer. I had been demanding of God. I had claimed health as my right. Furthermore, I had never, for one moment, stopped rebelling against tuberculosis or against the invalidism it had induced. I had not faced reality. The right way, then, must be the only way left—that of submission and surrender to the situation as it was.

Privately, with tears eloquent of the reality of what I was doing, I lay in bed and prayed, "Lord, I've done everything I've known how to do, and it hasn't been good enough. I'm desperately weary of the struggle of trying to persuade You to give me what I want. I'm beaten, whipped, through. If You want me to be an invalid for the rest of my life, all right. Here I am. Do anything You like with me and my life."

There was no trace of graciousness about the gift of my life and will, nothing victorious, nothing expectant. I had no faith left, as I understood faith. Nevertheless, a strange deep peace settled into my heart.

In the early hours of the next morning something awakened me. The luminous hands of the clock on my night stand said that it was 3 A.M. The room was in darkness, that total darkness known only to the country, where there are no street lights. My mind was active, chewing on the spiritual adventure of the day before. I, who had deliberately surrendered all hope of health, now discovered an active, newborn hope in my heart. Whence it had come, I did not know. Story after story from the New Testament narratives came to my mind. There was the one about the man born blind; the one about the man at the Pool of Bethesda, who had been incapacitated for thirty-eight years; the one about the man with the withered hand. I saw that all of these cases had one thing in common. In each instance, Jesus told the man seeking healing to *do* something, and *as he obeyed*, he was cured. Obedience was apparently the test of real faith. That man at the pool, who did not even think he could stand up, had to get up anyway and roll up his mat, and as he made the effort, he was cured. The one with the useless hand had to try to stretch it out, and as he did so, it became normal. The blind man was told to go and wash in a pool, and as he obeyed, his sight returned.

"Suppose," I mused, "I could talk to Jesus, as those people did, and ask Him to cure me, I wonder what He would tell *me* to do?"

My imagination supplied dramatic possibilities—Jesus might tell me, for example, to appear downstairs for breakfast with the family the next morning. I could picture their surprise and mingled delight and alarm.

Suddenly, with new resolution, I almost sat up in bed. I had no sooner breathed the question, "Lord, what *would* You ask me to do?" when it happened. Past all credible belief, suddenly, unaccountably, Christ was there, in Person, standing by the right side of my bed. I could see nothing but that deep, velvety blackness, but the bedroom was filled with an intensity of power, as if the Dynamo of the Universe were there. Every nerve in my body tingled with it, as with a shock of electricity. I knew that Jesus was smiling at me tenderly, lovingly, whimsically—a trifle amused at my too-intense seriousness about myself.

"Go," He said, in direct reply to my question, "Go, and tell your mother. That's easy enough, isn't it?"

I faltered. What would mother think? It's the middle of the night. She would think I had suddenly gone crazy.

Christ said nothing more. He had told me what to do. It was clear to me that I could take it or leave it, but that if I did not obey, the chance might be gone forever. In a flash, I understood the real freedom of choice God always allows His creatures. I also understood, on the other hand, why Thomas had knelt in adoration at this One's feet crying, "My Lord, and my God." There was supreme kingliness here, as well as a human personality more vivid, more compelling than that of anyone I had ever met. It would be difficult *not* to obey Him.

"I'll do it, if it kills me," I said, climbing out of bed, sensing even as I did so, the ludicrousness of my own words. Somehow, I knew that Christ's eyes flashed humor as He stood quietly aside to let me pass.

I groped my way into the dark hall to the bedroom at the other end, and spoke softly to Mother and Dad. Naturally they were startled. Mother sat bolt upright in bed. "What—what on earth has happened?"

"It's all right. Don't be alarmed," I reassured them. "I just want to tell you that I'll be all right now. It seemed important to tell you tonight."

"What has happened?" Dad repeated.

"I'm sorry to have wakened you. I'll tell you all about it in the morning. I promise. It's too long a story for tonight. Everything's all right."

When I returned to the bedroom, that vivid Presence was gone. I found myself more excited than I have ever been before or since, and more wide awake. It was not until the first streaks of dawn appeared in the eastern sky that I slept again.

The next morning that extraordinary experience was quite as vivid as it had been during the night hours. The question was whether Christ meant that I had been healed instantaneously, or that recovery would come sometime in the future. I did not know. There was nothing to do but wait for the next X rays.

Meanwhile I wrote to Peter, telling him as calmly and reservedly as possible of that almost unbelievable occurrence. I had certainly never made any claims to mysticism. Yet, I well knew that this was the type of Christian experience which many people would tag "mystical" and promptly dismiss as only half-credible. Why it should have happened to me, I had no idea. But I also knew that what I had experienced was real. Peter's reply was equally reserved, "simply because," he wrote, "I just don't know *what* to reply." Years later, I found that he had carefully preserved that particular letter of mine, putting it with his most cherished personal papers.

As it turned out, the healing of my lungs came slowly, no doubt because my faith grew slowly. The next X rays showed, for the first time, definite progress. Thereafter, there was steady, solid healing, never with the least retrogression, until finally the doctors pronounced me completely well.

During the time of convalescence I learned that tuberculosis is a disease of lack, of deficiency, or malnutrition. Where real poverty is not involved, the malnutrition is often spiritual as well as physical. Physicians now recognize that certain temperaments and physiques have a proclivity for certain diseases. Patients in every tuberculosis sanatorium joke about the number of famous people who had had this particular malady—Francis Thompson, Robert Louis Stevenson, Anne and Emily Brontë, John Wesley, John Keats, George MacDonald, Katherine Mansfield, and in our day, Vivien Leigh, Betty MacDonald, and many another. It is not by chance that these victims of the disease were all individuals of a sensitive nature whose talents found expression in the artistic realm. The type of person who seems most susceptible to tuberculosis is one in whom the link between the spirit and the flesh is very close. To these people, particularly, would the Apostle John's words apply: "Our beloved, I pray above all things, that you may prosper and be in good health, *even as your soul prospers.*" The Bible takes for granted the fact that man is a threefold being—spirit, mind, and body—and that the health of each has a bearing on all. If, in a tuberculous patient, the basic spiritual deficiency (which is frequently present) is recognized and treated along with the physical deficiencies, the disease usually rapidly retreats.

In my own case, the real cause of my illness was a bad case of spiritual malnutrition. I had not known that my soul was all but starved to death, but it was. This might be a revelation to many laymen who believe that attending church once a week is quite enough spiritual exercise for anyone. In this instance, neither parental example nor a lifetime of church work, not even listening Sunday by Sunday to Dr. Marshall's inspired preaching had given me the necessary spiritual nourishment because I had not done my part during the week. Then when circumstances denied me even that Sunday service, I discovered the necessity of a day-by-day effort for myself. It was a hard lesson to learn, but an invaluable one.

Another step toward health was a sharp facing up to my situation. Jesus is supremely a realist, and He would have us be realists too. He led me to imagine the hated disease set out before me. I had to take a good long look at it, walk all around it, call it by name, and take the attitude, "So, you have tuberculosis. Is that so awful? There is nothing here that God cannot deal with." This changed my inner attitude from one of cringing fear to a healthy normality, and as the fear of the disease diminished, it lost its hold on my body.

Meanwhile, having discovered through experience in his own family that God can and does deal with health problems in this age, Peter could not but share this discovery with others. A new emphasis became apparent in his thinking and preaching. It resulted in a paper called "The Silent Keys" he read before the Inter-church Club, a group of ministers, and in a series of sermons which he called "The Lost Secret." Often it showed itself in his pastoral prayers. In the fragment of a prayer which follows, he was thinking of certain specific individuals in our congregation:

. . . . There are loved ones today, O Lord, for whom we pray. The prayers, even now, are being whispered before the Throne of Grace. We pray as we ask for something without any hesitation, knowing that Thou art disposed to give before we ask.

We thank Thee that pain has been removed, and sick have been made well. We thank Thee for askings that have been received, for prayers that have been answered.

We are so glad that, by Thy grace and mercy, broken bones have mended, and weak and struggling hearts have been made strong.

Hear us, this morning, as we pray for some who need stronger hearts. Thou art the Great Doctor who can do it. Wilt Thou strengthen the hearts of them whom we name even now?

We pray for some who are sick of tuberculosis. While human skill can do this and that and say, "Wait and rest," we know that *Thy* skill can heal lungs. Hear us, as we pray for that.

We think of some whose eyes need to see. Lord Jesus, Thou has not forgotten how to do that. Hear us, as we pray for these miracles today.

And there are some, who bereaved, still feel lonely, and have not even yet found joy—the joy of Thy resurrection—and the sense of the presence of loved ones who are with Thee. *For if they are with Thee, and Thou art with us, how can they be very far away?* But we would feel them near, we would somehow be persuaded that they still live; that they are happy; that they still love us, as we love them. May such assurances come to the hearts that need them today. . . .

People often ask the question, "How much should I do to help God answer my prayers, and how much should I leave to Him?" In his sermon "Why Worry?" Dr. Marshall gave his considered answer to this practicable question:

When faced with problems that worry us, we should, by all means, talk them over with the Lord.
We should, because He wants us to, turn the matter over to Him.
But God may insist on bringing up other matters as a prerequisite to His answering our prayers.

If we *want* to trust God,
    but feel that our faith is hardly strong enough for such a venture,
then we can, with every confidence, ask Him to give us the faith too,
    for faith is a gift of God.

What, after all, do I mean, when I speak of taking worries to the Lord and leaving them there?

Let me use the simplest illustration of which I can think.
Suppose a child has a broken toy.
He believes that his father can mend it.
He brings the toy to his father, saying that he himself has tried to fix it and has failed.
He asks his father to do it for him.

The father gladly agrees . . .
    takes the toy
        and begins work.

Now obviously, the father can do his work most quickly and easily, if the child makes no attempt to interfere, but simply sits quietly watching,
    or even goes about other business
with never a doubt that the toy is being successfully mended.

192

But what do most of God's children do in such a situation?
Often we stand by, offering a lot of meaningless advice and some
rather silly criticism.
We even get a little impatient, because it is taking so long,
    and try to help
        and get our hands in the Father's way, generally hindering His
        work.

Finally, in our desperation, we may even grab the toy out of our
Father's hands entirely, saying rather bitterly that we hadn't really
thought He could fix it anyway,
    that we had given Him a chance,
        and that He had failed us.

There are times when God does ask us to do something.
He may ask us to mend some broken relationships,
    to do something to make the way straight before Him.

But never forget that His plan may include simply turning over your
problem
    doing nothing else . . .
        just shutting out all doubt and worry.

This is the kind of solution that God loves because it glorifies Him.

And we are glad to say:
    "I didn't do anything but just believe.
        God did it all.
            Give *Him* the credit!"

Why not give Him the chance with your problem?
God can fix it for you.
He is eager to do it.

In this sermon, Dr. Marshall told a story, to illustrate his point,
"of a certain family during the war, who were in a desperate plight
over the help situation." "The certain family," as many people in
our congregation suspected, was our family.

The story begins in the late summer of 1944, when I had been ill
for many months. We were spending our vacation in a rented cottage on Cape Cod. Soon the time would come when, normally, we

would head back to Washington—Dr. Marshall to pick up his heavy fall and winter schedule, I to continue my quiet invalid's life in the big, cheerful front bedroom of the Manse.

But we just could not face the prospect of another year like the last. There had been a procession of fourteen maids through our house in the last fifteen months. All of them had been lured into better paying government jobs, which they also considered far more glamorous than housework. As a result of the constant upheaval at home, our four-year-old was showing signs of insecurity, my recovery was being retarded, Dr. Marshall's work was suffering. Moreover, much of our good china had been broken, furniture had been scratched and linen ruined, silver had been lost and broken.

We had already tapped all of the usual sources for maids, but to no avail. When employment agencies, ads in the papers, and the help and advice of many friends failed, then we tried ads in church papers and periodicals. We even wrote to orphanages, thinking that we might secure the help of an older girl. The time eventually came when there were no more bright ideas to try. It looked as if the only thing left to us was temporarily to separate as a family. I would go to a rest home, Peter John to my parents, Dr. Marshall to a hotel or club.

In this extremity, we turned the problem over to God. We told Him that if He wanted us to close up the Manse until I got well—and no one knew how long that would be—we would bow to His will. "But," we added, "if You want us to stay together, then we will trust You to send us someone to take care of our household by the day we return to Washington for the winter. The problem is now Yours, in all its ramifications. We promise to be hands off."

This, we knew full well, was a daring prayer. I still marvel not only that we had the courage to pray such a prayer, but that we kept our part of the bargain and made not the least effort to secure a cook or housekeeper for our imminent return to Washington for the winter.

Our answer was a spectacular demonstration that God's help in practical matters of this kind is very real; that He never does things halfway, but does them richly, gloriously, beyond our fondest expectations.

One of the most fascinating things about the way God overrules human lives is the way He makes the circumstances of several lives "work together for good," like intricate pieces of a jigsaw puzzle, with no waste, no lack, no surplus. That this is so became apparent as the answer to this particular prayer unfolded.

Our deadline was Wednesday, September 6th. On Friday morning, September 1st, Alma Deane Fuller, a Kansan, who was a newspaper reporter on Capitol Hill, decided to join the choir of our church in order to be sure of a seat at the morning service.

Miss Fuller had been in Washington for eight months. She had been attending New York Avenue Church regularly. For years, this girl had been groping to find God. That part of the story is best told in her own words:

> Like nearly everyone else in Washington, I thought Dr. Marshall was one of the most challenging and inspiring ministers I had ever heard preach. Sunday after Sunday, I would stand in line outside the church hoping to get a seat, only to get just far enough inside to have to stand throughout the service. Yet, hearing him meant so much to me, I wouldn't think of staying away just because I had to stand.
>
> For years I had been aware that religion was a very real and wonderful thing to some people, but not to me. I wanted it to be, but couldn't seem to get a grip on it.
>
> Dr. Marshall was one of the few people I knew who seemed close to God. He always talked about God as if God were his closest friend, as if they had wonderful times together. The sermons I heard him preach only intensified my spiritual hunger. I hung on his every word, as most of his listeners did, and prayed that somehow, someway, I could get to know God like that too.
>
> Another thing that bothered me very much was that I wasn't sure I was in the right job. It was a very interesting job, with the Senate as my beat. For a girl reared on a farm, there was a thrill attached to such a position, and the pay was average, but I had a restless feeling that I just wasn't in the right place. I had had two good jobs during the two years since I graduated from Kansas State, but in them too, I felt something important was missing. I felt that I belonged somewhere else, but I did not know where it was. It was like being away from home and not even knowing where home was.

On the first night that Alma Deane went to choir rehearsal, over one hundred young people from many different parts of the United States were present. During the announcement intermission, Mr. Beaschler, our director of music, told them about having spent part of his vacation with us on Cape Cod. "By the way," he added abruptly, "do any of you happen to know of a maid or housekeeper who would like a good job for the winter? The Marshalls will be back in town next Wednesday, and I heard them say that if they hadn't found really reliable help by then, they would have to close up the Manse and break up the family for a while. If you have any constructive suggestions for them, you will not only be doing the Marshalls a favor, but the whole church."

At that moment, God started answering both Miss Fuller's prayers and ours. "Suddenly, I had the strangest feeling," she said later, "that Mr. Beaschler was talking to me and to no one else. In fact, I just *knew* he was talking to me! I didn't know the Marshalls personally. I didn't even know that Mrs. Marshall was ill, but every-thing Mr. Beaschler said stood out in my mind like boldface type or neon lights. I became very excited. Over and over, I heard in my mind, 'A. D. why don't *you* go?'"

The idea did not appeal to Alma Deane at all. She did not like housework and did not know how to cook. "How," she argued with herself, "would I be of any use to the Marshalls? How could I live on a housekeeper's wages? How would I ever explain such a strange, rash move to friends and to my family, who are so proud of my job on Capitol Hill interviewing Senators and Cabinet officials?"

But the idea persisted. That night she sat on the edge of her bed until two o'clock. She raised every possible objection, of which there were many, and could think of not a single good reason for want-ing to become a housekeeper. Nevertheless, the idea persisted. It drove her relentlessly. The next day, she looked up our address in the phone book, caught a bus, and came out to Cathedral Avenue. She walked up and down in front of the house, looking it over care-fully, just to assure herself that the whole thing was not a dream.

On Wednesday, the day of our deadline, Miss Fuller came to see me. As she sat by my bed, I saw a girl dressed in an unbecoming aqua-colored suit. She had beautiful, but restless, deep brown eyes, in which I saw instability, even fear. A. D., as she told me she liked to be called, was a little ill at ease, but was very frank. Quietly, she told me what had happened on Friday night at choir rehearsal.

"I am not qualified for the job," she insisted. "I don't really want it, but I had to come and talk to you, so I can begin sleeping again at night. Frankly, Mrs. Marshall, there's something about this that I don't understand at all. All I can say is, here I am, and I don't even know *why* I'm here."

At that point, I became just as excited as A. D. had been on Friday night. "I think I can supply the missing pieces to the puzzle," I volunteered. Then I told her about our knotty help problem, the way we had prayed about it at a distance of some five hundred miles, and that today was the date we had set for a decision on it.

The girl sitting by my bed looked astonished. It had not occurred to her that the insistent mental prodding she had felt was God's way of speaking to her. Since the whole thing involved revolutionary changes for both of us, we agreed to pray about it for two weeks, while I visited in Seaview. If, at the end of that time, both of us still felt that this was God's doing, A. D. would give up her job on Capitol Hill and come and live with us. She left as in a daze.

Subsequently, in a talk about the matter with her boss, she was told that to become a housekeeper would be to commit professional suicide. Nevertheless, at the end of the two weeks, the answer was clear to both of us. A. D. was convinced that, though to resign her job seemed a completely unreasonable move, it was nonetheless God's plan. For six years, she had pleaded for His help. She had asked and sought and knocked. This was His answer. She could not refuse to obey.

With as great a courage as I have ever witnessed, feeling like a parachutist taking a first leap, she resigned her position. She moved her possessions to the Manse on a Saturday night. As she set her things down in the room assigned to her, she had sudden proof that she had done the right thing.

"I suddenly knew for the first time in my life," A. D. said afterward, "what it meant to be in the right place at the right time. It was something like the way the horizon rights itself and stands still when you are coming out of a dizzy spell, and everything suddenly settles into place. All restlessness and uncertainty left me, forever. The peace of God has never left me since that time. I know now that obedience to whatever God asks of us brings peace and a sense of rightness with the world. There is no substitute for it. That night was the beginning of a whole new life for me."

A. D. thought she would probably stay for a few months. She stayed four years. She became not only a housekeeper, but a cherished friend whose steady, loving companionship alleviated my loneliness and hastened my recovery. Before our eyes, all the potentialities of beauty and character which had been lying dormant in her came to fruition. She became a poised and delightful person. Even her looks changed; she developed a flair for dressing fashionably. She acquired an artistry for homemaking, as well as rare qualities of leadership.

We, for our part, got a more wonderful answer to our prayer than we could ever have imagined. A. D.'s four years with us were a period of spiritual adventuring and growth for Peter and me, too. He and A. D. and I became a kind of team, each of us contributing much-needed help to one another. Even A. D.'s experience on Capitol Hill was of inestimable value to Peter when he assumed the Senate chaplaincy. Links were forged between the three of us that will last through all eternity.

Moreover, A. D. by no means committed professional suicide. In 1948, without even seeking it, she stepped into a fine position in the National Red Cross, at more than twice the salary of her old job on the Hill. That position seemed made just for her. It used every bit of experience she had ever had. Furthermore, after the interim with us, she was a lot farther up the professional ladder than she could have climbed had she spent the four years in journalism.

Peter and I never stopped thanking God for sending A. D. to us. This answer to prayer was but an additional undergirding to Peter's already rock-ribbed faith. Often he referred to the incident from the pulpit.

One of the excuses we offer for our lack of faith is the old cliché, "God helps those who help themselves."[4]
Rather, God helps those who trust Him to solve their problems.
My own experience substantiates the evidence of Scripture that our actions in any given situation are more important to God than our thoughts or intellectual belief.
Jesus was not being facetious when He said that even faith of the mustard-seed variety can win great things from God.
The greatest answers to prayer in our family have come at times when our faith was so small as almost to expect the worst.
Until we took hands off and really turned the problem over to God, He could not help us.

Do we trust God enough to put the ultimates of life—the things affect-
ing health,
    life, and death,
        basic economic needs—
into His hands?
If we do, that—in God's eyes—is faith, and He will always honor it.
Why not try it for yourself?

fifteen

*W*AVERLEY

I builded me houses . . .
I made me gardens and orchards . . . my heart rejoiced in all
my labour.

Ecclesiastes 2:4–5, 10

The Railway Express truck rumbled up Pleasant Road and stopped before an obviously new Cape Cod cottage. It was a gray-shingled house with green blinds, nestling atop a gently rising slope. The driver of the truck climbed out and began unloading a number of heavy cartons. Mr. Robert Ingraham, who had a summer home just up the road, stood watching with undisguised interest. Jeffrey, his red-brown cocker spaniel, having trotted after him down the road, stood by his side waiting patiently to see in which direction the long legs would move next. Presently, Mr. Ingraham flicked away his cigarette and sauntered up to the expressman.

"Say, you have quite a load there. Somebody must be moving everything he owns."

The driver chuckled. "All of these boxes are from Peter Marshall addressed to Peter Marshall. I'm fetchin' up his things. I hear in the village that he has bought this house."

"Never heard of him."

The expressman withdrew his head from the dark interior of the truck where he was hunting for more packages from Peter Marshall to Peter Marshall. He straightened up and looked in amazement at the tall man standing in the road. "You don't know who Peter Marshall is?" His tone implied that any fool *should* know. "Why he's the preacher at the church with the tallest spire in Washington."

Bob Ingraham walked on down the street with a somewhat laconic look on his face. He wondered how he was going to like having a preacher for a neighbor—tallest steeple or not.

No decision Peter ever made gave him such lasting pleasure or deep satisfaction as the decision to buy that cottage. Since we lived in a Manse, there was a great satisfaction in owning a home of our own. More important, once a year, for a few weeks, we could leave behind us the constant pressure and demands of life in Washington and live more nearly as we wanted to live. The man who, during his first year of married life, had vainly hoped for flower and vegetable gardens, a hammock under the trees, and a garage plaza where we could entertain our friends, for the first time saw some of these dreams materialize. The man who in Washington longed constantly for more time to be with his son, to plant a rose garden, to build furniture in a basement woodworking shop, finally managed some of these things during our more leisurely summertime life.

These were some of the reasons that made Peter always think of "Waverley" as his real home. He often spoke of it as the closest thing to heaven on earth he ever found. From September to July of each year he looked forward and planned toward the time when we would leave for our cottage. As September approached, he could hardly bear the thought of leaving "Waverley," for his heart, his fondest hopes and dreams for the future were centered there.

We had acquired the gray-shingled house in the summer of 1943, after having rented cottages nearby for five years.

Our first summer on the Cape had been quite enough to convince us that this was the ideal vacation spot for us. Peter saw no need thereafter of wandering around the country searching for new places. It was one of the paradoxes about him that such a vigorous man, with an exceptionally active, restless mind, nevertheless enjoyed developing certain ruts in his life. This particular rut became the best-loved of all.

During the 1930s the Cape was still largely unspoiled by commercialism. It had not been "discovered" as a casual vacation land. It still had an atmosphere all its own. As soon as one crossed the Sagamore Bridge which spanned the Cape Cod Canal, the air took on a new clarity, became fresh and cool, with the tang of the sea in it. The world of harrowing hustle and bustle was left behind.

Each village had its own charm and its own history. Everywhere were the low Cape Cod cottages, hugging the ground for protection against strong sea winds, their shutters painted unorthodox colors—lavender or yellow, chartreuse, mauve, or robin's-egg blue. Everywhere in late June, the time of our arrival, the white picket fences were covered with a gay luxuriance of rambler roses.

Driving into Sandwich Village was like returning to the tranquil nineteenth century. Settled in 1637, this village was named after Sandwich, in Kent, England, and an Old World atmosphere still clung to it. The village green with its town hall, its grist mill on the pond, its colonial church with its graceful Christopher Wren spire, its ancient towering elms looked much as they had during the famous glass-factory days of 1825–1888.

One day Peter and I took my mother and father to Sandwich. Mother had an avid interest in history. She also had a special fondness for roaming through ancient cemeteries, reading epitaphs. This always amused Peter.

On this particular day, Mother's historical perception was not up to par. We had showed her the three-hundred-year-old Hoxie House, with its salt-box roof. We had looked over the relics of Sandwich glass in one antique shop and had gone on to another, also filled with the glass which had made the village famous.

Suddenly Mother conceived a bright, new idea. She lit up like a neon light. "Do you know what I think," she exclaimed. *"They must have made glass here once."* The saleslady's mouth worked itself into a mechanical, condescending smile. Peter moaned softly and began backing away, as if he wanted no one to know that he had ever seen this woman before. That was an incident her son-in-law never let her forget.

It took only a few visits to antique shops like these to turn us into enthusiastic amateur collectors of pressed glass. Of course, some of it was not old. Amateurs like ourselves could always be fooled. But it was beautiful just the same. There was opalescent, like a dappled sky at sunset; cranberry which the old glassmakers took from the stain of the Cape Cod cranberries in the autumn; cobalt blue, like the color of the sea they knew so well; delicate green like their marshlands; peachbloom with the shadings and texture of a rose petal; and there were ruby reds, ambers, deep amethysts, and a thousand variations. Each year we brought home a few pieces, until finally, the windows of our sun parlor in Washington glowed with our little collection.

Both of us enjoyed the Early American interiors which abounded on the Cape. We were not modernists in taste. We discovered that maple and chintz, pressed glass and old pewter, hooked rugs and Hitchcock chairs created an atmosphere that spelled home for us.

But the thing that Peter liked best of all was that nowhere on the Cape could one escape the sight or the sound of the sea. Though he had been forced to relinquish his early ambition to go to sea, the call of the sea was still in his blood. He liked nothing so much as to watch the ocean in all its moods. The fogs at night made him feel at home. The long heaving surfs and the white mists of the mornings delighted him. There, on that tiny peninsula, at its widest but twenty miles across, the sea and its influences were always at one's elbow. There were four hundred miles of white sandy beaches offering infinite variety. On the south side, off Vineyard and Nantucket sounds, the tides were gentle, the beaches perfect for tiny children. But off Chatham, Orleans, and Truro was the open Atlantic, with pounding surf and treacherous shoals.

However, even if Cape Cod had not had all these attractions, that of summer nights, cool enough to enjoy an open fire and to sleep under blankets, would have been enough for Peter. The man who almost had a complex about hot weather had not hoped to find such a summer climate west of Scotland. Every day, when he bought the Boston paper at the village store, the first thing he read was the temperature reports from different cities.

"Look at that, Catherine," he would say gloatingly, "Washington, New York, and Boston, all having heat waves. It was 97 in Washington yesterday, and *it was exactly 64 here this morning.*"

If Washington's temperature was less than 95, he seemed just a trifle disappointed. The most cruel blow of all was to receive a letter from some friend in the District of Columbia reporting "amazingly cool weather in Washington. Would you believe it? We slept under a blanket last night." This practically ruined his day. I think that some of our friends finally caught on and doctored their weather reports accordingly.

My husband's idea of a real vacation was to go to some spot as far away from all mail deliveries and telephones as possible, where he could dress in slacks and a sports shirt, and give his razor a rest at least every other day.

At first Cape Cod met these requirements. The world outside seemed quite remote. Seldom did we see anyone we knew. Then gradually, over the years, the Cape seemed to change. More and more Americans discovered its superb summer climate and its many charms.

One rainy day we decided to drive to Hyannis, the shopping center of the Cape. This was prior to my illness when our custom was to save antiquing and shopping for these rainy, no-beach days. Peter was wearing gray, creaseless slacks, a blue sweater (a bargain which he had picked up in Scotland), a sloppy raincoat, his favorite battered Cape Cod hat, and a two days' growth of beard.

We were browsing through one of those combination gift and book shops when, across the room, Peter spied someone he knew. It was one of his colleagues from Washington, a nationally known minister. This particular clergyman was the type who, had he been marooned on a South Sea island, would even there have worn the proper thing and said the proper thing. Even on his vacation he was wearing "the cloth" and a clerical collar.

Peter managed to get behind a very tall bookshelf where he appeared to be engrossed completely in the titles before him. At that moment a saleslady came up. "Can I help you?" she asked brightly. Then she noticed the books at which he was staring so intently—*Don Sturdy with the Harpoon Hunters, The Outdoor Chums in the Forest*, and *The Bobbsey Twins in the Country*. The lady gave him a long, searching look. "Ah ... er ... just looking, thanks," explained Peter lamely, noticing for the first time that he was in the juvenile section. "My son, you know ... He—enjoys adventure stories." (Wee Peter was then exactly two years and seven months.) Then, noticing that the clergyman's back was turned for an instant, Peter slipped out the side door.

After we had put a breathless block between us and the bookstore, Peter spoke again. "Catherine," he said mournfully, "Cape Cod is getting overcrowded!"

No house and yard ever received more loving planning than "Waverley." We had most of every year in which to dream up improvements, only two months to work at them. Moreover, I was forced to find devious ways of furnishing the house from my bed. This was largely accomplished by mail order and by telephone.

We thinned out our household furnishings in Washington, and sent all duplicates and everything we could spare to the cottage. Peter shopped for a suite of bedroom furniture and selected blond maple, with low posts on the beds. Whenever the Scotsman bought furniture, he wanted to be sure it would last a long time. "I couldn't shake the chest of drawers, Catherine," he reported about the blond maple suite. That made it all right.

From an antique-dealer friend in Washington, I bought a day bed for the living room, a small maple chest, a walnut washstand, four little black-painted chairs, and some antique lamps. "Honestly, Kate," chided my husband, "I never saw such a passion. If you were in your coffin and spied a sign reading 'Antiques' out the hearse window, you would rise up to have a look."

Of course antiquing is really the art of finding some other use for old things than the use for which they were originally intended. We became singularly adept at this. Thus an old wooden cranberry picker became a magazine rack. A sugar bucket, painted and decorated with the Peter Hunt type of decoration, doubled as a wastebasket. An old wooden churn made a fine umbrella stand. Christmas lights, small buckets of blue, amber, and opalescent glass—the nineteenth-century forerunners of electric Christmas decorations—were most attractive filled with vines.

Peter was always turning up with a picture which he had had framed for "Waverley." They were, of course, always seascapes, with two exceptions—landscapes of Scotland and a series of gay Scottish regimental prints. I started making braided rugs in color schemes to go with each room. Mother and I labored over hundreds of yards of ruffling for white organdy curtains.

When all of this was put together, it spelled home. Every article in the house had been thoughtfully acquired; every article had a history. In addition, planning for the house gave me something definite to do during the long years in bed, and undoubtedly aided and abetted my recovery.

My husband considered the yard and the outside of the house his exclusive responsibility. When we bought the cottage, the shutters were green. That just wouldn't do! As quickly as possible Peter painted them a deep, bright "Chatham blue." In Scotland, as a teen-age boy, he had grown beautiful roses. Ever since, he had longed for another rose garden. That, he planned, would be at the side of the house, and would have as its background against the woods a Rose of Sharon hedge. Across the front of the property he wanted a low picket fence, covered with rambler roses. There would be a perennial border just inside the fence. He would have tall spires of delphinium in all the shades of blue and mauve he loved best, phlox, day lilies—lemon and orange—gaillardia, Kaempheri iris, and Shasta daisies. In Scotland he had loved hollyhocks, carnations, the shy fragrance of wallflower, privet hedge. These he would have in our yard.

All of this was planned on paper. Then came the doing in consultation with a local landscape gardener. Gradually, bit by bit, year by year, all of Peter's dreams were realized. In the poor, sandy soil at the side of the house, to which topsoil and fertilizer had to be hauled, he staked out his garden and dug neat beds. His hybrid teas should have fresh manure, he thought. He sought it out in local pastures, "waiting on the cows," as he said, pronouncing it "ma'-nure," which seemed to make it not only respectable, but positively genteel. Of an evening, worn out from digging, he would pore over nursery catalogs and the garden pages of the Sunday paper, which he religiously saved.

Words like "floribunda" and "mulch" were often on his lips. He went around talking about "Divine," "Enchantment," "Desirable," "Fantasia," "Pink Dawn," and "Mrs. Miniver." That did not mean that he was completely bewitched by Greer Garson. Those were just the names of rosebushes he was ordering.

He was delighted when he found a rose named "Katherine Marshall," only this one was "Katherine T. Marshall," named after Mrs. (General) George Marshall.

The day finally came when the first rosebud appeared on the new bushes. I was lying on the day bed in the living room, when Peter appeared, bearing triumphantly in one hand a perfect salmon-colored bud. I knew that he had hated to cut it, but that this particular rose was a symbol of something very important in his life. His shyness about revealing his real sentimentality gave his gesture a touch of formality and Old World courtliness. He presented the rose to me as if he were laying his heart at my feet, as indeed he was.

It became a family custom for Mother and Dad to spend a month each year at "Waverley." Peter looked forward to their coming as eagerly as I did. No family ever enjoyed a more harmonious relationship or had more fun together. Long ago, my parents had received Peter into their hearts as their own son. He, in turn, gratefully accepted them as bringing something into his life that he had lacked.

Though my father is a minister too, he has always been a fine carpenter on the side. Since my childhood, when he fashioned for me a set of doll furniture—a bed, dresser with glass-knobbed drawers and a swinging mirror, chairs, a table, and a glass-doored cupboard—carpentry has been his hobby. On the other hand, Peter's experience in work with his hands had been limited to metalwork in the Tube Mill.

At first, as they undertook together to work their way down my lists of projects, the two men worked like a team of horses pulling in opposite directions. Peter was forever slowing Pop down, to the latter's voluble exasperation. "Now why do you want to do it *that* way?" Peter would ask. Or "Dad, that just won't do. We'll have to take it out and begin all over."

As projects multiplied from year to year, and the two men built window boxes, a rose arbor, a lattice fence to hide the utility area, an umbrella table for the yard, a blanket chest, a bookcase and a vanity-table stool, they became quite a working team. In the beginning, Dad had most of the know-how, but Peter learned rapidly and supplied an attention to detail that Dad had lacked. Every joint had to be perfect. There could never be a rough edge or a poorly driven nail. And, of course, everything had to be *sturdy*.

The blanket chest turned out to be so sturdy that it was all Peter, Dad, and our across-the-street neighbor Bill Johnson could do to get it up the stairs and to its place under the eaves. I'm sure it will be there as long as the house stands.

Perhaps the masterpiece was the ladder the two ministers built. It would be nice, they felt, to have a tall ladder around the place to use in cleaning out gutters and inspecting roofing. "And," said Peter, "commercial ladders are so flimsy." He, therefore, insisted on making this one out of heavy two-by-fours. It was a beautiful job. There was only one difficulty. It was so heavy that the two men together could scarcely lift it off its hooks in the garage and get it to the side of the house. They would stagger futilely under its weight, until one of the neighbors saw their plight and gave them a hand. That ladder is probably the only one of its kind in the world.

Peter and Dad not only worked together; they also played together. Their specialty was the old-fashioned game of Parcheesi. To Peter's abiding annoyance and exasperation, his father-in-law was a killer at that particular game. Dad's one technique, on which he staked everything, was to send everyone else "home" whenever he got the chance. He refused to be merciful, even if it temporarily impeded his own progress. Moreover, for a preacher, he threw a wicked pair of dice.

"You can kiss that man good-by, Peter," we would hear, as we listened in from the kitchen. "He's going home. A seven will do it. That's all I need." He would go through an elaborate ceremony of blowing on the dice. When he rolled, lo, there would be the seven.

This irked Peter. It always irked him to lose. Moreover, he never took a beating docilely. "Man, you're in league with the devil," he would fume. Then he would try psychology on Father. "Now, look, Dad, *that's* not the way to win, sending everybody home right and left. What fun is there in that?"

But the more he argued, the more stubborn Father became, and the more often he won. Parcheesi was the only game that baffled Peter.

During one lunchtime, Peter was in a very jocular mood. He was feeling expansive. He had needled each member of the family in turn, keeping up an endless patter of nonsense. Through all of this, Dad, who was not feeling quite so expansive that day, sat in complete, profound silence.

"What's eating you, Dad?" Peter finally queried. "You haven't made a single comment since we sat down."

Intoned Dad with great dignity, "So far I haven't heard anything worth commenting on."

"Well, *excuse me,*" Peter said, promptly sliding out of his chair and getting all the way under the table. He stayed there until he heard Dad laugh.

Though X rays of my chest showed much remaining trouble, by the summer of 1945 I began taking short walks. This getting out of bed on faith in response to a sure inner prompting seemed to speed up the natural healing process that had remained dormant for so long. After more than two years in bed, I found endless delight in all the simple everyday things that most people take for granted.

I took short walks in the pine-scented woods, hunting for wild cranberry vines, sweet fern, and bayberry. I liked to go to the beach and walk, with bare feet, along the edge of the cool water and feel the sand slipping from beneath my toes in the receding waves. I basked in the sun and seemed to absorb happiness along with its warmth. It was good to be alive again in a beautiful world. Gratitude flowed out of me and returned to bless and to heal.

There were certain times when the beach was deserted. Then I liked it best. I would lie on the sand with the wind rippling over me, watching the circling seagulls and the playful tripping sandpipers. Listening to the rhythm of the waves, I knew, in some indefinable way, that at last I was in tune with the rhythm of God's universe, and that I was getting well. The old, haunting, ever-present tiredness was slipping away. Life was returning to my devitalized body, and it was good.

Close by the beach we found patches of blueberries and huckleberries. The two Peters spent hours picking them, looking forward to blueberry muffins and juicy deep-dish pies. We picked beach plums and, as of old, I made jelly of them. It was the color of the most beautiful glass the skilled glassmakers of old Sandwich had ever turned out—a blazing cranberry shade.

One afternoon I was lying on the portable chaise in the yard reading. A bronze-colored cocker spaniel wandered into the yard and came directly to me. At first I did not recognize him. I had never owned a pet as a child, had never been fond of cats and dogs, or they of me. This little cocker looked me over carefully with soft, brown eyes, seemed to approve, nuzzled my hand, and settled himself contentedly at my feet. I was surprised. No dog had ever treated me so before. The following afternoon the same thing happened.

On the third day, we were on our way to the beach when Hazel Ingraham called to us. "Our dog Jeff seems to be quite fond of you folks," she said. "We love the poor wee lamb devotedly, but we're having to do a lot of traveling and are finding it hard to take care of him. We wouldn't think of giving him away unless we could find a really wonderful home for him. Would you like to have him?"

Her offer astonished me. I had thought the Ingrahams irrevocably wedded to Jeff. It took the two Peters a flat sixty seconds to decide. When we left "Waverley" that fall, Jeff went with us, a full-fledged member of the family.

If vacations are to re-create, they must refresh spiritually as well as physically. This our Cape Cod vacations did for us. Though Peter always worked hard at "Waverley," there was also time for spiritual stock-taking.

Family prayers, just following the dinner hour, were always more leisurely there. Each member of the family, even our guests, took turns conducting them. Our son, by the time he was five or six, took his turn, though he had to be coached a bit ahead of time. At the cottage, Peter often tucked our son in bed at night and heard his prayers. Often he read to him—books like *The Wind in the Willows* or *The House at Pooh Corner*.

There was time for long, satisfying discussions on religion or theology as we lay on the beach or sat in the yard sipping cool drinks of an afternoon. It was at such times that Peter's amazing spiritual humility frequently revealed itself.

Neither professionally, nor as a husband and father, nor in his own spiritual development did Peter ever think of himself as having arrived. Years before, when he had been pondering the call to Washington, most of the Atlantans, who pleaded with him not to accept it, had used as their chief argument, "If you go, you will have reached the top professionally. There will be nothing more for you to strive toward or to look forward to." But that had not turned out to be true. In Peter's eyes, the possibility of real success lay only within himself, not in the recognition of men or what congregation he served. That success he never felt he had achieved. He well knew that, as God rates things, the most strategically located congregation in America might not be in Washington or New York, but in some obscure little country church in the hills of Pennsylvania or the Valley of Virginia.

Always in these conversations there was revealed Peter's one great fear that he might fail his people. He would think of those vast, hungry-hearted congregations who came to hear him, of their problems, of the way they leaned on him and depended on him spiritually. "I get sort of panicky sometimes," he would say, "for fear I will go back empty-handed and have nothing for them. I ought to be reading those books I brought up and writing sermons, rather than working in the garden. The summer is slipping by *so fast.*"

The next day he would come in from the yard, resolutely pick a book out of his box, and stretch out on the day bed to read it. What usually happened was that, after reading a few pages and making careful marginal notes, he would go to sleep with the book open on his chest. Afterward, he would feel more conscience-stricken than ever.

Still, he never felt that the sermons he wrote at the cottage were good. By the time he got back to Washington to preach them, they no longer excited him. They seemed cold, lifeless. This was probably because Peter's best sermons rose out of the soil of emotion in his own heart. That emotion had to be a present, valid reality. He could not conjure it up.

Peter preached sometimes in the Pilgrim Congregational Church at Harwich Port. At those times the little church, with its simple white interior and its forest-green carpeting, would be crowded with summer folks, among them our neighbors on Pleasant Road.

It had not taken Peter long to win the respect and love of the little shore colony. A preacher who deeply believed and tried to live what he preached, who had a sense of humor, who was always good company, could scarcely fail to be an irresistible combination. Thus it was that whenever Peter preached on the Cape, his neighbors, regardless of denominational leanings, were always in the congregation.

"Who's Peter Marshall?" Mr. Ingraham had asked the expressman.

A few years later he had the answer.

"Why he's my neighbor. He stole my dog and incidentally, my heart."

sixteen

PREACHER'S WORKSHOP

I charge thee. . . . Preach the word . . . a workman that
needeth not to be ashamed. . . .

II Timothy 4:1–2; 2:15

he snow, which had made timid sallies during the night, was
falling rapidly now. It was an unusual sight in Decatur,
Georgia. The young men inside the towering Gothic building,
struggling with Hebrew, and listening to lectures on homiletics and
theology, kept watching the fluffs of white slipping past the window.
But in one class, in the next to the last row, Peter Marshall had found
something far more interesting than snow. He was listening intently
to a sentence which he would remember for the rest of his life.

"Gentlemen," the professor was saying, "in writing your sermons, I beg of you, *use a sanctified imagination.*"

A sanctified imagination! An imaginative faculty dedicated to
Christ. That was to become the keynote of Peter's preaching, his
own peculiar contribution to the art of sermon making.

Whereas most ministers write a sermon to develop an idea, Peter
wrote his sermons to paint a picture and to arouse an emotion.

Wrote Frank S. Mead in an article for the *Christian Herald*,[1] in
November 1948: "What Peter Marshall says, you never forget. . . .
But it isn't *how* he says it, so much as *what* he says that goes in like
a knife. He has a gift for word pictures, for little dramas and folk-
sie incidents; he takes you out on the road to Galilee and makes

you think you belong there, and he brings you back sharply to Main Street. He never preaches over your head."

Peter used the medium of the pictorial sermon to transport Galilee to Main Street, to bring his people face to face with a living Lord, to dramatize human problems.

This was a natural technique for him to use because he thought in pictures.

Was he discouraged? "His discouragements," he said, "had come in a melancholy procession to sit down in dejected rows in the chapel of his heart."

Was he unable to recall someone's name? Then he would "send the librarian of his mind back into the stacks to find it."

"The waters of the oceans of God's love," he suggested, "do come up into the tiny bays of our unbelief."

New Year's Eve he described as "the narrow isthmus between two years."

Our doubt in prayer is like "cobwebs in the corners of the room. The broom of our faith cannot get into the corners. That takes Divine Grace."

"The use of the right word, the exact word, is the difference between a pencil with a sharp point and a thick crayon."

Peter believed that the use of the sanctified imagination, the painting of word pictures, using the vehicle of a story, was Jesus' way of teaching. It will forever be, he believed, the most effective method.

He stated his conviction about this to a group of young ministers just starting their careers:

Pictorial preaching is the most effective because it is easier to get at the average mind by a picture than by an idea.

An Arab proverb puts it this way: "He is the best speaker who can turn the ear into an eye."

Preaching on characters in the Bible or incidents in their lives demands pictorial preaching with imaginative treatment in a dramatic setting. It is a piece of life . . .
a film from the world's big drama . . .
a newsreel from the Scriptures.
You must sketch your situation as if you were painting it.

For your colors you have words . . .
Your sermon outline provides the lines of your picture.
Your brushes are gestures and the modulations of your voice.
Your shadows and highlights are your own expression and the tone
of your voice. . . .

The task of the preacher, gentlemen, is "to see clearly and tell what
you see in a plain way."[2]

Thus, in sermons like "The Rock That Moved," "Letters in the
Sand," or "Up a Tree," Simon Peter, the nameless woman taken in
adultery, or the little publican quisling Zacchaeus reached out warm
human hands to us across the centuries.

Suddenly we understood in a deeper way than any moralizing could
have taught us that these were men and women quite like us, with
the same fears, the same weaknesses, the same sins, the same potentialities, and—the same Lord. If Christ had solved *their* problems for
them, He could also solve *our* problems.

The lasting impression on those who heard these sermons was
the effect of having seen a vivid motion picture. Yet the minister
had used no medium except that of language.

A tired Washington radio newscaster, who had to rise at 5:30 each
Sunday morning and work till four o'clock, started coming to New
York Avenue for the Sunday evening service.

The first Sunday I heard Dr. Marshall [he reported], I knew nothing
at all about him or his background. I wondered how I was going to
stay awake, but during the sermon I forgot my fatigue. I marveled at
his clear diction. At first my attention was held completely by the
way this man was saying things. Then my interest shifted rapidly to
what he was saying. . . .
It was obvious that God was near and real to him. He used vivid word
pictures. . . . His wonderful speaking ability, his power of expression—
I found out as time went on—always seemed to reach its greatest
height in the Lenten season. He could describe Christ, the disciples,
the events and persons around them as graphically as a special-events
broadcaster on the scene. . . .

Inherent in the philosophy behind this kind of preaching was Peter's conviction that emotion, not reasoning, is the real springboard under the will to action.

By emotion he did not mean emotionalism, for which he had contempt. He heartily disliked a shaky tremolo voice, or the "ministerial tone" once associated with the sawdust trail. Carefully he avoided sticky adjectives, the slack and sloppy affectation that ruins true reverence. He felt that terms like "Dear Jesus," "Lovely Lord," "Sweet Saviour," "Beautiful Holy Spirit" are quite alien to the robust language of the New Testament.

Nor did this mean that Peter disparaged scholarship or human intelligence, or that he believed that one's mind ought to be parked outside the church door. Not at all. It was rather his oft-reiterated statement that "Christianity is a matter of perception, not a proof."

By emotion, Peter meant that truth in every generation generates its own peculiar passion; and it is a virile, not an insipid, passion.

Of course, every preacher hopes to stir his listeners to action, so that they will "do something about it." Most ministers hope that this can be accomplished by appealing to intelligence and common sense.

It is interesting that Clarence Darrow, a self-styled atheist, but one of the most effective criminal lawyers this country has ever known, based his courtroom technique on the same proposition, that emotion, not intelligence and common sense, is the strongest motivation. "The most important thing," concluded Darrow, "is to make the judge *want* to decide things your way—then give him a point of law that will give him a reason for doing what you have made him want to do."

Clarence Darrow's courtroom victories, internationally publicized, attest to the fact that this insight into human nature was accurate.

And the amazing influence for good in people's lives that Peter's preaching wielded underscored the effectiveness of his preaching technique.

This influence reached into a wide variety of places. Some Congressmen and Senators attended New York Avenue regularly—Wherry of Nebraska, Angel of Oregon, Hobbs of Alabama. There were many secretaries to important men who were members of our church—one in the White House, the secretary to Admiral Leahy; the secretaries to Congressman Hinshaw of California, to Congressman Judd of Minnesota, to the Assistant Secretary of Agriculture.

There were high-ranking judges, several people in the State Department, the president of the Marjorie Webster Junior College, professors in the English and chemistry departments at George Washington University, the head of the music department in the District schools, and so on and on.

Because Peter's preaching was so far from the bookish tradition, his sermon ideas did not come in the usual way, that is, if the usual way is sitting in a secluded study, poring over commentaries, Bible dictionaries, and theological exegeses.

This greatly troubled me, just after Peter and I were married, when the academic influence of Agnes Scott College was still fresh upon me.

"How," I wondered, "can Peter ever be a great preacher if he doesn't read widely, study for long hours, meditate for more long hours?" So I tried—in a gentle, diplomatic, wifely manner—to pour my husband into a dry and studious mold. But he was an individualist; he would simply not be poured.

His professors at Columbia Theological Seminary had already discovered that Peter was an individualist long before I came on the scene. Having seen that, they might have discouraged or even killed the very thing in their young student that was to lift his preaching out of the mediocre. But the consecrated men on Columbia Seminary's faculty were too wise for that.

Early they realized that Peter's instinctive approach to sermonizing was different from theirs—different from the method they taught. Of course, techniques can be tested only by results; Peter's results were clearly good. Therefore, their conclusion was, "do it your own way, Peter."

Many years after Peter's graduation, he wrote to one of his beloved professors:

> I shall never forget how you encouraged me to be a preacher; how you wisely insisted that I be myself, that I try to develop by God's help whatever talent He had given me. . . . It was you who saw to it that it was Peter Marshall that graduated and not a student trying to imitate somebody else.

Most of the time Peter got his ideas for sermons from life, from the needs of the people on Main Street as he uncovered them through conferences, pastoral visits, and reading (usually periodicals), which revealed national trends. This resulted in very down-to-earth preaching.

A United States Senator once humorously commented that he liked Peter Marshall's preaching because "he hits us where we're at."

Peter gave this advice to the boys at the Gettysburg Theological Seminary:

> You must root your preaching in reality, remembering that the people before you have problems
> doubts
> fears
> and anxieties
> gnawing at their faith.
> Your problem and mine is to get behind the conventional fronts that sit row upon row in the pews. . . .
>
> Consider, for example, the needs of the people who will come to hear you preach.
> Use your imagination as you try to deal with the problems that are most real to them. . . .
>
> If, when you write your sermons, you can see the gleaming knuckles of a clenched fist . . .
> the lip that is bitten to keep back tears . . .
> the troubled heart that is suffering because it cannot forgive . . .
> the spirit that has no joy because it has no love. . . .
>
> If you can see the big tears that run down a mother's face . . .
> If you can see these things—preach them . . .
> preach for them—
> and get down deep.

Trying to "get down deep" and answer the real questions of real men and women is harder than expounding theology or a pet idea. But that was the ideal Peter had set for himself, and mostly he hewed to that line. It resulted in wartime sermons like "A Mother's Question" and "God in Wartime," dealing with the problem of why a loving God allows war; in "how-to-do" sermons like "Where Do I Begin?" "Steps toward God," "The Wandering Sheep of Prayer"; in sermons like "Christ and Sex" and "Mr. Jones, Meet Jesus"—the latter on social drinking.

Many a preacher gets ideas for sermons in unlikely places—places that would surprise the laymen. Peter's sermon called "Acrophobia of the Soul" is a good example.

One night he was reading the *Literary Digest*. He saw an article there on phobias. Said the article:

> Joan Crawford has twin phobias—nyctophobia (fear of darkness) and acrophobia (fear of heights). . . . Acrophobia is a term to apply to friends that swear that "nobody will ever get me up in an airplane."

There it was. That was all Peter needed. He used twin texts for this sermon—Ecclesiastes 12:5 and Colossians 3:2. The sermon was an analysis of the tragedy of personalities content with mediocrity and conformity. It was a plea for an end to fear of the highest ideals, thoughts, and ambitions.

A series of Sinclair gasoline ads once gave Peter the idea for a sermon for young people. The manufacturer claimed that the potential (kinetic) energy of one gallon of his gasoline would lift the largest ocean liner, the pyramids of Egypt, or the Empire State Building.

This ad gave Peter the idea for a sermon about the unused power in our souls, our unused resources in Christ, the church's lost secrets; what could happen if consecrated young people harnessed God's power and claimed America for Christ.

It was typical of Peter that some of his best sermons were inspired by movies or radio programs. A wartime radio program, *We Hold These Truths* by Norman Corwin, gave him the idea for his "The American Dream" sermon—called by Tris Coffin "one of the great documents of recent times."[3]

When Peter wrote such sermons he was squarely up against the creative process of the writer. That is, an idea had to work up from his subconscious mind, stir his own imagination and emotion, and be captured in words that would, in turn, kindle imagination and emotion in his congregations.

This is in contrast to the more usual method of writing a sermon: whereby the preacher builds a careful intellectual structure with three points, cemented together by assiduously collected illustrations.

Peter enjoyed talking himself into a sermon. The idea would develop as he talked. When some of us listened to this, we realized that the structure, the outline, sometimes even the three points were there all right. But just as the skeleton of the human body is covered with flesh, so the outline of a sermon, Peter felt, should not be in evidence. His artistry would not permit him to say, "And secondly" or "Now in the third place."

The dinner-table conversation in our home on any Wednesday night was likely to be the Sunday morning sermon. That was because the church bulletin went to press on Thursday. Invariably Peter would interrupt this sermon colloquy with, "But what shall I *call* it?" There the sermon languished until the right title was forthcoming. By Thursday morning he might not know precisely what was going to be in the body of the sermon, but if he had a good title, he was happy.

A flare for memorable titles was one facet of his gift for clipped and pungent phraseology. Every Saturday night he methodically read and evaluated "the agony columns," as he called them, the church pages with the sermon topics of all the preachers.

A list of some of his sermon titles tells its own story:

"One Star Was Not Neutral"
"The Art of Moving Mountains"
"The Dice of Death"
"Noah Was Drunk"
"Life's Rosary"
"Prove It!"
"Christ's Incredibles"
"The Man with the Bowler Hat"
"The Grace of Stepping Back"
"You Can't Postpone the Sunset"
"Why Don't We?"
"The Key to the Miraculous"
"Through a Kitchen Door"

The titles which he gave the "Doctor and Mrs. Jeremiah Zimmerman Lectures on Effective Preaching" at Gettysburg Seminary are typical of him. He called them "Selected Shorts on Preaching":

"The Man"
"The Message"
"The Vision"
"The Method"
"The Setting"

or, "if you prefer less stilted titles":

"The Producer"
"The Script"
"Lights!"
"Camera!"
"Action!"

I should not give the impression that Peter proudly flaunted his individualism in respect to sermon writing. On the contrary, the methodical, scholarly techniques of some of his best friends always made him feel inferior.

Peter was forever questioning other ministers about where *they* got *their* sermon ideas and how *they* met *their* pulpit deadline. He was particularly envious of one good friend, who made a practice of outlining his sermons for a year ahead and of keeping a separate file of material on each projected sermon. But Peter just couldn't work that way.

The preacher's workshop was his office at the church. This was a tiny room on the second floor whose windows looked out on New York Avenue, right in the heart of downtown Washington. Books lined two sides of the room almost to the ceiling. As Peter sat at his desk, he faced a wall all but covered with etchings—all seascapes. There was also a model of a clipper ship under glass, and a beautifully detailed model of John Knox's house in Edinburgh. There were a few framed Lincoln mementos. A wine-red rug and some leather chairs completed the picture.

This workshop had certain disadvantages. If Peter raised the windows, he had to concentrate above the roar of the traffic, the rumble of ancient streetcars, the ear-splitting staccato of inevitable pneumatic drills. If he closed the windows, he suffered with the heat—which he was certain had been sent as a Scotsman's personal cross.

He worked under great pressure. Over and over, the telephone interrupted his determined effort to meet his deadline. He would type a page, call to his secretary from the top of the stairs, and the sheet would go fluttering into the downstairs hall. Then, while he worked on page two, she would be typing page one into the unusual form of the complete manuscript from which he always preached.[4] (The sermons included in this book are printed exactly as the original manuscripts were typed.)

A lot of Peter's sermon-writing pressure came from the fact that people and their needs always had priority on his time.

One Saturday he still had two sermons to write. He had given strict orders to a new secretary that he was not to be disturbed.

It was during World War II, early in 1945. One of our church boys, a Marine fighter pilot, was on his way overseas for the second time. He found himself back in Washington with a few hours between trains. He had anticipated an encouraging and stabilizing visit with his minister.

When he got to the church, he found that the new secretary did not know him. "Sorry," she said firmly. "Dr. Marshall is not available for callers today."

"I'm on my way overseas," the pilot explained patiently. "I wanted very much to see him. Is he in his office?"

"Yes—yes, he is. But he just can't be disturbed. I'm sorry."

"Thanks," the boy said, as he turned away, "I understand." But he was terribly disappointed.

On the street outside he met Dodson, the church sexton. He was one of Dodson's "boys." Dodson gave the young man a warm, grinning welcome, his gold front tooth shining in his dusky face.

"You've seen Dr. Marshall, of course—"

"I couldn't, Dodson—couldn't get past the new secretary. She said he just couldn't be disturbed. Guess he's writing his sermon."

Dodson's face wrinkled up, as he pondered this. Suddenly he had an inspiration. "Wouldn't be surprised but what Dr. Marshall's wastebasket need emptin'," he said. "I'll be right back. You wait here."

A moment later Peter came bounding down the stairs, all smiles and welcome. As he grasped the young pilot's shoulder and the two of them turned to go back up the stairs, Peter paused and smiled at the bewildered secretary.

"Marines don't always follow all the rules, thank heavens," he said. "*Now* I'm not to be disturbed. I'll be in conference."

They met a grinning Dodson on the stairs. He had forgotten to empty the wastebasket!

The conference turned into a bull session that lasted for two hours. It meant a lot to that young pilot. In fact, it literally saved his life during the terrible October 1945 typhoon in the Pacific, when he was trying to find the five-mile strip of volcanic ash that is Iwo Jima, and land in a 200-mile-an-hour wind. But that's another story.

Allowing such interruptions was typical with Peter. He was always overriding his own rules when he felt that people needed him. It was necessarily a little confusing to secretaries.

Like most ministers, Peter was not the best judge of his own sermons. Almost invariably when he thought he had written one of his best, the rest of us did not rate it so highly. And, when on Saturday night he was bemoaning a "terrible sermon," he could be pretty sure his congregation would think it terrific. How other people rated his sermons was a constant source of astonishment to him.

"That's what keeps me humble," he often said.

seventeen

$\mathcal{V}$ALIANT HEART

Wait on the Lord: be of good courage, and he shall strengthen thine heart. . . .

Psalm 27:14

$\mathcal{A}$ ll up and down Cathedral Avenue, the forsythia was in full bloom. "It's almost exactly the color of the breakfast-room curtains," mused A. D., as she glimpsed the bush by the kitchen door. She was silent though as she placed Peter's boiled egg before him. He was consuming the sports page of *The Washington Post*, along with his tea and toast, and was much too engrossed in the pre-season prospects of the Nats to be interested in conversation.

It was a beautiful Sunday morning. Tomorrow would be April 1st. The trees were a lacework of delicate green. Brilliant dancing sunlight gave no hint that this Sunday would be different from any other.

Peter looked as if he had slept well. He had gone bowling the night before. He bowled every Saturday night with the Methodists, Dr. John Rustin's team. Midnight had seen him putting the finishing touches to his evening sermon. He was going to talk about faith.

It was necessary those days to have two identical morning services. This had seemed the only immediate solution to the increasingly embarrassing problem of overflow crowds. Loudspeakers had long been installed in the downstairs lecture room, the Lincoln Chapel, and even the church office, but still, there were long lines, and people constantly being turned away.

Peter put the paper down abruptly, took the last gulp of tea, and rose, looking at his wrist watch. It was 8:20. Hurriedly he put on his dark gray topcoat and started down the basement steps to the garage. His sermon about Caiaphas was neatly typed, waiting in the black notebook under his arm. His voice came floating back up the stairs, "Thanks for the breakfast, A. D. See you and Catherine at eleven. I've got to rush. I'm almost late now."

At ten o'clock the telephone rang. It was Mary, my sister-in-law, who was also Peter's efficient private secretary, calling to tell me that Peter was not feeling well.

"He will probably not be able to preach at the eleven o'clock service," she explained. Her voice was quiet and level, as it always was. "Don't worry now. One of the men will soon drive him home."

Questioning revealed that severe pains in Peter's chest, radiating out into his arms, had forced him to cut his nine o'clock sermon short. All at once he had interrupted himself to say to the congregation, "I'll have to ask you to forgive me for the way I'm delivering this sermon. I'm not feeling well and may not be able to finish."

He had tried to continue, then suddenly had clutched at his heart and leaned heavily on the pulpit.

"Is there a doctor in the church? If there is, I'd like to ask his help."

Somehow Peter had managed to pronounce the benediction. By then, several men had rushed to the front of the church. Two of them were doctors, one in the uniform of a Navy Commander. They had helped Dr. Marshall off the rostrum and up the stairs to his study. Mary finished by saying that he was resting there in the red leather "lazy-boy" chair.

A. D. and my sister Em, with Peter John close behind them, stood in the bedroom door listening to my side of this conversation.

When I had hung up and had relayed Mary's report, A. D. commented, "Peter has been complaining of pains in his arms for two days, hasn't he?"

I nodded. We had thought the pain merely muscular. Now with a sickening, deadly persistence, one thought kept recurring. I tried to ignore it, but it could not be dismissed. It just wasn't possible, though,

I argued with myself. My husband had one of the strongest physiques I had ever seen. No one of us would voice the thought; but as we waited, watching for the car bringing Peter home, the two words might as well have been written on the wall in neon lights—Heart Attack.

At 10:25 the telephone rang again. This time it was Bob, my brother. His news was that Peter had been carried on a stretcher across the street to George Washington University Hospital, and was now resting comfortably there. He said that Mr. Burroughs, our associate minister, would preach at the eleven o'clock service. Bob tried to be reassuring. He, too, avoided using the words "heart attack."

"I'll be down to the hospital immediately, as soon as I can get a cab," I said hastily, as I hung up.

When I arrived at the hospital, I found Bob and three of the church officers waiting for me. They were standing in a little cluster on the sidewalk, in front of the old red-brick hospital, talking in low voices.

Mr. Blake came forward with outstretched hand. He was trying rather too obviously not to show me his real concern.

"I had a little trouble with *my* heart thirty years ago, Mrs. Marshall, and look at me now. I'm still going strong. Dr. Marshall has a strong body—all we Scotsmen do. We were nourished on Scotch porridge, you know. Don't worry. . . ."

I found Peter's room very dark. He stirred a little as I tiptoed in, and put out one hand to greet me.

"You shouldn't have come, Catherine. You're not up to it . . ." his voice trailed off. It sounded weak and distant.

I felt humbled and touched that Peter would be thinking about *my* health at such a time. The hypos had made him very sleepy. He needed to rest. I stayed only a minute, breathed a silent little prayer, and slipped out.

In the hospital corridor outside, information as to Peter's real condition was dismayingly meager—"Complete, absolute rest," was the instruction given to the special nurse whom the doctor had already secured. Peter's pulse was reported to be regular but "distant." The doctor promised me that he would himself make a cardiograph the next morning. Then we would have the whole story of the nature and extent of the attack. The cardiograph would reveal whether or not the attack was a simple muscular spasm, which would not be so serious, or a coronary thrombosis, which would be very serious indeed.

Until then, there was nothing to do but wait and pray. Even as I caught a cab and started back home, I was conscious of spiritual resources—resources I did know I had—rising within me to meet a dangerous situation. I knew then that the last three years, those quiet, difficult years in bed, had not been wasted. I had been busy storing up reserves of faith. Everything God had taught me, everything I had read of other people's spiritual discoveries was sorely needed now. I wondered what on earth people who have no such resources do in times of sudden personal calamity. . . .

Even so, I realized how pathetically little I and most of my friends really knew about prayer. But the indelible memory, which stands out above all the dramatic events of the next forty-eight hours, is prayer . . . prayer . . . prayer.

On Sunday afternoon, as soon as little Peter was tucked in bed for his afternoon nap, A. D. and I knelt down together to pray. We asked God to take away our icy fears and show us *how* we should pray for Peter.

All afternoon the telephone rang incessantly—friends and members of the church were, of course, eager for news. Our only reports from the hospital, however, were the terse "Resting quietly. Pain somewhat subsided. Still using hypos."

The long afternoon, heavy with uncertainty, lagged unbearably. About four-thirty, three friends came to pray with us. The five of us knelt in the living room of the Manse. One of them especially, Bob McLeod, who loved Peter as if his minister were his own brother, seemed quite broken up. As he tried to pray, Mac's voice kept breaking with little half-sobs. He was indicting himself for what he regarded as his failure to help Peter carry his heavy burden of responsibility at the church.

But when we had finished, we still had no peace of mind. Our prayers seemed unsatisfactory—too scattered, not sufficiently clearcut. We were not sure that they had gone beyond the ceiling.

Down at the old church, after the young people's meeting, about a dozen of the group slipped upstairs to Peter's little cubicle of a study to pray for his recovery. Only a few weeks before, their minister had finished a series of sermons called "He Brought Good News" or "The Lost Secret." Those three sermons had been on God's healing power. They seemed now almost prophetic. The young people's prayers in his study that night showed how surely his points had gone home.

Later, as people were streaming out of the evening church service, the newsboy at the corner of 14th and New York Avenue was shouting at the top of his voice above the noise of traffic: "Doc-tor Pe-ter Mar-shall coll-ap-ses at Noo York Avenoo Chur-urch!!" The story had already been carried on the morning radio newscasts.

The long day was at last drawing to a close. A. D. shared my feeling of the incompleteness and inadequacy of our prayers. We were still groping, confused in mind and heart.

As I got one last report from the hospital and tried to go to sleep, I wondered what tomorrow would bring. Tomorrow, though I could not know it, would bring an even graver crisis.

The real impact of the seriousness of Peter's condition fell about one-thirty in the afternoon on Monday, April 1st. Peter's doctor, who had heard that I was just emerging from a long illness, was apprehensive as to the best way of breaking the news to me. He held a hurried conference with Bob and Mary and Mr. Burroughs. They decided to give me the news piecemeal. Bob and Mary were to come out to the house and tell me a little. Then I was to call the doctor to learn the rest. He sent me his own private phone number, one unpublished in the directory, so that I could reach him day or night.

The final news was grave indeed. It was as the doctor had feared—thrombosis—one artery to the heart completely blocked. Peter's temperature was rising; his blood pressure was going down; the attack was continuing unabated. That's what was causing his pain in breathing; that was why they had put him in an oxygen tent.

"I simply must know the truth," I said. "Tell me, how much a chance does Peter have?"

"Mrs. Marshall," the doctor answered, "it's time to be frank with you. Dr. Marshall has been hard hit. The very most I can give him is a fifty-fifty chance. We are doing absolutely everything we can. We can do no more."

The conversation ended by my saying, "If there is the *least* change in Peter's condition, will you promise to call me, day or night?" He promised that he would.

I put down the telephone receiver mechanically, feeling like some-one made of stone. Several other people were in the room; I was only dimly aware of them.

"It's just about as bad as it can be," I said to no one in particular. Then, "I'd like to be alone awhile." I knew that the time had come to roll up my prayer sleeves and pray as I had never prayed before. If there had previously been any doubt as to what we were to ask God for, there was none now. At last the issue was clear-cut, it was simply—life or death.

After everyone had gone, I sank down on the floor beside the lit-tle blue bedroom chair. I did not shut my eyes. I was looking out at the tops of the trees slowly swaying in the mild spring air, without really seeing them. It was as if I had put off my shoes and stepped out on Holy ground, into the majestic presence of God Himself, the Sovereign Ruler of Heaven and earth. Nothing else in all the world seemed real now—nothing but God and Peter and me.

My first thought was that I must be sure that there was no bit-terness or rebellion in my heart over what had happened, because I knew that these were the particular blocks to my own healing for a long time. Nothing, nothing must block this petition. My inner searching, however, revealed no dregs of bitterness.

Then I tried to relinquish Peter to God, to take to Himself if that was His will. Somehow I could not feel that Peter's work was over. Nor could I discover any sense of fighting against God for Peter's life. The prayer of relinquishment, then, was apparently not the right prayer to pray at that time. Somehow, even after an hour alone in that quiet room, I knew that I had still not found "the prayer" God wanted me to pray. I would simply have to try again later.

Meanwhile the reports from the hospital added nothing to our peace of mind. The heart attack was still continuing. Somehow we got through the dinner hour.

Friends called incessantly, offering to help—"If there is anything we can do. . . ." "If there is anything. . . ." I longed to grab them by the arm and say almost fiercely, "There is only one thing: Pray, pray, pray."

But how many of us, we who had been in churches all our lives, knew how to pray? I did not. Seemingly a thousand times that day I had shut my eyes tight and demanded, "God, make him well. God, please dissolve that blood clot!" But that was not prayer, and I knew it. Tenseness and fear shut out God and I was afraid, desperately afraid. Suppose Peter *did* die. . . . How could I live without him?

I longed for the help of prayer veterans—people who had not wasted precious time as I had wasted it; people who had disciplined themselves to use ordinary run-of-the-mill days for spiritual research; people who knew *why* it was that some prayers are answered and some are not; people who were so filled with Christ's presence that they could be relaxed and calm, even in the face of coronary thrombosis.

Suddenly all former values that I had attached to my friends dropped away. I knew wonderful people who were specialists in nearly every field but that of prayer—trained musicians, engineers, lawyers, even doctors. But in a legal crisis, one does not call on an engineer. Faced with an emergency operation, one does not want just anybody who means well, but the best surgeon available. Why, then, I reasoned, not apply this same common sense to the art of prayer?

Therefore I sent an SOS to two prayer specialists. To my friend, Dr. Glenn Clark,[1] I sent a telegram asking for his prayer help; A. D. telephoned to Alicia Abrahamson, of Washington's Fellowship House.

Mrs. Abrahamson called back to say that all of her household and office staff had dropped everything to have prayers for Peter, that a large group was meeting there that night, and that Peter's illness would be first on their list. Dr. Warner from the National Cathedral telephoned to tell us that special prayers would be said for Dr. Marshall at St. Albans that evening. Telegrams poured in. All of them bearing the same message, "Praying for Peter." They came from New Orleans, Dallas, Tulsa, Chattanooga, Birmingham, Atlanta, Marietta (Georgia), Corinth (Mississippi), and even a cable from our friend Ernest Danly in Tokyo.

By Monday night, prayer for Peter was literally "rising like a fountain" all over the United States. Thousands of people to whom my husband had endeared himself, who felt that his ministry was still sorely needed, were gathered here and there in little groups praying.

Our church people were in a sober, chastened mood. The session of the church called a special meeting and passed a resolution asking each member of the three church boards to spend a quarter hour each evening between 7 and 8 P.M. in prayer for Dr. Marshall. Spontaneously, without anyone calling them together, a large group of

young people gathered in the Lincoln Chapel. Word of the continued seriousness of their minister's situation had spread. The chapel
was nearly full. After many articulate prayers had been spoken, some
of the young people stayed on, just sitting there, apparently praying
silently. One stalwart young man was still there long after everyone
else had gone.

Out at the Manse I was tucking Peter John in bed. Our son was
then six years old. He was very sober and concerned about his daddy.

I sat on the edge of his maple bed to hear his bedtime prayers.
"Peter," I explained, "Jesus has promised us in the Bible that if we
are sick and have faith, He will make us well. Why don't you and I
just ask Him to make Daddy well?"

There was dead silence. I could feel his little mind working on
this. "But, Mommy," Peter questioned, "will God keep His promise?
Does God *always* keep His promises?"

I knew this question had deep significance, and that I was on the
spot. After all, I had no medical assurance that Peter would not die
that night. If I said, "Yes, God does always keep His promises" and
our little boy's father died, not only would Peter suffer the loss of
his earthly father, but his faith in his Heavenly Father would have
been irreparably shattered. If I answered, "Well, sometimes God
keeps His promises, sometimes He doesn't," I would have played
safe as far as external results were concerned, but in our six-year-
old son's little mind, God would forever have been reduced to a
wishy-washy undependable source of help.

Then, in my dilemma, from somewhere deep inside me, out beyond
the icy fear still there, the answer came. It was spoken with confidence, almost as if other lips than mine were speaking, "Yes, Peter,
God does always keep His promises."

In just fifteen hours we were to have the visible proof of that
blind assurance.

How could I ever forget the hours that followed? I lay in bed rigid,
every nerve taut, absolutely unable to sleep. I was ashamed of this;
I knew it was dishonoring God, but I seemed to have no control over
myself. I told God every thought, every emotion, every fear. As long
as I lay there and prayed, I could keep relatively calm, but the minute
I stopped, icy fear choked me again.

I had the distinct impression that a titanic conflict was going on in the world of the spirit. I had never been so aware of an evil personality abroad in our world, call that personality what you will. It was as if the devil himself was putting up a terrific struggle for domination in Peter's body and for domination of fear over me—a fear that would make me let go my hold on God and slip into an abyss of hopelessness. I did not for a moment doubt God's power to heal my husband's heart, but I was so swept by emotion that I could not detach myself sufficiently from the situation to relax and let God in. Suppose, I thought, my fear and lack of faith make it impossible for God to work.

Finally I changed beds, thinking that might help. But it didn't. I held on by sheer will power and became utterly exhausted in the effort. God gave me one thought that helped. Into my weary, tortured mind there came the verses,

> Or what man is there of you, whom if his son ask bread, will he give him a stone?
>
> Or if he ask a fish, will he give him a serpent?
>
> If ye then, being evil, know how to give good gifts unto your children, how much more shall your Father which is in heaven give good things to them that ask him? (Matthew 7:9–11).

It was as if God were saying to me, "If you ask me for life for Peter, do you think I would deceive you and give you death?"

I held on to this for dear life, listening for the telephone summoning me to the hospital, thinking that the long night would never pass. Finally I heard the birds beginning to chirp. Dawn was coming.

At eight o'clock on Tuesday morning Mother and Dad arrived. They had been up all night.

I tried in vain to eat some breakfast. Food would not go down. I was almost suffocated with the physical symptoms of fear, a racing pulse, a churning stomach, and pounding heart.

While the others were eating breakfast I thought of Christ's promise to give peace, "peace not as the world giveth." I told Christ that I had absolutely no control over the tempest of emotion sweeping me on the inside, that I had tried all night to calm it and could not. I asked if He would simply, as a gracious gift, give me that peace right in the middle of my fears, in spite of all Peter's symptoms, as a sign that He would heal him.

Within fifteen minutes that request was granted. Tension and fear just left me; confidence and peace—peace rightly described as "The peace . . . which passeth all understanding"—flowed in. The butterflies left my stomach; the pictures on the wall came back into focus; other people came back into perspective. I knew then that my prayer and those of many others had been heard and answered, and that God wanted Peter healed far more than I did.

From that moment, without any effort on my part, I could stop asking God to spare Peter and begin thanking Him for healing him. It was sometime during the next hour, I learned later, that my husband's pain and difficulty in breathing left.

During that next hour I found myself longing to fulfill literally the directions given us by the Apostle James:

> Is any sick among you? let him call for the elders of the church; and let them pray over him, anointing him with oil in the name of the Lord:

> And the prayer of faith shall save the sick, and the Lord shall raise him up; and if he have committed sins, they shall be forgiven him (James 5:14–15).

I had never seen such anointing done. It seemed an almost fantastic thought. Yet I knew that it had been a much-used ritual of the church in apostolic times—however neglected in our day. The Catholic Church, I also knew, still used it as a preparation for death. But originally, anointing with oil was always a symbol of the *living* power of the Holy Spirit.

I sensed that the little ritual which I longed to perform for Peter would merely be symbolic of an already answered prayer—a prayer that had been answered at the moment that peace flowed into me— just as a marriage ceremony is but the outward symbol of the already existing love and union of two hearts.

"God," I prayed, "maybe this is just silly, but if you want me to do it, you will have to arrange for Peter's oxygen tent to be pushed back." I put a few drops of oil into a tiny bottle to take to the hospital.

At eleven-thirty that morning I walked into his darkened room. No nurses were anywhere in sight. *The oxygen tent was pushed back!* Peter told me, with a smile, that it had been removed just fifteen minutes before.

I bent over his bed and told him what I wanted to do. He smiled up at me and said quite promptly, "Yes, do, go ahead." As I timidly touched Peter's forehead with a drop of the oil, and prayed, thanking God for taking care of him, I had the feeling that He was smiling on us. This was what He had wanted all along. This had not only His approval, but His joy in it.

From that Tuesday morning, Peter made steady progress. That night he had his first truly refreshing sleep. Wednesday, his very low blood pressure went up. Thursday, his temperature, for the first time, fell below 100 degrees. Some time Thursday night it fell to normal.

Peter had a long convalescence ahead of him, a long period of enforced rest, but the crisis was past. There was no longer that dreadful hanging on the border line between life and death. We knew then that he would get well. We knew that God had spared his life for a specific purpose. The truth was that the most productive and significant period of Peter's life lay immediately ahead.

eighteen

THE DOMINIE

And ye shall be brought before governors and kings for my sake. . . .
For it is not ye that speak, but the Spirit of your Father which speaketh in you.

Matthew 10:18, 20

a few days after Peter was elected Chaplain of the United States Senate, he wrote to "Miss Mary" in Marietta, Georgia, to reassure this dyed-in-the-wool Southern Democrat:

January 16, 1947

My dear Miss Mary:

First, let me assure you that I have not sold out to the carpet-baggers! My election as Chaplain of the Senate does not really compromise me with the Republicans, although it might appear to do so, since they are in the majority. But I have just as many friends among the Democrats and will be praying for them too, since I dare to believe that God is neither Democrat or a Republican.

The whole thing came as a surprise to me—out of the blue—and I agreed to accept it, if it were a clear call, and if it came to me as a call of the Chief. So it did—and I could do no other than accept it. I was most uneasy about the flurry on the floor when the matter came up, but was assured that it was occasioned rather by the Bilbo affair than the merits of the case of the chaplain. . . . Not since 1879 has the chaplain been a Presbyterian, so they cannot say we are hogging things. . . .

Catherine and Peter are both well, although the little fellow is at home today with a touch of something or other. . . . He requests that

he not be called "Wee Peter" any more, since he is growing so big.
So he suggests that he be called "big Peter" and that I be called "ener-
mous Peter."

Our love to you always,
"Enermous" Peter

The move to nominate Peter as chaplain had indeed come as a surprise to him. The men spearheading the Republican conference had just quietly made up their minds that they would like to have Peter Marshall, the pastor of Abraham Lincoln's old church, as their chaplain. They had sought Peter out and challenged him with the opportunity of service to his country that the chaplaincy presented.

Peter's first and only brush with party politics followed. For him it was anything but a pleasant experience. His nomination touched off the first heated debate of the 80th Congress. The Republicans were in control of the Senate for the first time in almost two decades. The Democratic minority was therefore sharply on the defensive. They were righteously indignant that the Republican conference would want to replace the office of Senate Chaplain along with the other offices. They appeared to be horrified that there should be "any question of partisanship in the selection of a chaplain" (Senator Barkley, in the *Congressional Record*).

It took nine closely printed columns in the *Congressional Record* to record the debate that followed.

Mr. Baukhage, Washington news analyst and commentator, said: "But the Republicans had their majority, Dr. Marshall got the job, and as far as I can learn, nobody has regretted the choice."

Next morning most papers in the United States carried a story about it. Said *The Washington Post*:

DR. PETER MARSHALL ELECTED CHAPLAIN AFTER PARTY FIGHT. First fight on Chaplain. The Chaplain's job set off the first political debate in the Senate yesterday.

All of this was very painful to Peter. He was very embarrassed for Dr. Harris, then Senate Chaplain, a friend of his, and pastor of Washington's Foundry Methodist Church. It appeared that Dr. Harris had learned what was happening only by reading about it in the newspapers.

It was uphill going for Peter at first. He was immediately troubled by the fact that the Official Reporters of Senate Debates wanted a typed copy of his prayer before it was delivered each day. That meant that it was scarcely possible for him to pray extemporaneously, as he was accustomed to do.

One night, soon after his election, Peter had an opportunity to talk this over with Starr Daily. We had finished dinner at the Manse and had settled ourselves comfortably in easy chairs in the living room.

Peter was watching our guest with great interest. Starr Daily had a tall, spare frame, with skin stretched tight over high cheekbones, and alert, but gentle, almost luminous eyes. We had heard much of him, a once notorious convict, whose conversion was as cataclysmic and as miraculous as that of Saul of Tarsus.

The evening was turning into a memorable occasion. To be with Starr Daily was a fascinating experience. Peter commented later, "Starr Daily is the best living proof I've ever seen that 'a new creature in Christ Jesus' is not just the old man patched up, but an altogether new person living in the same body."

"It's a great opportunity you have there, Peter," said Mr. Daily in his flat Middle Western drawl. "If God can really pray those prayers through you, amazing things will happen."

"That's just the trouble," Peter retorted, "that brings up quite a point. I never like to write out public prayers. Yet, in the Senate, if I insist on giving the prayer extemporaneously, it will complicate things for the Reporters of Debates."

"So, you're afraid God can't direct a prayer which has to be composed ahead of delivery and read. Is that it?"

"Exactly. It gives me an uneasy feeling. I don't like it. In fact the atmosphere in the Senate Chamber makes it hard to pray anyway—shuffling papers, coughing, what not—a feeling of 'Let's get this over quickly so we can get on with important things.' It's like standing up and trying to pray in Griffith Stadium on the opening day of the Nats' baseball season, just before the President tosses in the first ball. I find that the Senators appreciate my prayers in inverse ratio to their length."

Mr. Daily grinned but said nothing for a moment. He seemed quietly to have withdrawn himself for deep thought. Finally he said,

"Peter, you know I wouldn't worry about writing out those prayers. Under the circumstances I really think God can tell you better what to pray as you sit quietly in your study, than He could if you waited until you got to the Senate Chamber. Let's ask God right now to write those prayers through you." So the two men quietly claimed, for Peter, God's promise that if any man lacks wisdom, "let him ask of God, that giveth to all men liberally, and upbraideth not; and it shall be given him" (James 1:5).

Peter seemed relieved. Thereafter he worried no more about writing out the Senate prayers. Moreover, the prayer request made that night was granted. God *did* write and pray those prayers through Peter.

Immediately the public press all over the United States began to note their brevity, their pungency, their sharp relevance.

An article in the *Kansas City Star* noted:

A CHAPLAIN THEY LISTEN TO
PRAYER MORE THAN A ROUTINE IN THE SENATE NOW

Not without reason are the prayers of the Rev. Peter Marshall, Chaplain of the Senate of the United States, attracting national attention. . . . Even the Senators are now listening to the prayers that open the session. . . .

A feature article by Robert Burkhardt in *The New York Times* suggested that the "Solons' Shepherd" had a "spirited way of being spiritual." Three examples of the way the prayers fitted the situation followed:

. . . During the debates on the appointment of David Lilienthal to be chairman of the Atomic Energy Commission, one of Dr. Marshall's prayers included:

Teach us that liberty is not only to be loved, but also to be lived. Liberty is too precious a thing to be buried in books. It costs too much to be hoarded. Make us to see that liberty is not the right to do as we please, but the opportunity to please to do what is right.

Later, on June 17, a day of varied business in the Senate, including a brisk argument on a resolution to authorize the Committee on Civil Service to investigate the appointment of first-, second-, or third-class postmasters, Dr. Marshall's prayer asked:

> Since we strain at gnats and swallow camels, give us a new standard of values and the ability to know a trifle when we see it and to deal with it as such.

At the time when Secretary of State Marshall left Washington to attend the Council of Foreign Ministers, the Senate Chaplain gave voice to the prayers of many when he asked:

> May Thy Spirit move them, that there may be concession without coercion and conciliation without compromise.[1]

Commented the *Chicago Sun-Times* under the headline, "A New Bite to Senate Prayers":

> The least heeded of any of the millions of words uttered in the United States Senate had usually been those of the chaplain, who opens each session with prayer. But now some observers are beginning to urge Senators to get there early enough to hear these utterances, for the new chaplain, the Rev. Peter Marshall, pastor of the New York Avenue Presbyterian Church, avoids the usual platitudes and is handing out some tart advice to the lawmakers. . . .[2]

Newspapermen, as well as the Senators themselves, put their own interpretations on how those tart morsels came to be. The most usual explanation was that Dr. Marshall must be assiduously studying the legislation under consideration and framing his prayers to influence it. What other explanation could there possibly be for their pertinence?—newspapermen asked.

Senator Arthur H. Vandenberg, the president pro-tem, joked: "I never know whether Dr. Marshall is praying for me or at me."
Life magazine had something to say about it:

> . . . When Dr. Marshall prayerfully addressed his God, he first took pains to throw the stuffed shirt into the laundry bag. "We confess, our Father," he prayed one day in the chamber of the United States Senate, "that we know we need Thee, yet our swelled heads and our

stubborn wills keep us trying to do without Thee. Forgive us for making so many mountains out of molehills and for exaggerating both our own importance and the problems that confront us. . . ."

Listening to such humorous and colloquial words from their chaplain, United States Senators often had the feeling that they were being prayed at as well as being prayed for. . . .[3]

Such was actually not the case.

Peter consistently denied the Press's assertion that he prayed to the Senators, in order to influence them or legislation, rather than to God.

"There is no politics in prayer," he said to a reporter of the *Omaha World Herald*, "and for that reason," the 45-year-old Presbyterian minister said, "I consider knowledge of the inside of Senatorial activities to be outside my pastoral duties."

Another reporter commented:

With characteristic humility, Peter Marshall views his assignment as that of intermediary, not a spiritual influence. His function is to talk to God, not to an audience. If there are others to join in the petitions, fine; that gives added strength, but a full house is not essential.[4]

The simple truth was that the pithy prayers often seemed so pertinent because God was praying through Peter. This was strikingly illustrated in one instance.

On the night of April 2, 1947, the Senate was in session almost until midnight. David E. Lilienthal had been nominated as chairman of the Atomic Energy Commission. His nomination was being hotly contested in a full-dress Republican attack, spearheaded by Senator Robert Taft of Ohio. At the end of over four hours of debate, when the men were exhausted and tempers were raw, Senator Kenneth Wherry of Nebraska happened to have the floor. The *Congressional Record* records the first part of the little drama that followed:

MR. MORSE: Mr. President—

THE PRESIDING OFFICER: Does the Senator from Nebraska yield to the Senator from Oregon? . . .

MR. WHERRY: No, Mr. President; I desire to move that the Senate take a recess. I shall be glad to yield to the Senator for a question or for any observation he wishes to make respecting the unanimous-consent agreement, but I shall not yield to him for extended remarks. The Senator knows that. . . .

MR. PEPPER: Will the Senator yield?

MR. WHERRY: No; not just now. Mr. President, I inquire if there is objection to the request I have just made? . . .
Mr. President, then I move that the Senate recess until tomorrow at 12 o'clock noon.

THE PRESIDING OFFICER: The question is on the motion of the Senator from Nebraska.

MR. TOBEY: I suggest the absence of a quorum.

THE PRESIDING OFFICER: The motion of the Senator from Nebraska is not debatable. The question is on the motion. (Putting the question.)

MR. MORSE: Mr. President, I wish to be recorded as voting "no."

THE PRESIDING OFFICER: The "ayes" seem to have it.

So at almost midnight the Senate finally recessed. Senator Morse and Senator Wherry happened to get to the same door at the same time. Mr. Morse threw some papers he was carrying on a nearby desk, approached Mr. Wherry, upbraiding him for refusing to let him have the floor. Hot words were spoken, other Senators intervened and stepped between the two men. It was all over in a few minutes. Later Morse and Wherry were seen sitting beside each other in the little Senate subway car, talking in friendly fashion, heading for the Senate Office Building.

The papers, however, did not let the matter drop there. The next morning the Washington papers exaggerated the incident into a near fist fight. Somehow Peter did not see a copy of the paper before he left for Capitol Hill. He got to the Senate Chamber knowing nothing at all about what had happened. In any case, he had written his prayer for April 3 two days before.

That morning he prayed:

Gracious Father, we, Thy children, so often confused, live at cross-purposes in our central aims, and hence we are at cross-purposes with each other. Take us by the hand and help us to see things from Thy viewpoint, that we may see them as they really are. We come to choices and decisions with a prayer upon our lips, for our wisdom fails us. Give us Thine, that we may do Thy will. In Jesus' name. AMEN.

As he left the Senate Chamber, Senator Wherry followed him into the corridor. Assuming that Peter knew all about the midnight disagreement of the night before and had beamed his prayer directly at Senator Morse and himself, he said, "Parson, I guess you know God pretty well. You know the Catholics believe in having a father confessor. Will you be mine? I'm awfully sorry for what happened last night. . . ."

Peter was puzzled. He had no idea what Senator Wherry was talking about. It was not until later that he found out. Only God could thus have written a prayer which so perfectly fitted the situation; only God could have used that prayer so appropriately for His own purposes.

Being guided by God so specifically in what he would pray or preach was nothing new to Peter, however difficult it might be for some people to believe. Many examples of this might be cited. On Sunday, December 7, 1941, Peter was to preach to the regiment of midshipmen in the Naval Academy at Annapolis.

All the preceding week he had been haunted by a strange feeling that he should change his announced topic and preach a particular sermon. It was a feeling he could not shake off. On Sunday morning he confided it to Chaplain Thomas.

"If your feeling about it is that strong, follow it by all means," was the chaplain's advice.

So Peter preached on the text, seemingly a strange text for young midshipmen:

For what is your life? It is even a vapour, that appeareth for a little time and then vanisheth away (James 4:14).

In the chapel before him was the December graduating class, young men who in a few days would receive their commissions and go on active duty.

As we were driving back to Washington that afternoon, suddenly the program on the car radio was interrupted. The announcer's voice was grave. His apparently routine words throbbed with emotion: "Ladies and Gentlemen. Stand by for an important announcement. This morning the United States Naval Base at Pearl Harbor was bombed in a surprise Japanese attack. . . ."

Instantly we knew that we were living through one of history's dramatic moments, that fateful December 7th, "the day that would long live in infamy."

Within a month many of the boys to whom Peter had just preached would go down to hero's graves in strange waters. Soon all of them would be exposed to the risks and dangers of war, and Peter, under God's direction, had preached to them—young, vital, alive as they were that morning—about death and immortality.

Since April 1789, the American Congress has always been opened with prayer asking God's blessing and wisdom for our highest legislative body. Sometimes Americans have regarded these prayers as merely a perfunctory gesture and the office of Chaplain as just another useless political plum.

In fact, in 1854 there was a strong movement to abolish Congressional chaplaincies. "We are opposed to having chaplains to the two branches of our national legislature," cried the old *Washington Sentinel.* "We hope the last of them has been elected. . . . Short as the prayers are, they are bores. . . ."

Though the anti-chaplain movement was defeated, and has not since been revived, today some people, if they ever stop to consider the matter, might still wonder if those prayers are more than just a bit of parsley garnishing the political platter.

Peter himself regarded his election as chaplain as "a great honor, but not for myself." He meant that it was a chance for him to do Christ's work in a new setting.

The particular concept which he longed to give his Congressional flock was that God was not only concerned about American policy, but that he could tell the individual legislator how to vote. It was not that Peter wanted to influence legislation; but he did want God to have the chance to influence it.

How well he succeeded in this primary objective is best told by the Senators themselves and by the newsmen who watched and listened. Senator Lucas commented: "Peter Marshall exercised a spiritual influence and moral guidance felt by every member here. While he had no voice in determining policy . . . no vote . . . his prayers carried weight in our heart and many times moved us in the right direction. . . ."

Tris Coffin, in his *Washington Times-Herald* column, "The Day Book," called Dr. Marshall "The conscience of the Senate. His voice was soft and gentle, but his words cut cleanly through the pompousness and demagoguery on Capitol Hill." Mr. Coffin went on to describe how he watched the Senators after one of Peter's prayers: "The Senators sat quietly, a little humbled, as they always were by the sincerity of the young chaplain. . . ."

Commented Senator Harley Kilgore of West Virginia, "Peter Marshall expresses more feeling and says more in his short prayers than all the Senators put together the rest of the day."

An editorial in *The Washington Post* said, "The Presbyterian minister opened the ears of the bowed Senators to his words of prayer and he put those words alongside their subsequent speeches. The prayers were novel out of the mouth of a minister, pointed in their application to the business at hand . . . charged with a hortatory spirit that carried conviction. His voice had a vibrancy, his word a Scot's tang, his presence, a manliness that enabled his elocution to linger in the Senatorial memory."[5]

Newspapermen are not given to becoming lyrical over preachers; therefore those were words of high praise. In spite of them, however, Peter was often discouraged in the beginning of his chaplaincy. At first there were few Senators there to hear the prayer. Those who were there seemed to Peter to be cold and indifferent. There were days when the new chaplain was convinced that he was just wasting his time on Capitol Hill.

Then things began to happen. One day the Senate was engaged in an important debate on the Sugar Bill. One of the Senators approached Peter at the close of his prayer. He had a quizzical look in his eyes. "Dr. Marshall," he said, "I've been listening pretty closely to what you've been saying in your prayers. You seem to think a man can get specific guidance from the Lord about his work." He paused, then went on a bit diffidently. "Tell me now, do you really think God could tell me how to vote on the Sugar Bill?"

"I certainly do," Peter replied promptly. "Of course, God may not send you a telegram. My own experience backs up what Abe Lincoln said once, 'When God wants me to do or not to do anything, He can always find a way of letting me know!'"

Such sincere seeking on the part of any Senator thrilled Peter. It made him feel that at last he was succeeding in his primary aim of pointing the men to a higher wisdom than their own.

More and more Senators began leaving their offices and committee rooms early in order to hear the opening prayer. Visitors in the gallery, pressmen, even the page boys began looking forward to those prayers.

Fan mail began coming to Peter from far-flung readers of the *Congressional Record*. There was even talk of putting the invocation after quorum call, so that more of the Senators could manage to be present.

Of all the appreciative listeners, none was more enthusiastic than Senator Arthur H. Vandenberg. The Senator from Michigan explained, "Rev. Peter Marshall was Chaplain of the Senate for two years while I presided as president pro tempore.... Thus it was my daily privilege to greet him each noon when the Senate convened and to present him to my colleagues for his daily prayer. This duty swiftly became a precious privilege for me, and this routine swiftly became an inspiration, and my chaplain became my intimate and priceless friend...."

This meeting each noon became a time to which both men looked forward. Peter's routine was to go first to the office of the Official Reporters of Debates, pass the time of day with the reporters, leave his hat and coat there, and then go to Senator Vandenberg's office. The two men usually spent about ten minutes talking, and then walked slowly together into the Senate Chamber.

There was nothing stuffy about their relationship.

"Come on, Dominie," Senator Vandenberg would say, "it's one minute to twelve—time to throw you to the wolves."

Often the Senator whispered some brief comment to Peter at the conclusion of his prayer.

At the time of the convening of the 81st Congress, Peter prayed a thirty-three word prayer for his tired, overburdened Senatorial flock. The prayer ended with the words, "Lord . . . have mercy upon them."

That was too much for Senator Vandenberg. He couldn't resist the aside to Peter, "Now I know just how a condemned man feels!"

Commented Mrs. Vandenberg, "You know, 'Pop' just thinks of Peter Marshall as one of his little boys."

It was typical of Peter that he made just as many friends among the newspaper reporters, the page boys, the Capitol guards, and elevator operators as he did among the Senators.

One morning my husband started out the Manse door with a checkerboard and a small wooden box under his arm.

I was puzzled. "I'm curious to know, Peter, why you've started taking games to the church office."

"It's my chess set. I've got a date to play chess with Gregor Macpherson, one of the reporters on the Hill. I'm going up early today."

"Gregor Macpherson, good Irish name," I volunteered.

"Huh!" Peter retorted.

The chess tournament was played in the reporters' office. The other men were greatly amused by it. They hadn't thought Dr. Marshall would really take time off to keep the date. Little did they know Peter, the G.G.P.

"He lost," Mr. Macpherson said afterward. "He was only an average chess player, but I never saw anybody take a game so seriously or work so hard at it."

Another one of the Official Reporters of Debates volunteered, "How I admired his straightforward way, his freedom from all cant and hypocrisy, his unusual, impelling diction, his sturdy personality. . . ."

Clearly, it was just this ability to endear himself to other men that was giving Peter the beginning of a new ministry, a ministry that went far beyond his public prayers.

"Immediately," commented Senator Saltonstall of Massachusetts, "we felt the impact of Dr. Marshall's prayers, so we wanted to know him better."

The opportunities to know their chaplain better often came at times when Peter acted in the capacity of a pastor to the Senators and their families. There were occasions on which he married their children, called when they were ill, comforted them in times of personal bereavement.

Peter had the imaginative ability to put himself in other men's shoes and thus to sense their real needs.

"It is part of my task as Senate Chaplain," he said in a newspaper interview,[6] "to articulate the needs that all these men in the Senate feel. . . ."

In the main, therefore, the Senate prayers fell into two categories.

There were those whose aim was to deal with the Senators' personal difficulties, like this one aimed at the problem of pressure:

Lord Jesus, as we pray for the Members of this body, its officers, and all those who share in its labors, we remember that Thou wert never in a hurry and never lost Thine inner peace even under pressure greater than we shall ever know.

But we are only human.
We grow tired.

We feel the strain of meeting deadlines, and we chafe under frustration.

We need poise and peace of mind, and only Thou canst supply the deepest needs of tired bodies, jaded spirits, and frayed nerves.

Give to us Thy peace and refresh us in our weariness, that this may be a good day with much done and done well, that we may say with Thy servant Paul, "I can do all things through Christ, who gives me strength." AMEN. (June 12, 1948)

Then there were those prayers that held up a virile patriotic idealism, a patriotism in which Peter's gratitude for America was always dominant:

Help us, our Father, to show other nations an America to imitate—not the America of loud jazz music, self-seeking indulgence, and love of money, but the America that loves fair play, honest dealing, straight talk, real freedom, and faith in God.

Make us to see that it cannot be done as long as we are content to be coupon clippers on the original investment made by our forefathers.

Give us faith in God and love for our fellow men, that we may have something to deposit on which the young people of today can draw interest tomorrow.

By Thy grace, let us this day increase the moral capital of this country. AMEN. (June 11, 1948).

It is news when Senators look forward to prayers, when newsmen consider them worth publishing; when periodicals with such varied approaches as labor magazines, *The Reader's Digest,* and *The New Yorker* repeatedly quote them.

An answered prayer is worth recording. Few who followed Dr. Marshall's chaplaincy could doubt that the petition which Starr Daily and Peter quietly prayed in our living room was abundantly granted. In the pages of the *Congressional Record* stands the proof—the vitality and timelessness of living, God-inspired words.

nineteen

⫟OGETHER

Endeavouring to keep the unity of the Spirit in the bond of peace.

Ephesians 4:3

⫟he years brought many changes for Peter and me. Into our marriage came an ever-deepening fusion of heart and mind, though never a static peace. It was a harmony growing out of diversity in unity, the most melodious harmony there is.

I had successfully weathered the difficulties involved in accepting my share of responsibility for Peter's career. Even my three years in bed had contributed to our partnership. During those years, when I was necessarily shut out of the organizational work of our church, I found a more important field of service behind the scenes, at the very heart of Peter's life and ministry.

His job was constantly to pour himself out for the hungry hearts of men and women. My job was to try to feed him spiritually, to strengthen him, to supply understanding and encouragement, so that he would always have something to give to others.

We came to see this oneness between us as the open door by which the Spirit of God poured into our lives and work. When that agreement was missing, the door was closed; we were "on our own"; our work was self-managed, fruitless.

When Peter and I could stand shoulder to shoulder at the center of our congregation, the unity between us extended into the life of our church, and God's blessings rained on our flock.

It was the same invaluable lesson that the apostles had learned at Pentecost. Like those first disciples, we discovered that the results of real accord could be breathtaking, limitless.

During these years we collaborated on some writing for the Board of Christian Education of the Presbyterian Church. Together we wrote *The Mystery of the Ages,* a Bible study on Ephesians and two issues of the little devotional magazine *Today.* This collaboration not only proved to be rewarding, but was also fun. Not even our closest friends could tell where my husband's writing left off and mine began.

Increasingly we thought through and talked through Peter's projected sermons together. Frequently I did the spadework, the research, and he, the final writing.

Often he would telephone me from the church office, "Catherine, I'm working on a sermon. I'm stuck. Let me read you what I've written so far. See what you think."

Peter once confided to a friend, "You know, I think my most effective sermons have been the ones Catherine and I have worked on together; and the trips to preach away from home that have brought the greatest results are the times when I have felt no tension on leaving Catherine against her wishes. I don't see why it can't be that way all the time. *I have to accept those calls to preach.* God called me to preach; that call hasn't been revoked. If He wants me to live, He'll see to it that I do. How *can* I make Catherine see that?"

Inherent in these remarks was the greatest proof of the reality of our union. It was the pain each of us experienced when there was the least pulling apart. The one point on which we had still not achieved perfect agreement was this matter of Peter's out-of-town preaching engagements. Always we had a somewhat divergent point of view about it. Peter's heart attack drew that divergence into sharp focus. It was no longer simply a question of the advisability of this policy or that. Peter and I both knew that his life was probably at stake.

My husband's heart, the doctors told us, had been severely damaged. Nevertheless, they had promised him, after a long rest, a 90 to 95 per cent return to normal activity.

That long rest he had taken—ten weeks in the hospital, two at the Manse, three months at "Waverley." For such a vital, vigorous man, he had exhibited a disciplined patience which amazed us all.

As he resumed his ministry in September 1946, at first my husband was cautious in deciding how much activity he would undertake. Gradually, as he did more, apparently with no ill effects to his heart, he gained confidence. His natural vitality and exuberance flowed back. He looked well; he felt well. He enjoyed life as much as ever. He had a deceitful type of heart condition. The usual hampering symptoms—shortness of breath, pain, swelling of the ankles—were entirely absent. This encouraged him to do too much; it encouraged others to demand too much of him.

The tempo of his activity steadily accelerated. A year after the heart attack, those of us close to Peter knew that he was once again treading on dangerous ground. The question was: What could we do about it? How could we stop him?

I mapped a veritable campaign in an effort to deal with the frightening juxtaposition of a seriously damaged heart and a not-to-be contained spirit in one man.

First, I tried a direct approach—that of trying to persuade Peter to a quieter way of life. I found all my arguments and pleas unavailing. It was like reasoning with a closed door. There was in my husband a quality of iron determination to pursue his own course.

Many friends, some at my suggestion, also had long talks with him. They tried to convince him that a physically geographically limited ministry, with more time for reading, study, and prayer, could in the end be a more fruitful ministry. They got no further than I had. Peter could simply not see it that way.

My next approach was to enter into a living conspiracy with Peter's secretary, members of his church staff, and many friends. All of us tried to shield him whenever we could, with or without his knowledge. Mostly he simply resented what he regarded as coddling.

In June of that year, the annual Sunday School picnic was held at Marshall Hall on the Potomac. To everyone's consternation their minister insisted on taking part in a baseball game.

Dr. Marshall was at bat. He swung and hit a long drive to left center.

"Dr. Marshall, let me run for you," one of the men pleaded.

"Not on your life," yelled Peter as he started for first base.

Several of the men were frightened, and actually ran the bases beside him. Peter got to third base and made it home on the next hit. He simply scoffed at the solicitude of his friends.

I saw then that Peter had tried to face up to the kind of life and ministry he would have if he decided to slow down, to protect himself as we wanted him to. He could not abide what he saw—a studied neurotic prepossession with self, a ministry geographically circumscribed, limited to Washington, an increasing curtailment of all activity. It would mean a narrow, limited life while he was still a young man at the very height of his powers. No, that was not for him, and he knew it.

Therefore, he made a bargain with his Lord. He put himself completely in God's hands. His part of the bargain was that he would continue to give his best to the ministry, leaving the result, including his health, entirely up to God. When that transaction was completed, the only unsolved problem in Peter's mind was the task of persuading me to his point of view. He knew perfectly well that I was still trying to protect him, still trying desperately to find another way out of our dilemma.

Perhaps, I reasoned, my prayers for Peter had not been answered, because I had asked God for too little. Perhaps God wanted to cure Peter's heart, so that he would not have to live a limited life.

Once again, as I had done during the crisis of Peter's first heart attack, I sought the help of prayer experts. This was done with Peter's full knowledge and cooperation. Yet those prayers were not answered in the way we hoped they would be. That door too was shut in our faces.

In the end, I did come to the relinquishment which Peter had wanted all along, but not until I had tried everything else.

Jesus said, ". . . if two of you shall agree on earth as touching anything that they shall ask, it shall be done for them of my Father which is in Heaven" (Matthew 18:19). I began to feel that this agreement between Peter and me in relation to his health was of primary importance, and that unity could be achieved only by a giving in on my part. I knew from my own experience that the prayer of relinquishment often has great power. I hoped that in this case it would make it possible for God someway, somehow, to save Peter's life

for many years. Perhaps God would have to change his tempera-
ment in order to do that, but I knew that God could do even that.

That was how it came about that in late September 1948, I turned
Peter over to God for better or for worse. We were driving to Rich-
mond when I told Peter about it. He seemed vastly relieved. Practically speaking, this simply meant to Peter that I was saying, "Preach
as often as you feel God wants you to. I'm hands off now."

So he did preach, more and more frequently, with ever-increasing
power and authority.

And I stood by, loving him, alternately proud of him and desperately afraid for him, utterly helpless, with a wistful heart.

Peter's whole attitude about his own health problem can finally
be understood only when viewed against the background of his attitude toward death. There was in him no fear of death.

He preached many a sermon on immortality. Yet his attitude on
the subject was sometimes quite misrepresented, as when *Time* (in
its February 7, 1949, issue) said of him: "Dr. Marshall . . . frequently
ended services by saying, 'If I am still here, I'll be with you next
week.'"[1]

I cannot remember Peter's ending any service with such a remark;
nor did he who enjoyed life so much do any straining at the leash
of mortality.

At the same time, Peter was exceedingly realistic and consistently Christian in his attitude toward death. In his mind, the soul
and the body were two completely separate things. "You and I *are*
souls," he reiterated frequently, "living *in* bodies."

One fall as we were returning home from Cape Cod, we drove
over a viaduct which arched over a large New Jersey cemetery. "Nice
straight plantings down there," Peter said admiringly. A. D. and I
recoiled at such callousness, but Peter laughed at us and refused to
retract. He knew that I, up to that time, had never really faced up
to the fact of death in human experience, and that *my* attitude was
the unhealthy one.

> Why are we so afraid to think of death? [he asked once in a sermon]
> Why do we shun it so?
> We try so hard to disguise the fact of death.
> And we are so stupid about it.

We rouge the cheeks of the corpse, and dress it up in its best suit.
And then we say with ridiculous gravity: "How natural he looks. . . ."

We, who call ourselves Christians, act in a very pagan way.
We gaze upon the lifeless, human clay . . .
We touch the cold cheek . . .
We line up to pass by the casket and "view the remains," as the stupid phrase has it,
    as if we had never heard of the soul, and never understood what personality is.

If this thing that we call death were some leprous calamity that befell only a few of us . . .
If it were something that could be avoided, then we might enter into a conspiracy of silence concerning it.
But it is inevitable.
Death comes to every man—to every woman.

It is life's greatest and perhaps its only certainty.

Peter Marshall believed in immortality more surely than anyone I have ever known. As a very young preacher he had been curious about the details of the life we human beings are going to live "behind the curtain."

During the years of his Covington ministry, he ferreted out everything in the Scriptures about immortality, pored over books on spiritualism, including Sir Oliver Lodge's *Raymond* and *Phantom Walls.*

Yet in the end, he rejected spiritualism as dangerous, unworthy of Christians, and not having the approval of Christ. Thereafter, though his curiosity remained, he left spiritualism strictly alone.

One evening at the Manse we received a telephone call telling us that a woman in our congregation had just died. She was a dear friend. She had been desperately ill for a long time, so that her death was not unexpected.

Peter came away from the telephone slowly and sank down in his favorite chair. His mind seemed far away.

"Gertrude died about ten minutes ago," he said thoughtfully. "I wonder what thrilling experience she's having at this very moment."

There was a young student at Davidson College to whom Peter Marshall was a veritable hero. This boy was killed in action in Japan in World War II.

One Sunday morning at the close of the service, the young soldier's mother spoke to Peter to tell him of her son's death.

Some time later she had occasion to tell me about Peter's reaction to the news. "Dr. Marshall gripped my hand and said, 'You'll see him again!' Of course I had believed that, but as Dr. Marshall spoke that one sentence with such depth of feeling, warm sweet comfort flowed into my lonely heart."

Ever since Peter's own brush with death at the time of his heart attack, there had been an added note of authority in his preaching that went straight to the heart of things. After that experience, Peter saw precious human life only in relation to time and eternity, which is its true perspective.

It was as if on his journey through life, Peter had mounted to the top of a plateau, where his own ultimate goal was clearly visible on the horizon. As he feverishly planned and worked on the details of New York Avenue's building program, he seemed to have a premonition that he would not be with us when the spire of the new church rose skyward. Already, he saw himself as just another name in the long list of ministers who had served New York Avenue Presbyterian Church.

In an after-dinner talk made to those who had helped in the building campaign, he had said:

Think of all the history these walls know . . .
How administrations have come and gone.
Wars have broken out in all their fury and have rumbled into silence
But the church goes on . . .
    Gurley
      Mitchell
        Paxton
          Bartlett
            Radcliffe
              Sizoo
                Marshall

And those who come after us. . . .
The church will go on.

The church has gone on . . . not always the same, thank God, changing, adapting itself to meet new conditions, testifying in every age to
the Spirit of the Living God through a new flaming forth of that spirit
in new forms.
No other institution has such a record, living on through the centuries, utterly dependent upon human faith and divine grace.

Nothing reveals quite so clearly Peter Marshall's own clear-eyed
humility about himself as a little incident which took place soon
after his heart attack. In the fall of 1947 when he had resumed work
again, a minister friend from Hagerstown, Maryland, dropped in on
him at the church office.

"Well, Peter," the friend asked, "I'm curious to know something.
What did you learn during your illness?"

"Do you really want to know?" Peter answered promptly. "I
learned that the Kingdom of God goes on without Peter Marshall."

twenty

EE YOU IN THE MORNING

Jesus said unto her . . . whosoever liveth and believeth in me shall never die. Believest thou this?

John 11:25–26

t was Monday, January 24, 1949. About noon the telephone at the Manse rang. The masculine voice at the other end had a strange, Italian accent.

"Dis iss Toni Gallupi . . . Iss Missus Marshall der?"

Immediately I spotted an unmistakable trace of the land of heather and mist behind the "Italian."

"Peter, you goof," I laughed, recognizing one of my husband's favorite tricks. Often he tried to deceive me with various assorted accents.

"Kate, how'd you know it was I?" he asked.

"Darling, don't you know I'd know your voice anywhere, anytime?"

"I've just gotten back from giving the Senate prayer," Peter explained. "I'll have a bit of lunch downtown, write a couple of letters, and come home some time between three and four. Remember, I have a date with Peter Dookums."

Yes, I remembered. Peter's date with our young son was the promise of a trip downtown which had been fitted into a busy schedule by a little boy's persistence. One of the engines in the train set was no longer pulling its share of the load. The two Peters had long considered the possibility of trading the locomotive in for a new one.

New York Avenue Church had no monopoly on tradition; even the trains had a tradition. The now-decrepit engine was part of a train set that had been presented to their new minister by a group of the church men on Christmas, twelve years before. Hadn't Mr. Marshall said that all of his boyhood he had longed for two things, a bicycle and a train? The men figured it was a little late for the bicycle, but they decided that an electric train would make a delightful surprise Christmas present.

The men who gave the present subsequently enjoyed it almost as much as the minister. Every Christmas saw a few of them out at the Manse, down on hands and knees on the third floor, setting up track, testing built-in whistles, building control panels, talking and laughing, looking a trifle sheepish when they came back down the stairs. Later, when our son turned six and cared not one whit for airplanes, but developed a little boy's passion for trains, his father gave him the set for his very own.

On Monday, Wee Peter, armed with all of his well-marked Lionel catalogs, was in the lower hall, patiently waiting. The green Oldsmobile had scarcely come in sight before he had flung open the door and was out on the porch, Jeff beside him, joyously leaping and barking, as he always did when Peter came home.

Twenty minutes later, the realistic worm-driven locomotive tender, with its eight drivers, the crane, green gondola, and long red caboose were neatly packed in a little brown suitcase. The two boys gaily told me good-by and climbed into the car.

They headed for the Mayflower Electric Shop down on L Street. The trains were on the second floor up a flight of long, steep stairs, not an easy climb for a man with a tired heart.

It turned out that the man who handled the trade-ins was in New York and would not be back for another week.

"Can *you* give us any idea what we'd get for this?" asked Peter, opening the little suitcase.

The man behind the counter picked up the locomotive. "Let's see. This is for an 072 series track, isn't it? Well, of course, I can't say exactly. Probably—well—maybe about $18."

Wee Peter's face fell. He had marked at least $50 worth of equipment in the catalog.

His father turned to ask him, "Peter, how do you like that? Would that be a good trade?"

His answer was prompt; he was the son of a Scotsman. "I don't like it. Cripes—heck—well, gee-whiz, I'd say we ought to get more than that."

Peter smiled. "But you can never get as much as you think on trade-ins. I doubt if we'd get a better deal any place else."

"If you want to come back next Monday," the clerk interposed, "you could leave the stuff here, packed just as it is."

Peter nodded. "Let's do that." And the clerk handed him a tag to fill out.

But the next Monday Peter could not come back. He was never to complete that transaction. As he wrote his name and address in his neat, careful handwriting, the "P" with all its curlicues, the "M" with its flourish, he would have smiled a slow, whimsical smile had he known that even that little tag would some day be precious to his son. Peter John would cherish that small soiled piece of cardboard as a reminder of the last good time he ever had with his father. For although we had no intimation of it then, the strength of Peter's heart was fast ebbing away. He had just fifteen hours left.

About three-thirty on Tuesday morning, Peter awakened with severe pains in his chest and arms.

He had only to speak my name once to arouse me; for some reason I had been lying there awake for some time.

"Catherine, I'm in *great pain*. Will you call the doctor for me?"

Immediately, I knew from Peter's tone of voice that this was a major crisis. As I sat up and reached for the bedside telephone, I could hear my own heart pounding. The doctor answered on the first ring, and agreed to come right over.

While we waited for him, Peter lay there trying to pray, but he was in such great pain that he could scarcely move his lips. Seeing his effort, I began to pray out loud for him. Not only did I ask Jesus to take away his pain, but I asked Him to bring good out of this, our latest difficulty. "Lord, will You overrule all this, so that one of these days both Peter and I will have reason to thank You that *even this* happened."

It was a strange prayer to make at such a time. "What good could *possibly* come out of *this*?" Peter asked quietly.

Sometimes in moments of crisis, our spiritual eyes are open to realities usually hidden from us. After that prayer, somehow we both knew that our Lord, full of love for us both, was standing there in the room beside us. Almost immediately the pain began to sub-side. Soon it was completely gone, and Peter said softly, "Thank You, Lord." Then, "Catherine, *you* thank Him."

By the time the doctor got there, he found Peter's condition rather good. He sat by his bed awhile, watching him closely. Meanwhile he made studied small talk in an effort to divert us.

Suddenly the pain returned. It was then the doctor decided that Dr. Marshall must be taken immediately to the hospital.

Peter frowned, then smiled wryly. "I take a dim view of that. What a revoltin' development this is!"

As I stood by the bed, holding Peter's hand, I sensed his feelings. I, too, hated the thought of his being taken to the hospital. It would be impossible for me to leave our son all alone in the big empty house and go with Peter in the ambulance. Somehow I could not even bear to let go his hand. Peter understood, and relayed his own little secret message of reassurance with his finger tips, while the doctor was taking his blood pressure on his other arm.

"Is there anything you want me to do for you—any plans? What about the Senate prayer tomorrow?" I asked.

"Call Mary, but don't tell anyone else about this yet. I don't want to alarm anyone. They'll find out soon enough. You might ask Cranny[1] to take the Senate prayer tomorrow."

After the ambulance had gone, I went back upstairs and knelt by my bed. But before I could speak a word, there surged through me, over and around me, as a great wave, an overwhelming experience of the love of God. It was as if the Everlasting Arms were literally enfolding me. It seemed unnecessary to ask God for anything. I simply gave Peter and myself into the care and keeping of that great love. At the time, I thought this meant that Peter's heart would be healed here on earth. Of course, God knew what I did not know. There, in the lower hall, just before the ambulance left, I had seen Peter alive for the last time.

It was at eight-fifteen that morning that Peter stepped over into the Larger Life. At eight-twenty the doctor telephoned to tell me. Little Peter had been making final preparations for school. He was by the phone as I got the news, and burst into a flood of little-boy tears. I was much too stunned to weep.

Later, I sat for an hour by Peter's hospital bed. He had been dozing and had slipped away very peacefully.

I felt that I knew just what had happened before I got there. All
at once, Peter had *seen* his Lord, and later, his own father, whom
he had longed all of his life to know. There had been moments of
quiet adoration and of glad reunion. Then suddenly, Peter had realized. *He was dead!*

"You know, this will be hard for Catherine," he had said. "What
can we do for her?"

And Jesus had smiled at Peter, "She'll be all right. We can supply her with every resource she needs."

So, they had waited for me there. That was why, when I opened
the door and stepped quietly into the bare little hospital room, it
was filled with the glory of God and with two vivid, transcendent
Presences. Peter was not in the still form, but was hovering near in
tenderness and in love.

I sat for a long time by the bed holding his hand. After a while
there came a gentle tap at the door. It was A. D. I beckoned her to
come in. Her eyes seemed glued to my face. Days later, I learned
why—what she had seen there. She stayed just a minute, then left.

There came a specific time, exactly fifty minutes by my wrist
watch after I had entered the hospital room, when those two luminous Presences left me. Suddenly, the room was empty, cheerless,
cold, and I shivered. It was time for me to leave too.

As I rose to go, I knew that this was farewell to the earthly part
of this man whom I loved; farewell to the touch of his hand, to his
warmth, his gaiety, his flashing smile.

"'Till death do us part," we had vowed on our wedding day, as
we had stood before the flower-banked altar. And that physical tear-
ing apart is very hard for us who are still so human, who are still of
the earth, earthy.

When I got back to the Manse, I found several friends already gathered, washing up the breakfast dishes, making the beds upstairs,
answering the telephone and doorbell. Messages of sympathy and
offers to help began to pour in from all over the city, all over the
country. The news traveled so fast by radio and newspaper that, even
as we sat down to make a list of people who had to be notified, tele-

grams and long-distance phone calls began arriving from those very
people.

Within an hour most of the members of New York Avenue had
heard the news. It seemed unbelievable. Peter had preached at both
services on Sunday and in the National Cathedral in the afternoon
and had seemed especially vigorous and well.

The news was sped across the Atlantic, by cable, to Scotland to
our white-haired mother, to whom it would be an almost devastat-
ing blow. Bob phoned my Mother and Dad in Seaview, Virginia, to
tell them.

Out in California, in a cottage in San Fernando, Ruby and Willard
Daughtry, our friends of so many years, heard the news over the
radio. Willard buried his head in his arms and suddenly his shoulders heaved with great sobs. He felt as if he had lost a brother.

On a street corner in New York City, Bob Ingraham, our next-
door neighbor on Cape Cod, casually bought a copy of *The New
York Sun*. While he waited for the traffic light to change, he glanced
at the headlines. His eyes caught the words, "Dr. Marshall," and
involuntarily he caught his breath. It couldn't be true; but there it
was. "Dr. Marshall Dies. Senate Chaplain." Stunned, he folded the
paper and crossed the street, thinking that he must immediately
telephone his wife in Providence, Rhode Island.

The news was whispered through government offices, and many
a little government clerk who had never met Dr. Marshall, but to
whom his very name had come to stand for something solid and
substantial and fine, like "the shadow of a great rock in a weary
land," felt a sense of personal loss.

In South Africa, a few days later, Peter's cousin, Jim Broadbent, the
man who had "staked" him to the United States many years before,
would get the message by air mail.

In his suite at the Wardman Park Hotel in Washington, Senator
Arthur Vandenberg heard the news over the radio. Almost immediately he sat down at his battered old typewriter and wrote out of
an overflowing heart:

My Dear Mrs. Marshall:
   *Having just heard the unbelievably sad news about Peter's sud-
den passing, I would come to you immediately in person were it not
for the fact that I am temporarily "interned" myself under doctor's*

*orders. . . . I want you to know how deeply I share your grief over the
loss of a very precious friend whom I have come intimately to know
during the past two years when I was serving as President of the Senate and he as Chaplain. We had a very beautiful relationship, a most
intimate one, in which I am sure he gave his heart to me as I gave
mine to him. I never knew a more rugged character. I never had a
more delightful companion. To me he was the embodiment of "Onward, Christian Soldiers." To me he was the personification of pur-
poseful religion. His prayers were eloquent and real. He lived his
faith. . . .I shall greatly miss him—tho' my loss is as nothing com-
pared to yours. I send you all my sympathy and prayers. I know, by
experience, how dark it can be in the Valley of the Shadow. Thank
God for His promise of the Great Reunion. . . . If I can ever be of the
slightest service to you, please do not hesitate to let me know. I feel
an intimate responsibility to Peter's memory. May his great soul rest
in peace.*

Most sincerely yours,
Arthur H. Vandenberg

But for a few days at least it was *not* dark in the Valley of the Shadow.
My path was lit by celestial light. Around me was all the glory of heaven.
It was as if Peter, joyously stepping over that invisible boundary that
divides this life from the next, had left the curtain pulled aside, letting
heaven through so that we, who were left here, could share a little of
his joy and understand better what was happening to him.

For the first time, I was actually living in the Kingdom of God on
earth. Many decisions had to be made. There was perfect guidance
for each of them. No groping to know God's will on this or that was
necessary. There was just a sure, immediate, inner knowing of the
right thing to do.

Though I did not sleep at all that first night, in the morning every
detail of the funeral service was clear to me, even in the Scripture
to be used. All our congregation knew how their minister had felt
about the pagan attitude most people, even Christians, have toward
death. Peter's "graduation," as he had so often called it, would have
to be what God wanted in every detail, no matter how unconven-
tional it might seem.

I knew Peter would not want me to wear black. I would just wear
my usual brown Sunday costume. The service would be at eleven
in the morning, the hour when our people were accustomed to wor-

ship under their minister's leadership. I would sit in the pastor's pew as I always did, and there would be the usual congregational singing. The theme of the service would not be eulogy of Peter but thanksgiving for the incredible way in which God had led and used this immigrant boy in His service. This was the time to give God's message to our congregation to help them meet this crisis in our church's life. I knew that Peter wanted the funeral to be a service of rededication for all of us.

Such sure direction was not the only sign of the Kingdom of Heaven around us. There was also a perfect oneness among all concerned. No bitterness or rebellion was in us—rather a great love for everyone. For the first time in twelve years, Washington seemed like a small town. There were no drawn shades in the Manse. Hundreds of friends came and went, bringing food, and flowers, and love. They found there such an atmosphere of harmony, quiet beauty, and peace that each of them was reluctant to go away again.

I knew Peter would want Harry Bryan from Bessemer, Alabama, and John Land from New Orleans to share his graduation with us. But they were far away. I hesitated to ask them to travel so far. Even as I pondered this, a wire came from John, saying that he very much wanted to come if I needed him; a wire from Harry informed us that he was on his way.

Bill Kerr, an elder in our church, and a Scotsman, wanted to arrange for Mother Janet and Father Findlay to fly over from Scotland for the funeral. Immediately, I knew that would be wrong, though I did not know why.

Later we found out why the answer was "no." Father Findlay was even then ill. He was to die at 7:15 on the evening of February 1st, exactly one week after Peter's death.

That very morning Mother Janet, not realizing the seriousness of his illness, had written me:

February 1st, 1949

My dear Catherine,

It is now seven days since we got your cable with the sad news of our beloved son, and your beloved husband, and Peter's daddy. Of course, it came as a great shock to me. I was stunned for a few moments as Father Findlay read out the cable. Then as I said, "Thy will be done, O Lord. Help me to keep calm," somehow I felt I was surrounded by the loving peace of God. I knew He was very close to me, and that that same Peace of God would keep you, Catherine. His precious promises will not fail us.

To you my dear Catherine, I really don't know what to say. I am thinking of you all the time. . . . I hope you will be able, and Wee Peter. He is a big boy and will always remember his daddy. . . .

Father Findlay has been in bed with a very bad cold and shortness of breath. So the doctor has said he must keep to his bed another week. . . .

Mother Janet was right. God's promise did not fail. He just lifted me up and carried me through the next few days. I was not myself; something quite above my ordinary human capacities had been added. It was what the theologians like to call "the grace of God." It enabled me to think of our bereft congregation and of what I could do to sustain them, rather than of my own loss.

It gave me such complete freedom as to be able to say at dinner that Tuesday night, "Isn't this a shame? Turkey and angel-food cake, two of the things Peter liked best, and Peter not here to share them with us!"

It enabled me to answer fully all our son's questions. Each night at his bedtime, we talked until his questioning mind was satisfied.

"When will we see Daddy again?" he asked.

"We'll see him either when we die or when Jesus comes back to earth, whichever happens first," I replied. "You see, if Jesus comes back to earth, while we are still living, He will bring Daddy with him. That will be when Jesus will really reign in the world. For the first time everything will be done right. Folks will treat each other as God wants them to. There won't be any more wars."

Peter seemed electrified. "Mommy," he interrupted, "do you mean to say that some day all wars will stop, that there won't be fighting in Palestine any more or in China? Why that's simply wonderful! I'm going to use that for my current events in school!"

I would not give the impression that I did no crying during those days. I did. There were times when I wept copiously. But there was no bitterness in the tears, only emotional release, and betweentimes God gave me a quiet mind and a steady heart.

For the first time I understood why the Bible speaks of God's love as a refiner's fire which burns us clean but does not consume. The pain of parting was like a burning flame in my heart, but it was a cleansing, refining action, consuming the dross and leaving the imperishable part of me intact and stronger than ever before.

Meanwhile extraordinary tributes to Peter were appearing in almost every newspaper and periodical in the country. There was something about him and about his story that had captured the imagination of Americans everywhere. An editorial in the *Washington Evening Star* said:

> Living and working in Washington only eleven years, the Reverend Dr. Peter Marshall nevertheless has left his mark upon the whole city. He was a man of contagious spirit, eager and alert, quick to see opportunities of service and to meet their challenge. Within a few months after coming here he had made himself an influence throughout the entire community. Wherever he went, whatever he did, the result of his presence was constructive. In classic language, he was a builder of the Kingdom of God on this earth.
>
> Perhaps one explanation of Dr. Marshall's power might be found in the fact that he was a son of the people and kept his touch with them even when he had risen to high station. Born and reared against a bleak and uncongenial background, he earned his bread as a laborer in his youth. His formal education was limited to a mechanical and mining college at Coatbridge in Scotland and the Columbia Seminary at Decatur in Georgia. Most of his scholarly achievement he owed to his own inquiring mind. The magic of his eloquence was a native gift which he shared with Burns and Carlyle, Hugh Miller and John Buchan. But he was a great preacher because of an inner genius, a force of faith which demanded expression in human ministry.
>
> His decade at the New York Avenue Presbyterian Church was a period of progress which soon will find fulfillment in a new religious center on the site long ago hallowed by the presence of Abraham Lincoln. Dr. Marshall will not see the building program finished, but his association with its start will be an asset always. He is certain of remembrance, too, at the Capitol. Able interpreters of the Word preceded him in the chaplaincy of the Senate, and he contributed notably to the tradition which they established. His final prayer for government "above party and personality, beyond time and circumstance, for the good of America and the peace of the world" was a masterful utterance which well may be regarded as his testament to the country he adopted and dearly loved.[2]

In Peter's mind, no high words of praise spoken on the floor of the Senate, expressed in the hundreds of letters which came to me or in editorials in magazines like *Time, Life,* or *Newsweek,* were half as much tribute as that paid by a small boy in our Sunday School.

His name was Donald. He was just a little boy with a freckled face, pug nose, and tousled hair. His home was on H Street, just across the street from the church. Donald had been the star of New York Avenue's Community Club's Christmas play. He had made a perfect "littlest angel."

His minister's nice smile, the touch of his big warm hand, were still fresh in Donald's memory. Dr. Marshall always stooped way down to talk to him, until he seemed no taller than he, so he could look right into Donald's eyes. And now his mother said that Dr. Marshall was dead, that he would never see his minister again.

"But I've gotta see him again—just gotta," Donald thought, hugging the idea to himself.

At the supper table his parents did not talk about much, except what had happened to Dr. Marshall. "His body is lying in state in the church," his father commented. "All afternoon there has been a continuous stream of people going in and out."

"Donald, you're not eating much," his mother said. "I wish you had a better appetite."

"If I clean up my plate, can I go out on the sidewalk?" the little boy asked.

"Yes, if you eat every bit."

Donald ate every bite. This, he knew, was his chance.

A little while later a tiny figure slipped into the sanctuary of the New York Avenue Church and down the long aisle. The organ was playing softly. There were pretty flowers. Some people were sitting quietly in the pews, as if they were thinking very hard about something.

Donald got to the front of the church and stood on tiptoe to look down into the face of his friend. Dr. Marshall looked as nice as ever, only not so gay as usual. He had on his robe and that nice red hood, the same one he had worn when he gave his Christmas talk to the children in the Lincoln Chapel. It was a pretty color, Donald thought. He stood there a long time, not even noticing the two Scots' guards in kilts on either side of the bier, or how moved they were by the adoration on a little boy's face.

That night at bedtime, Donald thought he'd better tell his mother how he'd disobeyed. His Sunday School teacher had said it was always best to be truthful.

"Mom," he admitted, "I saw Dr. Marshall this afternoon. I just *had* to, Mom. Please don't tell Daddy I crossed the street alone."

Peter must have liked that. But the obituary he would have liked best came spontaneously from one of the Senate page boys: "You know, Mrs. Marshall, Dr. Marshall wasn't just the Chaplain of the Senate. He was our friend."

Apparently most Washingtonians felt that they had lost a friend. As one of Peter's colleagues in the ministry commented, "There has not been a death in Washington since President Franklin Roosevelt's that has stirred the interest, concern and comment which attended the passing of Peter Marshall. . . ."3

Though the funeral service was held at a difficult time for office and business people, hundreds of them took leave and came. In death as in life, there were long queues outside the church. The ushers seated 1,600 in the sanctuary, the Lincoln room, the Lincoln Chapel, the parish hall, the lecture room downstairs, and then had to turn people away.

Even as the congregation gathered, Baukhage was broadcasting just up the street from the church:

> Baukhage talking. I might say here that something very sad to Washingtonians took place just as I was coming to the studio. Up New York Avenue, the funeral of Dr. Peter Marshall, Chaplain of the United States Senate, was taking place from his own church, the historic New York Avenue Presbyterian. I knew him. He was a remarkable man. A wonderful preacher. Noted for the brevity and sapience of his prayers.
>
> He was only 46 years old, but he had a heart ailment. . . . I wish that Peter Marshall might have been spared for us a little longer.

The Vice-President of the United States and many of the nation's notables were there. Close beside them were the church's Negro janitors, William and Dodson, and the boys from the Capital Garage across the street where Peter always parked his car. Those boys had slipped over still dressed in their overalls.

The service was simple and sweet beyond all description. Not only did Dr. John Land and Harry Bryan have a part in it, but Peter's good friends, Dr. Cranford, Mr. Bryden, Mr. Merker, Dr. Rustin, and Dr. Pruden. The choir sang some of Peter's favorite numbers: "God Is Ever Beside Me," "The Twenty-third Psalm" from the Scottish Psalter, and that one that Peter had learned to love at the time of his first heart attack:

> O Rest in the Lord, Wait patiently
> for Him,
> And He shall give thee thy heart's
> desire. . . .

Mr. Robert Bridge, the associate minister at New York Avenue, presided and said:

This is a funeral service which is to be different from the usual funeral service. For example, there is no group of mourners at the front of the church. Mrs. Marshall, with her family, is seated in the minister's pew where she worships Sunday by Sunday.

Underlying all that we say or do there is of course very deep emotion, but this is not the time nor the place to express that emotion or to give way to it. . . . If our eyes are moist, let them be shining too. We are gathered in a service of rejoicing. Let me say in a few words, and in very simple words, try to express what we are trying to do this morning. We are endeavoring to establish a new relationship. We have known Peter Marshall in the flesh. From now on we are to endeavor to know him in the spirit and to know him in the spirit just as really as we had known him in the flesh. . . .

Peter Marshall is still, and will continue to be one of the ministers of this church, though no longer visible to us. The fellowship we have had with him will remain unbroken and may God give us vision, grace, and strength to join hands with him. . . .

Later in the service, Harry Bryan said:

On the day after Peter Marshall made his surrender to God, and decided that at all costs he would obey the strong Voice he had known for a long time, and prepare himself for the gospel ministry, he traveled in my father's car to begin his first year in the theological seminary. I was driving the car, going for my last year in the seminary. My father was to make the opening lecture. Peter was fresh in his conviction of absolute surrender to what God wanted him to do, no matter what the cost. He was going with faith that God had prepared a way for the first steps to be taken. Bubbling over with that confidence, he made a worthy counterpart to my father's steady faith of many years serving God. And that half-day ride 20 years ago started a deep and abiding friendship which I can treasure throughout all eternity. We studied and played and sang and preached together. God used my friend, and gave to him a joy in studying that proved that he outstudied us all; a joy in singing because he outsang us, for he sang from his heart; and a joy in playing, because he abandoned everything when he could play. The truth is he outprayed, outpreached, and outplayed us all. Why? Because he had sought and found delight in the doing of God's will. . . .

All that he learned and then taught us about God by his vital, fresh approach to all of the questions of life is not a dream. He has inspired us too deeply and pushed us to new frontiers of sacrifice and courageous living. We can never call it something uncertain. Too much has come out of us in faithless sin and unbelief. Too much has gone into us in victory over sin and steadfast assurance for us ever to be the same. It is that our friend, this prince of God, has received a new and wider sphere of life and service. He is free for such activity as will delight his soul.

That same grace of God that had carried me through the last two days took me through this service. I was able to smile, not a forced smile, but a genuine one. As my son and I walked back down the long church aisle following the casket, and I saw a friend's stricken face wet with tears, I could smile and whisper as I passed, "Chin up, Betty." We got outside to find the little park in front of the church and the sidewalks packed with people who had been unable to get inside—business people, government people, bareheaded, silent.

Later, much later, I began to question God's will in this seemingly premature death. The moment I did so I stepped out of the Kingdom of Heaven.

"Why, God, why did it have to end this way?" I asked over and over. We had sure evidence that Christ was with us that night when the final heart attack struck. But if that was true, why did He not stretch out His hand and cure Peter's damaged heart? We had believed in healing. We had seen it, witnessed it in our family. Why, then, was he not healed?

During those days of questioning, A. D., who saw the Gethsemane through which I was going, wrote me:

Catherine, my dear, my dear. . . .

I think this is the first time I have been completely helpless to help you with the major crisis of your life. Before, I could at least bring up your tray or take a quart of custard down to Peter's hospital room, but this time, all I can do is yearn over you, and that I do with all my heart.

I wondered tonight, after talking with you, whether you had considered this as perhaps the most conclusive proof that God chose the time and hour of Peter's death: the way you felt about it that hour you were in his room at the hospital.

I don't think you have any idea how transformed you were in that hour. I have never seen you look so beautiful. The smile that was on your face was my first glimpse of the heavenly glory which surrounded every part of Peter's going. I know you well enough to know when something has been added to you, and you were unquestionably filled by a newness and a differentness, and all the love in the world was in your eyes.

That room was filled with the same power that was in you. It was charged with it. I shall never be able to thank you enough for asking me to come in. It was in those moments that I learned what Christ's power over death is. Glory filled that room.

And this is my point: In those supreme moments when we knew Peter's living spirit and Christ's spirit to be there with us, probably more closely in touch with Him than we have ever been, and you, it seemed to me, were completely free of self, and free of fear and confident of Christ's power to do anything. Yet you were not filled with any great outcry of "No, no—it's all wrong. This was not the time for Peter to die. I know it wasn't."

In those moments when we entrusted Peter's future to Christ, I think you were like St. Peter walking on the sea. But the moment inevitably came when the strangeness of your new situation drew your eyes from Christ, and the sea of doubt engulfed you.

Of course, all of the deep, heart-searching questions with which I wrestled were not answered at that time. Some day they will be; some day we shall know "why."

Until then, I decided that all I could do was to pray as I had prayed with Peter that last night; so with all my heart I claimed for my son and for myself the promise that:

> We know that all things work together for good to them that love God, to them who are the called, according to his purpose (Romans 8:28).

And God heard and answered. Within a matter of weeks, the way opened for the publication of a book of Peter's sermons. That book was to become a best-seller.[4] Through its pages, Peter would preach to thousands of people, whom he could never have reached, were he still with us in the flesh. The blessing of his life would go marching on and on, a living testimony to the power and love of God.

That June, as usual, the little Cape Cod cottage beckoned. As we drove into the yard, we saw that the shutters were just as blue as ever; the rambler roses were just about to burst into bloom as they always had; a pair of bluebirds had built their nest in the old pine by the kitchen door. Yet there was a difference this year. Even a little boy could feel it. We tried to be gay with each other as we unlocked the door.

Our neighbor had very thoughtfully opened some of the windows, and the white organdy curtains fluttered in the sea breeze. The Highland Regiments still marched jauntily, with kilts swinging, across the living-room wall—The Queen's Own Cameron Highlanders, the Black Watch, and the Royal Scots Greys. By his favorite lounge chair sat Peter's slippers, just as he had stepped out of them, and on the table by the chair lay a pocket edition of *The Case of the Perfumed Mouse.*

Each room spoke of him; his presence was everywhere. In the hall closet was one of his summer hats, the one whose blue band had faded to an intriguing shade of lavender. Under his bed were his old white shoes, the pair he used for garden work, with a pair of blue socks still stuffed inside.

I held one of the shoes in my hand and thought, "Now I understand those words, 'O memories, that bless and burn,' O God, how it hurts!"

Later that evening, after the tempest of emotion had subsided a bit, I headed beachward.

The waves made gentle little lapping noises on the pebbled shore, and there was a path of silver across the water. The crisp sea air fanned my hot cheeks. Suddenly I remembered something, the last words I had ever spoken to Peter. Was it possible that God had prompted those words, seemingly so casual?

The scene was etched forever on my mind—Peter lying on the stretcher where the two orderlies had put him down for a moment, while the ambulance waited just outside the front door. Peter had looked up at me and smiled through his pain, his eyes full of tenderness, and I had leaned close to him and said, "Darling, I'll see you in the morning."

And as I stood looking out toward that far horizon, I knew that those words would go singing in my heart down all the years . . .

See you, Darling, see you in the Morning. . . .

Sermons and Prayers

F

Peter and the other disciples had come back from their preaching tour with their heads swollen with success.

Their talk was still of the crowds that had flocked to hear them,
and of the debates that had started everywhere they went.

They told, too, of wonderful miracles they had been able to perform—
and already some of them had adopted a boastful, almost professional air.
They discussed their difficult cases . . .
but mostly they had been successful.

It had gone—like wine—to their heads.
If this was to be the work of the kingdom, they found it good.
They liked it,
and in their enthusiasm they chattered like children.

The talk veered round again,
as it had so often lately,
as to who should be the greatest in the kingdom.
They were concerned about promotions.

Christ would look at them as they spoke, his lips closed and his eyes fixed on the speaker's face as if he read his very soul.

It was a disconcerting look that silenced the speaker even though Christ never spoke a word.

They were like a group of preachers
    returned from an evangelistic tour,
    reporting on their crowds and their converts . . .

or like a group of interns discussing their cases and their methods . . .

or like merchants discussing the state of the market . . .
    or salesmen discussing the trade.

It was not altogether pleasing to Christ, for one could see the shadows passing over His face and His sighs were more eloquent than any words He might have spoken.

In the evening, Christ went up into the mountain, and took with Him Peter
    James
        and John.

Mount Hermon is very high, and has three peaks that are covered with snow even in the hot season.
    It was to pray that Christ had climbed up the winding path that rose steeply from the hot and fetid valley.

The three intimates—Peter, the rock,
    and James and John, the sons of thunder, as the Master had
    called them, did not talk much.
They needed their breath for the climb, and something in Christ's manner silenced them.

They left behind them the other disciples still talking as they turned back to the village that lay sprawled across the road skirting Hermon.

All night long somewhere high up on the mountain, Christ had prayed.
    Seeking the reassurance that He needed, the confirmation of His mission,

and the strength He would require to set His face to Jerusalem,
He had the experience that is known as the Transfiguration.

For the simple fishermen, it was an unspeakable revelation.

Meanwhile much had happened in the valley below.
Early in the morning, the disciples had visitors.
They had been followed by people seeking healing;
   the curious also had come along,
      for sensational things had been done,
         and news traveled quickly.

A man had come seeking Jesus, bringing with him his son, who,
he said, was possessed by a devil.

The other disciples had gone out to where the trail branched off
to wind up the slopes of the mountain.
There they would await the return of the Master and the other
three.

It was a colorful picture.
The majestic heights towered above them,
   the snow-capped peaks gleaming in the sunshine
   that tinted the shadows a deep purple,
   while the shoulders of the hills were the color of copper.

Some of the men sat down on huge rocks that had been chiseled
by the frost, polished by the rain and the snow, and now lay where
the hills had thrown them down.

It was a lonely place at night . . .
   excellent hiding for robbers.

But it was warm in the morning, and bright with the
   "lilies of the field"
      the wild anemones,
         the purple iris,
            and the scarlet gladiolus.

The colorful robes, the intense blue of the sky made a startling picture.
But there were few if any who noticed it, or cared about it.
There was too much excitement.

Hearing the sound of incoherent moaning, punctuated every now and then by a wild shriek, the disciples turned to see what was the matter.

They found the father of a boy trying to hold him—as the poor lad struggled in his father's arms.
The boy's head fell from side to side,
	and his mouth twitched as the fit seized him.

It was a pathetic sight.
The father cried out for Jesus,
	imploring the Son of David to heal his son.

People ran to form a circle around them, and one of the women shouted that the disciples over there would help.

"They can cast out devils, even as Jesus does.
Ask them.
They will heal your son," she said to the man.

But the distraught father, without looking up, said bitterly,
"I asked them before, and they tried, but could do nothing.
What use are they?
They are only cheats, like all magicians.

"They have no power.
Only the Nazarene can help him now.
	Oh, where is He?
Tell me and I will go to Him."

The disciples were troubled when they heard what the father said, but they stood looking at the boy now writhing on the ground.

None of them spoke.

Thomas was shaking his head and muttering to himself.

There were tears in Philip's eyes and he turned to some of the others but what he said none of the bystanders heard.

Andrew, with an honest frown upon his face, bent over the father and spoke comfortingly.

Judas stroked his beard as if deep in thought.

But he did not make any movement.

Someone said: "We did the best we could."

Just then the poor boy broke away from his father and fell to the ground,

the crowd scattering to give him room . . .

The comments from the crowd were neither illuminating nor helpful.

Some ventured the opinion that the case was hopeless
for the boy obviously had seventy devils in him.

Others whispered to their neighbors that such could not be the case for there were times when he was quiet and seemed as normal as any of them.

But there on the ground lay the grim evidence of their failure.

It was almost obscene—

this horrible taunting failure in the bright sunshine.

Just then one of the disciples cried out—

"Here comes the Master,"

and the crowd opened up to let Christ through.

He was closely followed by Peter,

James,

and John.

By this time, the father had managed to get his son to his feet and was wiping his face.

"What are you discussing among yourselves?" Jesus asked,

278

and immediately there was silence.

Then the boy's father spoke:
  "Master, I brought my son to see you, as he has a devil, and
  is pining away.
  I asked your disciples to heal him, but they failed."

Jesus turned to His disciples.
  "O faithless generation," He said, "how long must I teach you?
    How long must I have patience with you?
      Bring the boy to me."

Several of the disciples went forward to lead the boy to Christ,
but as soon as they touched him, he fell into convulsions and again
rolled on the ground foaming at the mouth.

"How long has he been like this?" Jesus asked the father.

"Since he was a child," the man answered.
  "And often he falls into the fire or into water and tries to kill
himself.
  But if Thou canst do anything, have compassion on us and help
us."

Now the father is not to be blamed for putting it that way.
  There had been failure before.
  After all, the Nazarene's disciples themselves had confessed that
they could do nothing.

  Sometimes even Christ had failed.
  He Himself admitted that on some occasions He was not able to
do any mighty works.
  The father's doubts were natural enough, and certainly excusable.

  Then, too, the father had prayed about it.
  Offering after offering had been sacrificed with no apparent
results.
  He had consulted the rabbis.

With pathetic eagerness and hope he had gone to see one healer after another.

The years had brought nothing but failure
     and hopes had withered and died.

"If Thou canst do anything . . . ," the father sobbed. . . .
     "if Thou canst, . . .
     have pity on us and help us."

Christ immediately took up the *"if."*

It is a very little word . . . this conjunction . . .
               this particle of condition . . .
     a very little word.

God uses it frequently.
The "ifs" of God make a great study.

The "if" is proper enough,
     but in this case it was put in the wrong place.
There was an "if"—
     but it was not on God's part, but on the part of the man. . . .

It was not to govern God's ability to give . . .
     not to condition Christ's power to do . . .
but rather the father's ability to receive.

It was not a question of the ability of the door to open,
     but a question of the father's ability to use the key. . . .

So, Jesus said unto him, "If you have faith, everything is possible to one who has faith."

Christ spoke with so much kindness and conviction that the man cried out, the tears streaming down his face. . . .
     "Lord, I have faith . . .
     I believe; help Thou mine unbelief."

So Jesus held the lad,
the convulsions ceased, and the boy lay on the ground like a
corpse, so that many people looking at him shook their
heads and said,
"Well, it is all over. He is dead."

But Jesus took him by the hand and lifted him up and gave him
back to his father.

My! How much we need faith today!
faith in God's power. . . .
and, what is more necessary, faith in God's willingness to
help us.

Most Christians do not doubt that God *can* do something.
They rather seriously question God's *willingness* to *do* what
He can for *us.*

Notice the man's reply: "Lord, I believe, help Thou mine unbelief."

What did he mean?
Is he contradicting himself?

Let me make two suggestions.

(1)
The man knew that Christ's ability to perform miracles,
to heal the sick especially, had in some cases been defeated
by lack of faith on the part of those whom He might have
cured.

The boy's father realized that his own faith had suffered some
shock and severe strain that had weakened it.
He was willing to admit that his faith was not as strong as it once
was.

So he might have meant—"Lord, I know that some of my faith
has oozed away . . .

I admit that I lack something,
I know that this will take a lot of faith.
If I don't have enough, Lord, make up the deficit yourself by giving me your faith."

Faith is the gift of God, the Bible tells us, and the poor man was certainly right in appealing to Christ for more faith.
The disciples themselves prayed to Jesus:
"Lord, increase our faith."

(2)
However, I prefer this other suggestion.
I believe that our faith is like the mercury in a thermometer—
it expands and contracts.
In cold weather, we know that the mercury falls in the thermometer . . .
but no mercury has been removed.
There is still as much mercury in the glass tube as there was before.

It has simply contracted.
The frost affects it by causing it to shrink.

In hot weather, the mercury rises in the glass.
No more mercury has been poured into the tube.
It is the same amount, but now it has been caused to expand.

Now is not our faith like mercury in a thermometer?

It too can expand and contract.
Consider, for instance, the effect of ill health upon our faith.
When we are feeling bad, it is difficult to have a buoyant faith.

Constant pain or protracted weakness depresses our faith.
Our spirits fall,
our outlook is clouded—for there is a close connection between our physical health and our spiritual vitality.

The Lord knew that—and He remembers it still!

It is hard for people to have a robust, vital faith when they are feeling out of sorts.

Faith can be depressed too by disappointment.
Hope deferred maketh the heart sick, said the poet,
and he might have added, maketh faith weak.

Unanswered prayers also force the mercury of our faith to fall.

It is comparatively easy for us under spiritual emotion to feel that our faith is strong and ample.
In good health, with blessings for which to be thankful . . .
faith will normally expand.

When you have just heard good news—your faith rises.
When you are happy and have been moved by some lovely experience . . . faith has a way of enlarging itself.

When our spiritual fervor increases, our faith expands.

Faith is not strain—it is repose.
It is not wishful thinking—
it is not credulity.
It is not believing ideas in spite of evidence.

It is doing things in face of all obstacles.

Now if I were to tell you that by having faith you would never be sick . . .
or that by believing, you would never have any deep sorrow in your life . . .
if I were to say that by exercising faith you would be spared any unhappiness . . .
I would not only be insulting your intelligence, but doing violence to the plain teachings of the Bible and the gospel of Christ.

We have no authority in either Scripture or experience for any such claims for faith.

But I can and must say this:
*If you surrender your life completely to God and put your
trust in Him, you can obtain divine power by which you
can win over anything.*

The gospel is a message of helpfulness to people who have no
ability to help themselves.
The gospel never says to anybody, "Try harder."
It says, "Believe harder."

There are people in this congregation who are defeated.
They try to do something with themselves,
    but they fail.
They summon all their will power—
    but they find that all too weak at times.

They make good resolutions,
    but they don't have the strength to carry them out.
They have good intentions, but something always happens to
break them.

Whatever the reason, they are defeated, and go on being defeated.

The wonderful part of the gospel message is that when you know
something should be done,
    must be done . . .
and you can't do it, then all you have to do is to surrender yourself to Christ, and He will do it for you.

This is the message the church has to deliver in the heart of this
city.
This is the message for the United Nations, if only somehow we
could get them to listen and to try it.

This is the message for our own Congress as it soon will meet to
face bigger problems than ever.
This is the message for the tangle of labor–management relations
that imposes upon the whole country dislocation of essential ser-

vices, and real hardship in some cases, where men are determined to get what they want, no matter how it affects the rest of the country or the world.

Now if we were real Christians, we should be free of all anxiety and unhappiness.

If we really believed what we say we believe, we would never worry.

If we are truly Christians, we would believe that the Christ we worship is God of heaven and earth, with power over life and death, and that He is willing and able to care for us while we live, and to give us blessed immortality when we die.

We must believe these things, if we are Christians,
    for we have the assurance of Christ that they are true.
We must believe them so deeply that we will come to know that they are true—
    as we know that daylight will follow darkness,
        and as we know that two and two are four.

How, then, could we fear life or death?

If you knew beyond all doubting that Henry Ford and John D. Rockefeller loved you well enough to give their lives for you,
    and if these two had promised to care for you and grant any request that you might make, would you not greet each morning with a smile of contentment or a joyous shout of laughter?

Would not your faith in their power and generosity free you from all care and anxiety?

True, they could not take away the fear of death, but the Christian has no reason to fear it.

Suppose you have been crippled from birth and now have found a great surgeon, in whom you have absolute faith,

who tells you that an operation will make you sound and whole
as you never were before.
Would you enter the operating room with terror in your heart
and fight against the anesthetic?

Or would you surrender to sleep with a sense of security and peace,
comforted with the hope of a glad awakening?

How can a Christian fear a sleep that promises so much?

So in living day by day.
If you will quit trying to pull yourself up,
   if you will let yourself go,
      if you will just yield yourself to God,
         love Him,
         and trust Him,
            and believe in Him, He will give you the
peace and quiet that will take away your strangling sense of worry
and give you power that will turn your defeats into victories.

It's just like swimming.
You know perfectly well that you've got to yield yourself to the
water.
The water will hold you up when you relax.

You can't float if you are rigid.
You've got to trust God in the same way.

There is no halfway ground for the Christian.

Jesus is the Son of God or He is not.
His words are true—or they are untrue.

If they are untrue, then Christianity is a cruel hoax and one-third
of the earth's people are victims of a foolish superstition, and we are
all deceived—
   all of us here hoodwinked and tricked,

and the great pioneers of faith were nothing but fools . . .
　　all of them . . .
　　　　　　　　Francis of Assisi and Thomas Aquinas . . .
　　　　　　Adoniram Judson and David Livingstone . . .
　　　　Luther and Loyola . . .
　　　　　　Dwight L. Moody and John R. Mott
　　　　　　　　General Booth and Brother Bryan
　　　　　　　　　　Muriel Lester and Martha Berry . . .
　　　　　　Wilfred Grenfell and Robert E. Speer,
　　　　Cardinal Newman and Albert Schweitzer,
　　Martin Niemuller and Gypsy Smith . . .
an amazing universality of fools . . .
　　all captives of a beleaguering spirit . . .

　　　　can it be that they were all deceived?

If they were not deceived—
　　if they were not all fools—
　　　　if what they believed is true—
　　　　　　then it follows that the greatest folly in human
　　　　　　history is to disbelieve and reject the words of
　　　　　　Jesus.

For if they are true, there is nothing in life that matters, except
to believe and serve Him and keep His commandments.

　　Men would try to move mountains by faith,
　　　　if they really believed they could.

Jesus said they could.

HE AMERICAN DREAM

During the Second World War, I met on the train a lieutenant who had just returned from fighting in Italy.

He had been in the North African campaign.
    He had fought in Sicily.
        He wore the Purple Heart ribbon with his campaign ribbons.

I asked him what he thought of America.
It was a hard question to ask a man who had been gone so long, who had been fighting for his country . . .
    who had been wounded in action . . .
It was almost an impertinence.

He said that after what he had seen in North Africa and in Italy, he appreciated America more than ever.
He described the filth and the squalor of the cities he had seen . . .
He spoke of Tunis and Bizerte . . .
He told me of his impression of the Arabs and the natives of North Africa.
    He had been deeply impressed with their misery and their slums.

I asked him some rhetorical questions, not expecting answers but rather to make him think, and to divert his attention from the bottle of rum in his raincoat pocket which, he had told me, he intended to finish between Roanoke and Washington.
"What is America?" I asked.

"What were you fighting for?
Did anyone in North Africa ever ask you that question?
If they had, what would you have said?"

I venture to say that deep down in the hearts of the men who fought the bitterest battles—of them who died—there was a glimmering of an understanding that the things for which they fought were somehow all tied up in one bundle of ideals
    of concepts
        of principles
that we call the American Dream.
It is a Dream that has shone brightly at times
    and that has faded at other times.

World events today are forcing us, whether we realize it or not, to rediscover the meanings and the significances of the things that make America different from other nations . . .
    the hope of a world weary of war, heartsick and hungry.

What is the American Dream?
What is it that makes our country different?

Do you know . . . you who fought overseas . . .
        who braved the sniper in the jungle,
      who flew through flak-filled skies,
    who waded through the mud of Italy,
  who knew the heat of the desert sun and the cold of the
North Atlantic?

Do you know . . . you who made your speeches in Congress and waxed eloquent on the stump?

Do you know . . . you who boast of your ancestry and your membership in patriotic societies?

What is America?
Where is our country going?
Let no answer be lightly made. . . .

We cannot speak with any truth or realism about the future
unless we understand the past.
What has America to give the rest of the world?
If only grain
    or money
        or clothing
            or armaments . . .
then we have already lost the war and the peace . . . and our own
souls.

Ours is a Covenant Nation . . .
The only surviving nation on earth that had its origins in the
determination of the Founding Fathers to establish a settlement
    "to the glory of God and the advancement of the Christian
    faith."
That was what William Bradford and George Carver had in mind
when, beneath the swinging lantern in the cabin of the *Mayflower*,
they affixed their signatures to the solemn declaration which established the Commonwealth of Massachusetts.

They had come from the Old World and were seeking refuge in
the New.
    They had come from tyranny and oppression . . .
        They had come from fear and coercion . . .
            They had come from famine and from
            difficulty . . .
                from wars and threats of wars. . . .
And they sought a new life in a new land.

Religious liberty to worship God according to the dictates of one's
own conscience
    and equal opportunity for all men . . .
These are the twin pillars of the American Dream.

Now a Covenant Nation is one which recognizes its dependence
upon God and its responsibility toward God.
This nation was so born.
God was recognized as the source of human rights.

The Declaration of Independence says so.

A Covenant Nation is one which recognizes that God and His purposes stand over and above the nation . . .

that the highest role a nation can play is to reflect God's righteousness in national policy.

That is what Bradford and Carver certainly intended.

That is what Roger Williams sought, when he set up his settlement in Providence, Rhode Island.

That is what William Penn was striving after in Pennsylvania.

That is what they wanted in Maryland, when, in 1649, the Maryland Act of Toleration set it down in writing.

That is what Thomas Jefferson was striving after when he wrote the Constitution of the United States.

That is what they fought for too.

You can trace it from Bunker Hill

from Lexington and Concord

down through Valley Forge. . . .

They were concerned about rights.

These free men who had burlap wrapped around their feet, as they marched through the snow,

who carefully hoarded their gunpowder and clutched their muskets under their tattered uniforms to keep them dry. . . .

They were concerned about the rights of free men.

They made the first downpayments there—downpayments that have been kept up to this good day . . .

through Château-Thierry and the Argonne . . .

to Anzio and Cassino . . .

at Saint-Lô and Bastogne . . .

at Tarawa and Iwo Jima . . .

at Saipan and Guadalcanal. . . .

There have been periods in our history when the American Dream has faded and grown dim.

Today there is real danger that the American Dream will become
the Forgotten Dream.

For freedom is not the right to do as one pleases
    but the opportunity to please to do what is right.
The Founding Fathers sought freedom . . .
    not from law but freedom in law;
    not freedom from government—but freedom in
    government;
    not freedom from speech—but freedom in speech;
    not freedom from the press—but freedom in the press;
    not freedom from religion—but freedom in religion.
We need to ponder these things today.

Our standard of values is out of focus.
We boast that many of our national leaders came out of country
schoolhouses.
Yet the average country schoolteacher makes $1,500 a year, while
we pay Big League baseball players $60,000 to $80,000 a year.
I, for one, enjoy baseball, but is hitting home runs more important than giving boys and girls an education?

It is a strange commentary on our standard of values that lob-
byists who try to influence legislation get more money than the
men who write it.

There is something wrong with a standard of values that gives
a radio comedian a million dollars and a high school teacher two
thousand.
The reward is greater for making people laugh than it is for making people think.

Again, no nation on earth has more laws, and yet more lawless-
ness than this nation.
There exists a current philosophy which you and I have accepted,
more or less, that
    *if we don't like a law, we need feel no obligation to keep
    it.*

Any philosophy which thus makes the will of the people its norm for morality and righteousness is a false philosophy.

The test, after all, is not whether a certain law is popular but whether the law is based upon fundamental justice
        fundamental decency and righteousness
    fundamental morality and goodness.
What we need is not law enforcement—but law observance.
In a modern society there is no real freedom *from* law.
There is only freedom *in* law.

Our government is in danger of control by corrupt party machines, and even by gangsters—
        cynical
      ruthless
    self-seeking lovers of power . . .
a fact which should challenge every true patriot and summon all who love America to roll up their sleeves and make this once again a "government of the *people*
        by the *people*
      for the *people*." . . .

For what is freedom?
Is it immunity for the unreliable and the despotic?
Is it freedom to take what you want regardless of the rights of others?
Is it a matter of getting yours while the getting is good?

The story of the waste of this nation's riches, for example, is a sad story of the misuse of "freedom."

Consider the philosophy which for far too long pervaded the thinking of those who settled and developed our southland.
Their philosophy was "plow and plant
      plow and plant
    plow and plant, until the land is exhausted,
  and then we'll move farther west and repeat the process."

Consider the philosophy of those who went into our forests to cut timber, feeling no responsibility to replace what they took by reforestation, so that we cut into vast tracts of good timberland and left it open,
> with no windbreak . . .
>> with no barrier against erosion . . .

with nothing to prevent dust-bowl storms . . . and the removal of hundreds of thousands of acres of irreplaceable topsoil, which year after year was washed into the Gulf of Mexico.

Only now is the Department of Agriculture meeting with any success in persuading our farmers to adopt contour plowing
> to put in windbreaks
>> to sow crops, grass, shrubs, and trees

that will tend to hold the soil together, and keep on the face of America that irreplaceable fertility which, in the past, has been her wealth.

I needn't say anything about the extravagant misuse or abuse of our wildlife.

There are many of you who, as hunters, know perfectly well that only the stupidity and greed of so-called sportsmen are responsible for the elimination of so many duck and wildfowl, once so plentiful, now nonexistent. . . .

All because somebody said: "This is a *free* country. I have a *right* to hunt and shoot and kill."

Surely freedom does not mean that people can do as they like with the country's resources!

There are so many things that are wonderful about America—
> things that are gloriously right and well worth defending.

But there are also things that are deeply and dangerously wrong with America, and the true patriot is he who sees them
> regrets them
> and tries to remove them.

The Bill of Rights applies to all men equally . . .

Yet where is the man who considers others equal to himself . . .
    who feels that other men are his brothers . . .
        who is ready to agree that liberty, except for himself, is
        a good thing?

The modern man will hardly admit,
    though in his heart he knows it to be true . . .
that it is only by the grace of God that he was not born of a different race or creed.

"All men are created equal," says the Declaration of Independence.
    "All men are endowed by their Creator with certain unalienable
    Rights." . . .
And this applies to red men
    and yellow men
        and black men
as well as white men.

There is nothing in the Bill of Rights that says:
    "This applies only to men with white skins
    or to people from Virginia."

But we must confess with troubled heart that not yet are the black men in our land wholly free.
    They are even yet half-slave in this "land of the free and home of the brave."

A democracy that boasts of freedom and still keeps some of its citizens in bondage is not worth defending.
    Let the implication of this sink into every American heart.

Again, while we know that the lot of the workingman in America is better than that of the workingman in any other nation, yet we seem to have more difficulty in labor relations here than in any place else in the world.
    That is a paradox.
    It is something very hard to understand.

Now before you get me wrong, I want to make it clear that I was a member of a union.

When I left Scotland I was a mechanical engineer.

I have worked in machine shops, and for three years I worked alternately night and day . . .

one week day shift and one week night shift. . . .

I know what it is to be unemployed,
to be out of work because other men are on strike.

I know what it is to work on time rate.

I used to average 10.48 pence per hour by time rate.

I know what it is to work piecework.

I know about incentive plans, and I know about slowdowns.

I want it clearly understood that I not only believe in, but I am willing to defend labor's right to organize
labor's right collectively to bargain
labor's right to strike.

But I am also prepared to defend the right of a man to work, if he would rather work than strike.

I am also prepared to defend the right of an employer to hire whom he will, and to fire those who are no longer necessary to his operation, or who, by laziness or disobedience, or by any other cause, are no longer acceptable to his employ.

I am also ready to defend the right of a man to join a union, if he wants to, and also the right of another man to stay out of it, if he would rather.

I believe that is concerned with fundamental rights in the American Bill of Rights.

In the first few months of living in this country, I went to New York City to try to get a job on a steel-construction job.

They were building a skyscraper, and I was told that I could get a job, but there were two things I would have to do.

One, I would have to go to the hiring hall that night and join the union.

That was all right, I could do that.
And then I was told, "You see that guy over there and pay him $50."
If I would do that, I would be all right.
And I decided I would not do that.
I decided that that was not my understanding of the American
way of life,
> that I was not going to buy a job . . .
>> that I was not going to bribe anybody,
>>> nor was I going to recognize the right of one man
>>> to collect at the expense of other men who
>>> needed work.

The paradox is that labor in this country does not realize how
well off it is.
Nor do the leaders of labor unions seem to realize that with power
comes responsibility, and that these two things are joined together
by the eternal laws of God.

Apparently some labor union leaders, together with some employ-
ers, do not seem yet to have learned that to every right there is
attached a duty,
> and to every privilege there is tied an obligation.

We, in America, are today enjoying the greatest freedom the world
has ever known—
> a freedom that staggers all who will consider it—
> *for we are free in these days to ignore the very things that
> others died to provide.*

We are free, if we please, to neglect the right of franchise . . .
> free to give up the right to worship God in our own way . . .
>> free to set aside, as of no consequence, the church's
>> open door . . .
>>> free to let the open Bible gather dust.

We are free to neglect the liberties we have inherited.
Surely there can be no greater freedom than that!

Significantly, religious liberty stands first in the Bill of Rights.
It is the most essential, the foundation of all the other freedoms.
Take that away, and eventually all freedom crumbles.

But the Constitution and the Bill of Rights would seem to infer
that we *will* worship God *in some way.*

Now, this generation has distorted religious freedom to mean
freedom from religion.
We find our Supreme Court now declaring it unconstitutional to
teach our children that this nation was founded under God to His
glory and for the advancement of the Christian faith . . .
   unconstitutional to include in the curriculum of our
   children's education any knowledge of God.

Today 85 million Americans or 63 percent of our population are
without even a nominal connection with any church.
At least 30 million children and young people are entirely without religious training of any kind.

But our children are souls—made in the image of God.
These souls are immortal and will live forever, and the human brain
is but a tool and an instrument which the human soul shall use.

In the name of God . . .
   in the name of truth . . .
teaching about religion must be demanded and provided for the
children of today, if this democracy and this civilization are to survive.

The idea may be abroad in some quarters that democracy is the
thing that must be preserved . . .
   and that God is to be brought in as its servant.

We must not get the cart before the horse.

The plea of the church today is not that people shall call upon
God to return to democracy and bless it . . .
   But rather that we shall together cause our democracy to

return to God and be blessed.

Let us remember that we are a republic under God.
Let us remember that each of the metal coins we jingle in our pockets bears the inscription
"In God We Trust."
Is that just blasphemy?
What does it mean to trust in God?

Certainly no conception of trust in God can make any sense which assumes that He will prosper our ways or bless us,
until our ways become His ways . . .
until we begin to keep the conditions He has specifically laid down for national blessing.

The blessing of peace is *not* a product of politics—but a fruit of righteousness.
God's order is always righteousness and peace—
not peace and righteousness.
The Bible has been telling us that for centuries.
When will we learn it?

Desperately we need a return to government by principles rather than by politics.
But where are the principles evident in the events of this present hour?

Peace is not made by compromise.
It does not grow out of expediency.
Peace is not a flower growing in the world's formal garden.
It is rather a product of the blacksmith's forge—
hammered out on the anvils of sacrifice and suffering . . .
heated in the fires of devotion to righteousness . . .
tempered in the oil of mercy and goodness . . .
Peace is a costly thing.

Now, there are only two nations in the world today capable of shouldering world responsibility for peace.

One of them, the United States of America, shies away from it.
She does not want it . . .
   She does not seek it . . .
The idea is distasteful; her instinct is to withdraw.

The other, the Union of Soviet Socialist Republics, is eager for
it, plotting and planning for it, and has openly announced its intention to have it at whatever cost.

Now the choice is clear.
Either we withdraw and let the Russians do it, or we assume it,
unwilling and reluctant though we are.

But the price of world leadership is high.
Deep in our hearts we know that we are not good enough for it.

The call is therefore for Christian men and women, of every communion, to become fighters for peace
      practitioners of righteousness.

Every Catholic and Protestant, who owns the name of Jesus,
must fight together to make America good enough to lead the
world,
      to make the American Dream of equal opportunity for all
      men come true.

Nonetheless, I believe that the dream has been glimpsed by
enough people
      and is deep enough in the heart of the average citizen
to shape America's future and make the dream come true.

We have already done a great deal for the rest of the world.
Let no man minimize our gifts.
But they are not enough.

We have to give more, and I do not mean more dollars.
I do not mean more tractors.
I do not mean more guns.

We have to give more of the only thing, after all, that makes our life different from theirs, namely, our ideals
                        our faith
                    our philosophy of life
                our concept of human dignity
            our Bill of Rights
        our American Dream.

That is what we have to export—
That is what we have to give to the French
                        and the Italians
                    and the British
                and the Belgians
            and the Dutch.
That is what we have to give to the Czechs
                    the Poles
                the Bulgars
            and the Slovaks.

If we can somehow sit down with their governments and say, "Now, look here, rich American blood was poured out to make possible your establishing this kind of government.

We don't mean that you have got to copy ours, but you have to make it possible for a man living within the borders of Greece to have the same opportunities that a man has in the state of Missouri."

Three hundred thousand Americans did not die in the Second World War merely to see conditions develop again that will make necessary another war.

God forbid.

That is what we fought for, because we found out that if there is a denial of personal liberty in Athens,
                or in Prague
            or in Amsterdam
        or in Edinburgh,
there is a restriction of personal liberty in Boston and Charleston.

We found out that what happened on the banks of the Yangtze
River affects the farmer over in Stark County
    or the man who makes shoes in St. Louis or Massachusetts.

It affects Joe Doaks, with a cigar stuck in his mouth, sitting out
there in the bleachers in the ball park yelling for his club.

There are the things America has to export, and perhaps that is
the reason why Almighty God, with the hand of Providence, guided
this nation.
He has made and preserved our nation . . .
    maybe that is the reason . . .
in order that this Republic of forty-eight states, in a federal union,
might save the rest of the world, by giving back to them the new
life that was forged from the anvil of sacrifice and daring adventure
in this country . . .

America may be humanity's last chance.
Certainly it is God's latest experiment.

But we cannot fool God about our individual or national goodness.
Let us not be deluded into thinking we can fool ourselves.

And so I come to my text—2 Chronicles 7:14.
It is God's word for America today—

> "If my people, which are called by my name, shall
> humble themselves, and pray, and seek my face, and
> turn from their wicked ways; then will I hear from
> heaven, and will forgive their sin, and will heal their
> land."

Sanctify Our Love of Country

Lord God of Heaven, who hath so lavishly blessed this land, make us, Thy people, to be humble. Keep us ever aware that the good things we enjoy have come from Thee, that Thou didst lend them to us.

Impress upon our smugness the knowledge that we are not owners—but stewards; remind us, lest we become filled with conceit, that one day a reckoning will be required of us.

Sanctify our love of country, that our boasting may be turned into humility and our pride into a ministry to men everywhere.

Help us make this God's own country by living like God's own people. AMEN.

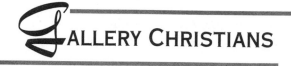ALLERY CHRISTIANS

I did not come to invite the pious but the irreligious.

Matthew 9:13[1]

t was 8:15 on a March morning. Jo Betts unlocked the door of his fish shop. The sign over the door read:

BETTS AND SON
Quality Seafoods, Wholesale—Retail
Serving Washington for Forty Years

Jo pushed open the door, which squeaked a little, strode in, and methodically hung his coat on a peg in the back room.

The place smelled of fish and brine.
Jo took a deep breath, whiffing it.
He had grown to like the smell.
It made him feel at home.

He had inherited the business from his father, who was dead now.
Betts and Son had almost gone under in the 1929 crash—but not quite. They had been one of the few fishmongers down on 7th Street, S.E., to survive the depression.
Now the business was thriving.
Later that morning, when business was in full swing, Jo suddenly looked up to see a strange man standing in the doorway.
He wore a quite ordinary-looking, blue-serge business suit.
But somehow, there was nothing ordinary about the man himself.

304

It was his eyes Jo noticed especially.
The fish merchant was no poet, but there was something luminous . . .
    yes, that was it—luminous—
and compelling about them.

Jo almost forgot for a moment where he was, what he was doing.
Then he recovered himself . . .
    "What can I do for you, sir?"

The stranger smiled . . . and beckoned . . .
"Jo—come on with me.
    I've been searching for you.
        I have an important job for you to do.
        No one else can do it."

Jo blinked and swallowed hard.
Surely he hadn't heard aright!
He'd never seen this man before in his life.
How *could* he know his name?
Was the stranger insane?

Jo had been in the process of opening a barrel of cod.
Deliberately he laid down the tool in his hand and almost as if mesmerized
    without a word of explanation to his employees
he just walked out the door and along the street with the stranger.

Jo Betts had never been a religious man . . .
He had paid no particular attention to churches.
But that is the story of how he became a disciple of the Lord Jesus Christ and, in after years, one of the greatest forces for righteousness in the nation's capital.

Now this story undoubtedly seems very strange to you.
There's something about it that doesn't quite make sense.
Would any man in his right mind walk away with a perfect stranger like that?

But don't you see what I've done?
I have simply used a little "sanctified imagination" to translate most of the details of the story of the calling of Peter and Andrew, as told in the fourth chapter of Matthew, into a modern setting.

Does that help you to see what an audacious
    daring
venturesome
thing it was that those fishermen did in forsaking everything to obey Christ's imperious summons?

Don't you see that it must have seemed just as crazy to their contemporaries
    to some of their friends and relatives
    as it seems to you in the story of Jo Betts?

I have often wondered—if *I* had been there—
    if *I* had been in their shoes
would *I* have had the courage to do what they did?
Would you?

Men found it hard to ignore Jesus of Nazareth.
There was something commanding about Him,
                    kingly,
              imperious.
The New Testament says that He "spoke with authority."

As with any man with a magnetic and compelling personality,
men reacted to Him almost violently.
    Either they loved Him devotedly
        or hated Him cruelly.
They found it difficult to be neutral.

There were, however, a few individuals who could never quite make up their minds to take the plunge . . .
    to become followers of Jesus.
He demanded so much.

He asked such unequivocal allegiance.

"He that loveth father or mother more than me is not worthy of me" (Matthew 10:12).

"Ye cannot serve God *and* mammon" (Luke 16:13).

"Not everyone that saith unto me, Lord, Lord, shall enter into the kingdom of heaven; but he that doeth the will of my Father" (Matthew 7:21).

It is of the men who never really became disciples of Jesus—
those borderline Christians
those "commuters into religion"—
that I want to speak.
How did Jesus affect those men?

There was Nicodemus.

Do you think Nicodemus ever forgot the night when he laid aside his work for the Sanhedrin, turned down the lamp, and went out under the stars to ask questions of the Galilean?

Every time the wind moaned or tugged at his robes, he would remember that musical voice:
"The wind bloweth where it listeth, and thou hearest the sound thereof, but canst not tell whence it cometh, and whither it goeth: so is every one that is born of the Spirit" (John 3:8).

We know that Nicodemus remembered, for we catch two glimpses of him later, in the narratives, in which we find him recognizing the Cause in which he had been invited to enlist—
the Cause that challenged everything good and noble within him—
and yet a Cause that he could not bring himself openly to espouse.

He did stand up in the Sanhedrin and speak a good word for Jesus. It took courage, and he did it.

307

But even so, he was still trying to be on both sides of the controversy.

He could not deny Jesus.

Neither could he confess Him.

He must have seen Jesus die, for he was there to assist in lifting down the broken body from the Cross.

He helped Joseph of Arimathea to bury the One Who had challenged him to the depths of his being.

And now He was dead.

Nicodemus must have thought, "Now it is too late."

He must have been tormented by the knowledge that there were many things he might have said while Jesus lived.

There were many things he might have done.

And I suspect that Nicodemus could never forgive himself for being too late, as he looked at the still face of his Friend, and the little smudges that his tears made on the white linen in which he was helping to wrap that broken body.

Then there was Pilate.

Many have speculated about Pilate.

Artists and poets alike have wondered about him afterward.

We cannot tell.

But I venture that he did not soon forget the Prisoner Who stood before him one morning—manacled

sleepless

beaten

weary and heartsick . . .

yet with eyes that shone, and an expression that was unforgettable.

The governor had sat forward in his chair, and almost without knowing it had said aloud: "What is truth?"

He did not wait for His answer. . . .

Perhaps the answer came to him every day for the rest of his life.

Perhaps he saw the answer every time he shut his eyes.
Perhaps he heard the answer in the silence of his own empty heart.

Pilate tried to wash his hands of Jesus.
I am sure he is still trying—to wash his hands—but he can never get them clean.

If you had been in Barabbas's shoes—in the death cell awaiting execution—
    and had been reprieved, because Somebody else was going
    to die in your place,
you would have wondered all the rest of your life why they put Him to death instead of you. . . .

And in your moments of quiet, you would have heard running round the whispering gallery of your soul the question:
    "Why did they consider Him more dangerous than me?"

Was the rich young ruler able to go on as if he had never met Jesus?

You remember how he came hurrying to Jesus one day, to ask Him what he must do to inherit eternal life.

There was enthusiasm there—of a sort.
There certainly was interest.

What he expected Jesus to tell him, we shall never know.
But the record does say that Jesus was attracted to him, for he had a most pleasing personality and was a young man of great promise.

He had every social and cultural endowment.
He had enjoyed fame and privilege.
He had great possibilities of usefulness in the kingdom.

But Jesus saw what the young man himself had never realized, namely, that he was trusting in the wrong things and was too much in love with himself and his position.

"One thing thou lackest," Jesus had said.
Could he ever forget that?
He never handled money again without hearing the quiet voice
of Jesus.

He could never forget the eyes that seemed to look into his very
soul,
    that seemed to weigh him in the balance and find him
    wanting . . .
"One thing thou lackest."

And we may be sure that with all his money he could never again
be satisfied, for he would be tormented by the thought that the one
thing he lacked was the most important thing of all.

Or what about the lawyer . . .
           the smart
     glib
   self-assured arguer,
who asked Jesus: "Who is my neighbor?"

Jesus answered him by telling him a story—
   the story of the Good Samaritan,
 and made a very simple application when He said, "Go, and do
thou likewise."
Upon this smug, self-satisfied man, there was laid the challenge
to *do* something,
   to *be* somebody.

But we are left to infer that the challenge was one he never met.
I wonder if he was forever afterward haunted by a picture of a
traveler on the Jericho road?

I have named only a few of those who were gallery Christians,
who stood on the edge of Christianity.

There were others—many others—but those whom I have named
have this in common:

They were not weaklings.

Some of them were rich.
Many of them were influential.
They were attractive, with great possibilities . . . men of promise.

The drifters in our day for the most part are like that.
That is the strange thing.
They too are influential . . .
                powerful . . .
            strong men and women . . . popular . . .
        attractive as far as their friends are concerned . . .
    well educated . . . cultured . . .
Why do they stay on the edge of the crowd?
Why don't they follow Jesus?

Do you ever puzzle over this?
    Do you ever wonder?

There is a text in Matthew that reads: "I am not come to call the righteous, but sinners to repentance" (Matthew 9:13).

As long as it remains in the language of the King James Version it is not likely to strike fire in the minds and hearts of sophisticated men and women.

Well . . . read it in a modern translation.
Goodspeed, for example, puts it this way: "I did not come to invite the pious but the irreligious."

Washington is full of drifters as far as Christ is concerned.

They are not anti-Christian . . .
    not antireligious. . . .

They simply don't care much one way or the other.
They are conscious of no great loss.
As long as life goes smoothly, they feel no sense of need.

They don't have *any* religion, as they themselves will tell you quickly and frankly enough.
This group is growing in America.
More than 60 percent of all American children are growing up without any religious training of any kind.
We are becoming a secular nation.

These irreligious people say, "I don't need the church.
    What could it do for me?
I'm a decent citizen . . .
    Never break any very big laws . . .
        Pay my taxes . . .
            Give some to the Community Chest.
What more do you want?"

Well . . . here is Jesus saying He came to invite them particularly.

Whether we church people like it or not, we must admit that Jesus made a strong appeal for this type of person . . .
    who never comes to church . . .
        never thinks of it . . .
and who will either lift an eyebrow or smile in that particular way when somebody talks about being at church . . . or coming to prayer meeting.

Yes, Jesus liked people—all kinds of folks—
    red-blooded folks . . .
for He himself was red-blooded.

We have had enough of the emaciated Christ . . .
    the pale, anemic, namby-pamby Jesus . . .
    the "gentle Jesus, meek and mild" . . .
Perhaps we have had too much of it.

Let us see the Christ of the Gospels . . . striding up and down the dusty miles of Palestine . . . sun-tanned.
    bronzed
    fearless.

312

Let us see the white knuckles of the carpenter's hand as He upset the tables of the money-changers and glared at the racketeers. . . .

Let us feel the terrific dynamic of the personality that walked clear through a lynching mob that sought to throw Him over a cliff.

He strode through them, and no man laid a hand on Him.
That's the Christ we ought to see.

Let's see the Christ Who called a spade a spade . . . and let the chips fall where they might.
Take Jesus out of the perfumed cloisters of pious sentiment,
and let Him walk the streets of the city.

Let's be honest.
We have nothing to fear.
Let us say boldly that the kind of people Jesus liked best are not the kind that the average church appeals to at all.

We classify people by the families they come from . . .
the clothes they wear
where they went to school
where they live
and how much money they have.
So that some people are our type—and others are not.
The average church member likes to have people of his own social level in his church.

I'm sure Jesus does not approve of that.
There were no such barriers
no such distinctions with Him.
All men of every race and color are God's children, and He came to invite them all to be His friends.

Inside the church itself, there are people who resent the intrusion of those whom they call "outsiders."
I hope they can justify that title before God, for someday they will be called to do so.

We erect barricades to keep people out—God help us . . .
God forgive us!

Think of the people whom Christ especially invited to be His
friends—
    Peter and Andrew, James and John—fish merchants . . .
      Zacchaeus and Matthew—unpopular tax collectors . . .
        Mary Magdalene—once a prostitute . . .
          Joanna—the wife of Herod's chancellor, a
          society woman . . .
            Saul of Tarsus—an aristocrat, a
            persecutor of the church.

The church people could not understand it.
It was a scandal.
"Why eateth your Master with publicans and sinners?" asked
the Pharisees (Matthew 9:11).

And Jesus answered, "They that be whole need not a physician;
but they that are sick. . . . For I am not come to call the righteous,
but sinners to repentance" (Matthew 9:12, 13).

At another time He said to the Pharisees:

> "I say unto you, that likewise joy shall be in heaven over
> one sinner that repenteth, more than over ninety and nine
> just persons, which need no repentance" (Luke 15:7).

There are thousands of people today who fall into just this category—the ninety and nine sheep whom the Shepherd came especially to find.

They seldom—if ever—come to church . . . oh, perhaps once a
year on Easter.
They contribute nothing whatever financially.
They use Sundays for sport and recreation.

They never read the Bible. . . .

They never pray.
They speak of God only in profanity.
They are a pagan lot more or less . . .
   red-blooded
      thoroughly sophisticated.

They like a good time . . . but have never discovered the secret
of true happiness.
   The pleasures of sin—as the Bible tells us—are very real
     and very attractive.

This is the life to which young people are exposed.
This is the life they are tempted to lead . . .
   and some of them are troubled about it.

There is a clash between the ideals in which they have been
reared and the standards they find generally accepted in society.

The church—this church—cannot be indifferent to the conflict.
We invite the sophisticates,
   the irreligious, to join the church,
and we extend to them our fellowship.

But that is not the all-important thing.
   The thing that really matters is that they will meet Jesus Christ,
and come into contact with Him Who alone can offer them the full
life,
   the abundant life
     the life that brings out the best in them,
   and give them a happiness and a peace of mind that cannot be
found anywhere else.

I wish I could convince you somehow that it is not the church I
am trying to present—*but Christ!*
   The church has its faults.
   That is because it is made up of people like you and me.
   We are far from perfect.

The wonder is that the church has as much influence as it has
... and is supported as well as it is.

There are a few hypocrites in our churches.
Of course—we all know that.

But there are hypocrites in your club too, and that doesn't seem
to bother you.
There are hypocrites in your lodge, and that doesn't keep you
away.
But hypocrites in the church seem to be such a stumbling block.

We are not offering the church—but Jesus of Nazareth.
The whole function of the church, after all, is to introduce peo-
ple to Christ.
That is our business and it is nothing else.
He Himself said: "I came not to invite the pious, but the
irreligious."

Perhaps that applies to some of you.
He is calling *you*.
Christ is here—a thousand times more alive than when He
walked in the flesh up and down the sun-baked trails of that little
land.

He is too big to be shut up in any church or cathedral.
He will burst the seams of any theological robe we tie around
Him. . . .

No creed can hold Him. . . .
No doctrine or dogma can tell all about Him.

No . . . He will stride out of here . . .
    and elbow His way through the city's crowds . . .
mixing with the irreligious . . . because He likes them.
They are His kind of men and women.
    He wants them.

Red-blooded they are . . . and He needs red-blooded men and women now.

Vigorous they are. They like life.

That's why He is so anxious that they should have life . . . and have it more abundantly.

They laugh and enjoy living . . .

He wants to hear laughter.

"A man of sorrows, and acquainted with grief"—that He was . . .
    but it was in order that our joy might be full.

Some of you have drifted long enough.

For a number of years now you have been a casual spectator Christian.

There have been times when you felt prompted to stand up and be counted with those of us who, acknowledging our own sins
        our weakness
            and our hypocrisy,
    and are ashamed of them, nevertheless keep trying, by God's help, to do the things Christ wants us to do.

Have you ever said to the Galilean, "I believe in You.
    I am with You, come what may"?

Have you ever told Him that?

If you have not, why not do it—now?

Make Us Willing to Share

Thou hast said, Father, "It is more blessed to give than to receive." Give us the grace today to think not of what we can get but of what we can give, that a new spirit may come into our work, with a new vision and a new purpose, that Thou wilt delight to bless.

Make our people everywhere in our land willing to share the good things they enjoy, lest in our selfishness our food should choke us, and in our indifference our blessings turn to ashes.

Help us to give according to our incomes, lest Thou, O God, make our incomes according to our gifts. In Jesus' name we ask it. AMEN.

$\mathcal{S}$IN IN THE PRESENT TENSE

$\mathcal{T}$he three chief causes of death in the United States are, in
statistical order, diseases of the heart
cancer
and disorders of the nervous system.

Two of the three are obviously diseases brought on by the strains
imposed on the human body by worry
anxiety
nervousness
and the tensions of life in our modern world.

Our lives are so geared these days that any contemplation is
difficult.
I have tried it on the top of Washington Monument and found it
impossible even there.

I well remember leaning out of one of the windows—550 feet
above Washington—wondering how the city must have looked in
the time of John Quincy Adams
or Thomas Jefferson . . .
when Pennsylvania Avenue was a muddy road, rutted with carriage wheels.

As I stood there, lost in reverie, trying to recapture Washington's
past, I was interrupted by a brusque voice at my elbow saying,
"Keep moving please . . . move right on round."

Try standing for five minutes anywhere on the main shopping
street of any city,
or on the loading platforms for streetcars during the rush
hours in the evening.

Observe the surging, seething mass of humanity flowing past
you.
    Notice the furrowed brows
        the faces lined with anxiety and worry
            the haggard, hurried look.

Above all, notice the tenseness of the people,
    the feeling of tension in the very atmosphere.

Its symptoms are obvious—irritation, short temper, frowns, nervousness, impatience . . .
    fighting to be waited on . . .
        struggling against time . . .
Everywhere is this tension that is just on the verge of hysterics
        bitter tears
        screams of impotence and rage
and actual conflict.

Now, at this moment, when you are quiet, you know in your
heart that God did not mean us to live like that.
We were not made for that sort of struggle for existence.
It is against every law of health, every law of God.

The essence and core of Christianity is *trust in God.*

As Christ traveled up and down the dusty roads of Palestine, He
was constantly amazed that human beings did not really trust His
Heavenly Father.
    "Why are you afraid?" He would say.
        "How little you trust God!
            "Why are ye so fearful?
                "How is it that ye have no faith?
                    "O men, how little you trust Him!"

By every gentle word,
    by every act of compassion and pity,
  Christ was trying to show men that God is not only all-powerful,
but also all-loving . . .

nearer to each of us than we know . . .
always ready and willing to make His power available to meet
our needs.

Christ was constantly admonishing men to trust this loving
Father, to pin all their faith on Him.
"Have no fear, only believe," He said to one seeking
healing.
"Have faith in God," He said to a distraught father.
"All things are possible to him that believeth" (Mark 9:23).

Now why was it that Christ considered faith—trusting God— so
all-important?
And exactly what did He mean by "trusting God"?

This is fundamental to Christian faith.
It has to do with our understanding of life.
It has to do with that basic selfishness, which is so often mis-
taken for grief.

If you are in financial straits and have turned to God for help,
as you are expected to do . . .
as God wants you to do . . .
but you still continue to worry and don't see how you can make
both ends meet,
then you are not really trusting God to help you.

Why do we worry about these material things?
Our Heavenly Father knows perfectly well that we need them
and is more willing to send them to us than we are to ask for them.
"If ye then, being evil, know how to give good gifts to
your children, *how much more* shall your Father which is
in Heaven give good things to them *that ask him*"
(Matthew 7:11).
God has pledged His word to supply all our needs.

Paul could testify that God keeps His promises.
I myself know that this promise is true.

God may not supply all your wants, because sometimes we want things that are not good for us.
Parents don't supply all that their children may want.
But you have every need supplied.
What more can we ask?

Why is it that Christ considered anxiety and worry a sin?
Because worry and anxiety are really lack of trust in God.
And this lack of trust shows that we do not really believe the promises of God.
We believe *in* God—but may not *believe God.*

If you doubt God's ability to help you in a given difficulty, you are doubting either His power,
    His ability to help you . . .
or you are doubting His willingness to help you.

To doubt either God's power,
    or God's love
is to say by our actions:
        "Lord, I do not believe your promises.
        I do not think they really apply to me.
        I do not think You will do it.
        It might have been all right for Palestine in the long ago, but Lord,
        You just don't know Washington."

Surely it is perfectly evident that to doubt God in that way is to sin against Him, and to cut ourselves off from His help.

Thus one of the greatest sins of Christian people is the sin of tension and worry.
It is characteristic of all our people, that we, as a nation, need to learn *how* to relax.

We have permitted ourselves to be stampeded into a life of unnatural and dangerous high pressure.
    We try to cover too much ground.

We are always in a hurry.

I gave my mother's address to some of our boys who were going overseas, in the hope that they might be able to call upon her.

Some of them did, and commenting on the first visit she received from these American soldiers, Mother said,

"They came in a jeep, and they were in a hurry."

That, I think, is a typical commentary on our American way of life.

We are always in a hurry.

We hate to miss one panel of a revolving door.

Some bright soul has defined a split second as "that interval of time between the changing of a traffic light from red to green, and the honking of the horn in the car immediately behind you."

Whereas our grandparents could make a gracious ceremony and devote a whole evening to a game of parcheesi, we now feel frustrated unless we can, in a single evening,

combine a dinner date

take in a movie

make a couple of telephone calls

visit somebody on the way downtown

and maybe do some shopping on our

way to the show.

We try to do too much in too short a time.

We are compressing our lives into capsules that are quite indigestible.

That this sin of tension is taking a terrific toll among the people of the nation cannot be denied.

The incidence of functional diseases,

neuroses,

mental illness,

and heart troubles,

increases year after year.

323

Medicine has made great strides.

It has learned how to combat infectious diseases, but what has happened is that we have merely exchanged the types of disease.

The citadel of disease has simply retired to other strongholds further in, and more difficult to root out.

Fewer people now die of infectious diseases, but more die of degenerative diseases.

The years of life which we have *gained* by the suppression of smallpox
> diphtheria
>> and scarlet fever
are *stolen* by the chronic diseases such as cancer
>> diabetes
> ulcers,
> and heart disease.

Thus, disease still has not been mastered.

It simply has changed its nature.

As modern medicine seeks the cause of all this, it has made some startling discoveries.

The British Medical Journal puts it this way:
> "There is not a tissue in the human body wholly removed
> from the influence of the spirit."[1]

In other words, we are discovering that there is a closer relationship between our minds,
> our emotions,
>> the state of our spiritual health, and our bodies,
than doctors thought possible a few decades ago.

To illustrate:

It is a well-known fact that the hyperacidity often leading to stomach ulcers is directly caused by emotional stress and, generally, a sense of frustration.

I can vouch for that out of my own experience.

But physicians are now discovering that the same thing is equally true of other diseases.

Dr. Loring T. Swaim of Boston, a nationally known specialist on arthritis, says that

> It has been increasingly evident, as pointed out by doctors everywhere, that physical health is closely associated with, and often dependent upon, spiritual health.
>
> No constitutional disease is free from the effects of mental strains, which are part of life. Rheumatoid arthritis is no exception.[2]

If tension and worry are the great sins of our day,
    and if they affect not only our spiritual health,
        not only our peace of mind and happiness—but even
        our physical health,
it is certainly worthy of our greatest efforts to learn how to overcome them.

This is where Christianity has the answer.

God has designed us for happiness.
He has created us for peace and joy.
It is His will for each of His creatures that life shall be free and lived to the utmost for His glory.

Now, worshiping and serving God is a solemn thing,
    but it can be happy.
We have confused being solemn with being sad,
    being dignified with being depressed.

Have you ever wondered why going to church,
        working in the church,
    taking part in its activities
is done with a sigh instead of a smile or a song?

Why is that so few people find in it fun,

fellowship

good company

good times

good humor

and happiness?

Christ's invitation into the Kingdom of God as a joyous affair is like an invitation to a feast of good things, and an invitation to happiness.

Does your religious experience fit into that?

If not, there's something wrong.

People refuse the offer of Christianity, because they never dream that what they want can be found there.

Christ offers us what we are really hungering for, but we don't believe it, because we mistake what we really want in life.

How often Jesus used words that make the new life as attractive as a feast!

> The prodigal son is received with music, dancing, and a banquet.

> The faithful servant is invited to enter into the joy of his Lord.

> The wise virgins go into supper with the bridegroom.

There is only one conclusion.

Either Jesus was wrong—

> or we have missed something.

Jesus did not intend that following Him should be sad.

It is true that He was "a man of sorrows, and acquainted with grief," but that was in order that our joy might be full.

> "Come unto me, all ye that labour and are heavy laden, and I will give you rest. Take my yoke upon you, and learn of me; for I am meek and lowly of heart: and ye shall find rest unto your souls. For my yoke is easy, and my burden is light" (Matthew 11:28).

The yoke He imposes is an easy one.

It does not chafe

or hurt
> or hold you back.

On the contrary—
It takes away pain,
> gives you freedom
>> drives you on to a fuller and happier life.

But we won't believe it.
We won't give Him a chance.
We prefer to attempt to carry our burdens and, as if we did not have enough, we try even to carry God's burdens also.

Now what shall we do, who are seeking peace of mind and heart? How can we find it?

First, let us try to clear our thinking about the nature of God. Let us make a study, a serious study—for it merits our best efforts—to find out the nature of God.

Most of our difficulties, our lack of trust in God, spring from our basic misunderstanding of what God is like.
We are dismally ignorant of the love and the power of God.
> No wonder we do not trust Him!

Have you ever set out to read your New Testament to find out about God?
How do you expect to know what God is like if you never read intelligently the only Book that professes to tell you these things?
Get a good modern translation, like Moffatt's or Goodspeed's, and read it intelligently.
Christ came to reveal God.
He said to one of His disciples:
> "Have I been so long time with you, and yet hast thou not known me, Philip? he hath seen me hath seen the Father" (John 14:9).

If you want to know what God is like, look at Christ.

Study what Christ said.
Notice what Christ did.
And remember—
He is "the same yesterday, and today, and forever."

Next, study the lives of some others who have been personally
acquainted with Him.
Read the letters, journals, and biographies of men like
Francis of Assisi
Thomas à Kempis
Wilfred Grenfell
George Müller of Bristol
Brother Bryan of Birmingham
William Pulmer Jacobs of
Thornwell Orphanage
and Dr. George
Washington Carver.
Find out how God dealt with them, and thus you will begin to
find out about God.

The second step is to become personally acquainted with God
yourself—
in your own way,
according to your own needs and circumstances.
"Practice makes perfect" in the realm of the spiritual, as well as
in other things.

You see, your real trouble is spiritual, so that the remedy must
be spiritual too.
All of which means . . . "Take your burdens to the Lord . . . and
leave them there."
"But how?" . . . you ask.

Get off by yourself . . . somewhere . . . and tell God your fears—
what you are afraid of. . . .
Tell Him what you are worried about. . . .

And then ask Him . . . very simply . . . to take care of you.

Let all your fears go—give them to God.
He will not let you down.
Try to let yourself go . . . to God.

If you feel that you haven't enough faith to do that . . . ask Him
to give you the faith too.
He will do that—exactly that.

He will give you what it takes.

The man or woman who really trusts God is not spiritually
rigid . . .

afraid of what may happen tomorrow . . .
rehearsing in imagination all the terrible things that could happen.
No, as believers in God, we must relax.

When you are weary and sit down in a chair, you do not sit rigid,
expecting that chair to collapse beneath you—that is, unless the
chair is an antique. . . .
When you lie down on your bed, you do not lie like a poker—
tense, rigid.
You trust the bed to hold you.
You do not worry about the possibility of your bed collapsing and
depositing you on the floor.
I have had that happen to me . . . and it's not so bad, really.

But you don't lie there speculating about the possibility of its
happening.
You don't lie there all tense . . . listening for the sound of a bur-
glar at the window . . .

or the crackle of flames from the basement . . .
or the smell of smoke . . .
or the trembling of the earth in a possible
earthquake.

If you did, you would not get much sleep.
You trust your bed.
You trust your precautions against burglars.
You trust the police force . . .
and the fire brigade . . .

and trust yourself to sleep . . .
which is another way of saying you trust yourself to God.

The believer trusts himself to God . . .
    believing that God will watch over him.
Will you relax spiritually today?

Will you leave with God—now—the troubles you have been carrying around for so long?
    Will you ask Him—now—to take them away from you?
        and let you relax in simple trust . . . just like a little child?
                    Will you?

"There was once a fellow who, with his father, farmed a little
piece of land.
    Several times a year they'd load up the ox-cart with vegetables
and drive to the nearest city.

"Except for their name and the patch of ground, father and son
had little in common.
    The old man believed in taking it easy . . .
        and the son was the go-getter type.

"One morning, they loaded the cart,
    hitched up the ox, and set out.
    The young fellow figured that if they kept going all day and night,
they'd get to the market by the next morning.
    He walked alongside the ox and kept prodding it with a stick.

"'Take it easy,' said the old man. 'You'll last longer.'

"'If we get to the market ahead of the others,' said his son, 'we
have a better chance of getting good prices.'

"The old man pulled his hat down over his eyes and went to sleep
on the seat.
    Four miles and four hours down the road, they came to a little
house.

'Here's your uncle's place,' said the father, waking up. 'Let's stop in and say hello.'

"'We've lost an hour already,' complained the go-getter.

"'Then a few minutes more won't matter,' said his father. 'My brother and I live so close, yet we see each other so seldom.'

"The young man fidgeted while the two old gentlemen gossiped away an hour.
On the move again, the father took his turn leading the ox.
By and by, they came to a fork in the road.
The old man directed the ox to the right.
'The left is the shorter way,' said the boy.

"'I know it,' said the old man, 'but this way is prettier.'

"'Have you no respect for time?' asked the impatient young man.
"'I respect it very much,' said the old fellow.
'That's why I like to use it for looking at pretty things.'
"The right-hand path led through woodland and wild flowers.
The young man was so busy watching the sun sink he didn't notice how lovely the sunset was.
Twilight found them in what looked like one big garden.
'Let's sleep here,' said the old man.

"'This is the last trip I take with you,' snapped his son.
'You're more interested in flowers than in making money.'

"'That's the nicest thing you've said in a long time,' smiled the old fellow.
A minute later he was asleep.

"A little before sunrise, the young man shook his father awake.
They hitched up and went on.
A mile and an hour away they came upon a farmer trying to pull his cart out of a ditch.
'Let's give him a hand,' said the father.

"'And lose more time?' exploded the son.

"'Relax,' said the old man.
'You might be in a ditch sometime yourself.'

"By the time the other cart was back on the road, it was almost eight o'clock.
Suddenly a great flash of lightning split the sky.
Then there was thunder.
Beyond the hills, the heavens grew dark.
'Looks like a big rain in the city,' said the old man.

"'If we had been on time, we'd be sold out by now,' grumbled his son.

"'Take it easy,' said the old gentleman, 'you'll last longer.'

"It wasn't until late in the afternoon that they got to the top of the hill overlooking the town.
They looked down at it for a long time.
Neither of them spoke.
Finally the young man who had been in such a hurry said, 'I see what you mean, Father.'

"They turned their cart around and drove away from what had once been the city of Hiroshima."[3]

Give to Us More Faith

Forgive us, O God, for our little conception of the heart of the Eternal, for the doubting suspicion with which we regard the heart of God.

Give us more faith. We have so little . . . we say. Yet we have faith in each other—in checks and banks, in trains and airplanes, in cooks, and in strangers who drive us in cabs. Forgive us for our stupidity, that we have faith in people whom we do not know and are reluctant to have faith in Thee who knowest us altogether.

We are always striving to find a complicated way through life when Thou hast a plan, and we refuse to walk in it. So many of our troubles we bring on ourselves. How silly we are . . .

Wilt Thou give to us that faith that we can deposit in the bank of Thy love, so that we may receive the dividend and the interest that Thou art so willing to give us.

We ask it all in the lovely name of Jesus Christ our Savior. AMEN.

ℒETTERS IN THE SAND

> I came not to judge the world, but to save the world.
>
> John 12:47

There are many startling verses in the New Testament . . .

This one for instance,
   "let us not criticize one another anymore."[1]

No more criticism of any kind?
Can you imagine living like that?
Yet that is exactly the spirit in which Jesus looked at men and women.
   He knew that even when one has sinned grievously . . .
      when things are desperately wrong in a human life
   it is love—not criticism—that helps
      and heals
         and redeems.

"But Christ *did* criticize the Scribes and Pharisees," you may say. Yes,
   He did . . .
      That is an exception . . .

But that was condemnation of an attitude of mind and heart.
It was a solemn warning of the wrongness of the spirit shown by
these religious leaders—
their self-righteousness
their hypocrisy
their concern about ritual and form
their making religion a legal matter.

You will remember what He said to the nameless woman who
was brought before Him by the very same Pharisees.
They had caught her in the act of adultery, and in the coldness
of their hard hearts they would use her case as a trap for Jesus.

I do not know the woman's name.
Tradition does not name her.
The incident takes place in the early morning in the temple court.
The eastern sun—already up—casts short purple shadows among
the great pillars.
Jesus is seated, teaching a large group of devoted followers gath-
ered round him.

Suddenly, a group surges forward, pushing their way roughly
through the morning worshipers.
Christ's face clouds for a moment, and pain looks out from His
eyes.

The Scribes and Pharisees thrust their way toward Christ.
In the midst of them is a woman—being dragged roughly by
strong men whose faces are hard and stern.

They are pulling her along.
She struggles feebly now and then.
She winces and cries out with the pain of their strong grip on her
arms.
With all the strength of their contempt they throw her down at
Jesus' feet.

Then they spew out their accusations . . .

335

In voices honed on hate they shout the vile names reserved for such women.

There are voices hot, like scorching blasts from a furnace . . . and others cold, as if they came from frozen hearts.

The woman lies before Christ in a huddled heap,
    sobbing bitterly
        trembling in her shame
shivering as she listens to the indictment.

Her head is bowed; her face covered with her hands.
Her disheveled hair falls over her face.
Her dress is torn and stained with the dust of the city streets along which she has been dragged.

His disciples look into the face of Christ and see in His eyes an infinite sadness, as if the load of all the sin since the world began has already been laid on Him.

His steady eyes take in the situation at a glance.
He sees what they try to hide from Him—
    the hard faces that have no pity or mercy in them
        the looks of satisfaction and self-righteousness with
            which they finger the stones they have picked up.
Every hand holds a stone and clutching fingers run along the sharp edges with malicious satisfaction.

Their shouting ceases as the piercing look of Christ travels round the circle questioningly, and they fall to muttering, as one of their group shouts out the accusation again.

The woman has been caught in the very act of adultery.

Christ looks beyond the woman sobbing at His feet,
    perhaps in search of the man who shares her guilt.
But the woman alone is accused.
There is no man sharing her shame.

It seems to His disciples that Christ does not look at her at all.

He is watching those men who try to hide the stones they carry in their hands.

They are ready—her self-appointed judges—to throw them at the poor defenseless creature on the ground, for it is the law—the sacred law of Moses—that such shall be stoned to death.

They have brought her to Christ as a vindictive, malicious after-thought, not for formal trial—for they have already tried her—but in a bold effort to trap Him, either by setting aside the plain commandment of the law, or by tacitly consenting to a public execution.

If He chooses to repudiate the law, the priest can accuse Him of being no Prophet.

He had said that He came to fulfill the law, not to *destroy* it.

If He permits the woman's stoning, He will clash with the Roman authorities.

In this little occupied country, Rome alone retains the power of life and death.

If the Nazarene condemns the woman, He will lose His popularity with the multitudes who love and follow Him.

"Be ye therefore merciful," He has often said to them, "as your Father also is merciful" (Luke 6:36).

How can He condemn the woman and still be merciful?

Every form of sin is repulsive to Him,
    and although at times it seems that He thinks the sins of
    disposition and attitude more to be detested than the sins of
    the flesh,
    yet He nowhere—at any time—condones evil and the doing of
wrong.

The circle of bearded men wait impatiently for His answer.

Will His verdict be justice—or mercy?

It is a clever trap.

Surely the Nazarene can find no way out of this one!

But Jesus stands there calmly, quite unruffled by the dilemma so
neatly framed.
He well knows that, in the eyes of the Pharisees, *He* is the real
enemy—not the woman.
Therefore, He will appeal the case to a Higher Tribunal.
He will lift the issue from the level of human law to that of Divine
law.
He will appeal to the bar of conscience.

He does not speak.
Stooping down, He slowly, deliberately, begins to write in the
dust at His feet.
This is the only time we know of His writing anything . . .
    and no one knows what He wrote.

Some ancient scholars believe that He traced there in the dust a
catalog of human sin.
Perhaps He looks up at a tall man, with graying hair and piercing blue eyes, and traces the word "Extortioner"—
    and the man turns and flees into the crowd.

Christ looks up into the faces of the men standing in the circle,
and steadily—with eyes that never blink—he speaks to them:
    "He that is without sin among you,
    let him first cast a stone at her" (John 8:7).

His keen glance rests upon the woman's accusers one by one.
Then He writes in the sand at their feet—letter after letter.
They watch His finger—fascinated, as it travels up and down—
    up and down.
They cannot watch without trembling.

The group is thinning now.
They think of the recording angel.
They think of judgment.
They have howled for it.
Now it has descended on them.

338

Looking into their faces, Christ sees into the yesterdays that lie deep in the pools of memory and conscience.

He sees into their very hearts, and that moving finger writes on . . .

Idolater . . .

Liar . . .

Drunkard . . .

Murderer . . .

Adulterer. . . .

There is the thud of stone after stone falling on the pavement.

Not many of the Pharisees are left.

One by one, they creep away—like animals—slinking into the shadows . . .

shuffling off into the crowded streets to lose themselves in the multitudes.

"He that is without sin among you, let him first cast a stone at her."

But the adulteress could not have been unfaithful had not a man tempted her.

There would be no harlots if men had no evil passions.

Another should have stood with her in condemnation, but she was alone.

The first lesson Jesus taught that day was that only the guiltless have the right to judge.

"Judge not, and ye shall not be judged."

"Forgive, and ye shall be forgiven" (Matthew 6:37).

But no stones have been thrown.

They lie around the woman on the pavement.

They have dropped them where they stood, and now she is left alone at the feet of Christ.

The stillness is broken only by her sobbing.

She still has not lifted her head . . .

And now Christ looks at her.
He does not speak for a long moment.

Then, with eyes full of understanding, He says softly:
    "Woman, where are those thine accusers?
    Hath no man condemned thee?" (John 8:10).
And she answers,
    "No man, Lord."

That is all the woman says from beginning to end.
She has no excuse for her conduct.
She makes no attempt to justify what she has done.
And Christ looking at her, seeing tear-stained cheeks and her
eyes red with weeping,
    seeing further into her heart,
        seeing the contrition there,
says to her:
    "Neither do I condemn thee: go, and sin no more" (John 8:11).

What a strange verdict for the Nazarene to pass . . .
There has been no doubt of her guilt, and likewise there is no
doubt about His attitude toward it.

What He here says is not that He acquits the woman, but that
He forgives her.
Not that He absolves her from blame, but that He absolves her
from guilt.
Not that He condones the act, but that He does not condemn her
for it—He forgives her instead.

His soft voice is like a candle at twilight,
    Like a soft angelus at the close of the day . . .
        like the fragrance of a rose in a sickroom . . .
            like the singing of a bird after the storm . . .
It is healing music for a sin-sick heart.

All is quiet for a while.
If she breathes her gratitude, it is so soft that only He hears it.

340

Or perhaps it is a silent prayer which He and the angels in heaven alone can interpret.

Perhaps He smiles upon her, as she slowly raises her eyes, a slow, sad smile of one Who knew that He Himself has to pay the price of the absolution.

And it may be that His finger writes again in the dust, tracing this time the outline of a cross or the shape of a hill—
a hill shaped like a skull.

No, we do not know her name
nor where she lived
nor who she was.
But of this we can be sure—she was never the same again.
She was a changed woman from that moment. Of that we can be sure.

She has looked into the eyes of Christ.
She has seen God.
She has been accused
convicted
judged but not condemned.
She has been forgiven!

And now her head is up.
Her eyes are shining like stars, for has she not seen the greatest miracle of all?

It is more wonderful than the miracles of creation . . .
more beautiful than the flowers . . .
more mysterious than the stars . . .
more wonderful than life itself . . .
that God is willing, for Christ's sake, to forgive sinners like you and me.

For we are *all* sinners . . . guilty of different kinds of sin, no doubt.
For there are sins of the heart,
and sins of the mind

341

and sins of the disposition
as well as sins of the body.

We, too, may be forgiven, no matter what type or kind of transgressions we have committed.
That we may be forgiven is the greatest miracle of them all.
God is willing to forgive us,
to cleanse us from all unrighteousness,
because the blood of Jesus Christ, His Son, cleanseth us from all sin.

That is the basis and the only basis for our forgiveness.

Therefore, "be kind one to another, tenderhearted, forgiving one another, even as God for Christ's sake hath forgiven you" (Ephesians 4:32).

We have no greater need today than this—the need of forgiving one another.
The whole world cries out for forgiveness . . .
Nations need it.
Society needs it.
Business, capital, and labor need it.

Homes need it.
Individual human hearts need it.
Friends need it.
Aye—and enemies too.
We need forgiveness—to be forgiven and to forgive—for without forgiveness, our troubled hearts can know no peace.

But there is a stern condition to be met, if you and I are to be forgiven . . .
There must be no malice in your heart against anyone in the whole world.
There must be no refusal on your part to forgive anyone else . . .
whatever he or she may have done . . .
no matter how wrong they were . . .

or how innocent you were.

If you hug to yourself any resentment against anybody else, you destroy the bridge by which God would come to you.

If you do not forgive other people, you yourself can never *feel* forgiven, because you will never *be* forgiven.

How can I be so sure about that?

Simply because Jesus said so . . .

"But if ye forgive not men their trespasses, neither will your Father forgive your trespasses" (Matthew 6:15).

Jesus was not sentimental about the alternatives.

He was blunt and honest.

In other words, if you will forgive others when they offend you, then your Heavenly Father will forgive you too.

But if you refuse to forgive others, then your Heavenly Father will not, indeed cannot, forgive you your offenses.

So—if you would have peace in your heart—

if you would know the forgiveness of God—

it is a case of forgive—or else.

We Confess Before Thee

Forgive us, Lord Jesus, for the things we have done that make us feel uncomfortable in Thy presence. All the front that we polish so carefully for men to see, does not deceive Thee. For Thou knowest every thought that has left its shadow on our memory. Thou hast marked every motive that curdled something sweet within us.

We acknowledge—with bitterness and true repentance—that cross and selfish thoughts have entered our minds; we acknowledge that we have permitted our minds to wander through unclean and forbidden ways; we have toyed with that which we knew was not for us; we have desired that which we should not have.

We acknowledge that often we have deceived ourselves where our plain duty lay.

We confess before Thee that our ears are often deaf to the whisper of Thy call, our eyes often blind to the signs of Thy guidance.

Make us willing to be changed, even though it requires surgery of the soul and the therapy of discipline.

Make our hearts warm and soft, that we may receive now the blessing of Thy forgiveness, the benediction of Thy "Depart in peace . . . and sin no more."

AMEN.

PRAYING IS DANGEROUS BUSINESS

few months ago I heard a talk by a university professor, who addressed a civic club.

When the professor had finished, the men were thoughtful and quiet.

They went back to their offices and their places of business in a chastened mood, for the professor had sketched a very grim picture.

He was talking about a formula a Jewish professor of mathematics had written on a blackboard in 1913 for the amusement of his students.

Einstein had written this:

$$E = MC^2$$

Energy equals mass multiplied by the square of the speed of light.

Of this formula, *Time* magazine, thirty-two years later, said that man could forget all that he had learned up until now, for this formula had changed everything.

This formula was the first key to the doors leading to atomic power.

The potentialities of this new power are such as to stagger the imaginations of men.

Clearly we are on the threshold of a new world . . .
    with terrific implications.

It all depends on how we use this new energy—
    whether for good or evil . . .
        whether for humanity or against it.

345

Man found fire when he learned how to make a spark.
Now fire can be directed by a flame thrower to burn human bodies—
> or it can be used as steady lights gleaming on tall tapers on an altar.

When explosives were discovered, the world shuddered in apprehension at the implications of this dreadful power.
Explosives can blow men to bits—when packed inside a shell casing.
> Or they can also be used in a coal mine to dig out coal to keep people warm in winter.

Gasoline drives a tank . . .
> It also drives an ambulance.

Electricity can toast your bread at the breakfast table.
> It is also used in the death house in Sing Sing.

> Because thieves have walked in darkness, shall darkness be called a thief?

Not a single one of the new powers discovered by man possesses any redeeming force.
> Neither fire
>> nor steam
>>> nor explosives
>>>> nor electricity
>>>>> nor atomic energy
can change his nature.

Man got one power after another . . .
> but they never turned him toward God or made him like God.

As Mr. Fulton Oursler said in a radio address on *The Catholic Hour:*
"It would take another kind of power altogether to make an unhappy man happy

a bad man good
a cruel man kind
a stupid man wise.

"Yet there is such power freely available in this world, and unless
it is used, the atomic bomb,
like all other useful inventions of man,
will be turned to evil.

"Every Christian knows that redeeming power.
For two thousand years it has been at man's disposal."[1]

The greatest force ever bestowed on mankind streamed forth in
blood
and sweat
and tears
and death on Calvary . . .
when Jesus of Nazareth was crucified on the cross.

It was a power so great that it shattered the last fortress—death.
It was a power so great that it made atonement for all the sin of
all the world.
It was a power so great that it provided for those who would
accept it the ability to live victoriously like children of God,
in fellowship with Him Who made the world and the sun,
the moon and the stars.

It was a power that would enable believers to do the mighty works
of Christ,
and to experience, flowing in and through their lives, the
energy of God.

Here is a power so tremendous that with it nothing is impossible;
and without it, nothing we do has any eternal value or
significance.

It is a power so simple that a child may use it . . .

347

Yet we reach for that power only when our hands are clasped in prayer.

The prayer of faith can move mountains.
It can heal the sick.
    It can overcome the world.
        It can work miracles.
            It "availeth much."

It is like the atomic bomb in at least two particulars:
    It may be just as dangerous . . .
        And it certainly is as little explored.
In very truth, prayer may be our only defense against the evil implications of the atomic bomb.

Prayer generally is an unexplored field.
Believers have not experimented with prayer, regarding it as an emergency measure or a conventional practice to be maintained,
    much as one's subscription to a series of cultural lectures.

It is culture—and not conviction—that keeps some people praying.

The whole field of prayer,
    and praying as laying hold on unlimited power,
  is unexplored, with the result that spiritual laws still lie undiscovered by the average believer.

There is an element of danger and risk in all exploration into new fields.
Every scientist knows that.
Every explorer into the realm of the spiritual will find it just as true.

In a little pamphlet, I saw a story about a former missionary who had been stricken by illness and bedridden for eight years.
    During these eight years, she had steadily and persistently asked God:
    "Why?"

She could not understand why this incapacitating illness should lay her aside when she had been doing the Lord's work.
There was some rebellion in her heart,
    and the drums of mutiny rolled every now and then.

The burden of her prayers was that the Lord should make her well in order that she might return to do His work.
But nothing happened.
    Her prayers seemed to get nowhere.
She knew that they were not answered,
    and they seemed to be rising no higher than the ceiling.

Finally, worn out with the failure of her prayers, and with a desperate sort of resignation within her, she prayed:
    "All right, Lord, I give in.
    If I am to be sick for the rest of my life, I bow to Thy will.
    I want to yield to Thy will more than I want anything else in the world—even health.
    It is for Thee to decide."

Thus leaving herself entirely in God's hands, she began to feel a peace she had not known at any time during her illness.
In two weeks she was out of bed, completely well.

Now why did this prayer unlock the very gates of Heaven,
    to put down blessings and health?
whereas the other three thousand prayers had produced no results?

The answer is that somewhere within this missionary's experience is revealed a little-known and rarely understood spiritual law, which, if followed, always works,
    just as the law of gravity works.

The spiritual law in this case is that we must seek and be willing to accept the will of God—
    whatever it may be for us.

349

Our prayers must not be efforts to bend God to our will or desires—
>   but to yield ourselves to His—whatever they may be.

We forget that God sometimes has to say, "No."
We pray to Him as our Heavenly Father, and like wise human fathers,
>   He often says, "No,"
>>   not from whim or caprice,
>>>   but from wisdom and from love, and knowing what is best for us.

Christ Himself, in the agony of the Garden of Gethsemane, prayed with the certain stipulation that God's will—not His—be done.

It is this factor of divine decision which the skeptic cannot comprehend,
>   and which the believer must accept,
>   that produces answered prayer.

It is this matter of the surrender of our wills to God's will that is hard for us.
It is this unknown factor—sometimes not knowing what *is* God's will in a particular case—that makes praying dangerous business. Usually we learn how wonderful God's will really is only through experience.

Starr Daily tells of a boy who was desperately ill with infantile paralysis.
The mother arrived at the church, weeping—full of fear.
Her minister, Pastor Brown, drew her to one side and asked: "If you knew that it was God's will, would you be willing to let Billy go to heaven?
Could you give him up, if you knew God wanted him?"

After a long struggle with her emotions, she said, "Yes, if I knew for certain it were God's will I'd be willing to release the boy."

Pastor Brown then lifted the child up to God in prayer, surrendering him completely to the mercy and wisdom of God. Three days later the boy was discharged from the hospital with no sign of paralysis left in his body.[2]

Dr. Glenn Clark, who had probably experimented more with this type of prayer—
    the prayer of relinquishment—
than any other contemporary, says that Starr Daily's story is not unusual.
The prayer of relinquishment has in it amazing power.

But, you see, it's a dangerous prayer in a sense.
Praying that kind of a prayer is a big adventure.
It's dangerous business.

Just as soon as we are willing to accept God's decision in the matter about which we are praying,
    whatever it may turn out to be,
then, and not until then, will our prayers be answered.
For God is always far more willing to give us good things than we are anxious to have them.

If we know spiritual laws and pray *with* them,
    instead of *against* them,
the results are certain.
But it is here that we enter into an almost totally unexplored realm.

Men who have explored and ferreted out the so-called natural laws . . .
    have harnessed them and used them even to making water run uphill,
        iron to float,
            and man to fly.

Very few of us have done any exploring in the hinterland of spiritual laws.

351

We do not know them . . .
    so that our praying, for the most part, is a hit-and-miss
    proposition.

Sometimes, in our desperation, we hit upon the right way to pray,
and things happen—
    our prayers are gloriously answered.
But for the most part, our praying is very haphazard,
    and the results are often disappointing.

It is also dangerous business to pray for something unless you
really and truly mean it.

You see, God might call your bluff,
    take you up on it . . .
and would you be surprised!

It is for this reason that it were better for most of us not to sing
some of the hymns we used to sing in Sunday School . . .
    or at revival meetings.

Do you remember when you sang, "I'll go where you want me
to go, dear Lord . . .
    over mountain,
        or plain,
            or sea.
I'll say what you want me to say, dear Lord.
I'll be what you want me to be"?[3]
Suppose the Lord had taken you up on that one!

Or here is another . . .
    a couple of lines in one of our hymns of consecration:
    "Take my silver and my gold;
    not a mite would I withhold."[4]

Probably you have sung that many a time.
What a shock it would have been if the Lord had taken you up
on that one!

Suppose He said, "All right, go, sell your property, cash in your bonds, and give Me that money to use for My needy children." Suppose He did!

Real praying—
     that is, talking with God—
and maintaining communications with Him as Director of your life and activities—demands real honesty.

If our prayers are to avail anything at all, we have to open up every corner of our hearts and minds to Him.
We dare not say one thing with our lips and mean another thing in our hearts.

Being really honest with God does not come easily to any one of us.
Sometimes we do not know ourselves very well.

A woman had been ill in bed for a long time.
She had constantly prayed that God would make her well.
She thought she wanted health more than anything in the world.

But one day, as she prayed, it seemed to her that God said, just as He had to the impotent man at the Pool of Bethesda—
     "Do you really *want* to be made well?"

As the woman pondered this strange question, suddenly she realized that there was a sense in which she had grown fond of her quiet life—
               no dishes to wash
          none of the petty details of living
     all the time she wanted to read and think. . . .

She saw that God's will for her was health all right, but that it was actually going to stretch her to attain it.

"Climb out of bed," Christ said to her.
     "As you take up active life again, you'll get well."

353

And she did get well.

Yes, it is very hard really to be honest.

But when we are honest with God, He is equally honest with us.

He will take any promises or pledges we make to Him at their face value.

He has a way of calling our bluff.

That is why praying is dangerous business.

I once heard about a man who knew that he needed patience more than anything else.

He knew that impatience was his worst fault.

And it kept him perfectly miserable.

So he began to pray for patience.

What do you think happened?

He secured a new secretary . . .
    and lo and behold, she was the slowest secretary the man
    had ever seen or heard of.
The girl almost drove him crazy.

The poor businessman was almost frantic when, one day, it occurred to him that this was God's answer to his prayer for patience.

And when he understood how God had answered his prayer, he began to learn patience.

But God—who surely must have a sense of humor—had used an exasperatingly slow secretary to teach the lesson.

The businessman learned patience all right.

He also learned that you had better mean what you say when you ask God for something.

Another reason why praying is dangerous business is that when God answers prayer, we have to follow His guidance
    or take the consequences.

A friend of ours in a nearby city had been out of a job for several
months.
Finally, there came an offer from a firm in Michigan.
They asked him to come out for an interview.
He decided to go.

Meanwhile, he prayed that if God did not want him to take this
position,
He would close the door in his face.
This was to be the sign.

Well, God heard the prayer and took it at simple face value. Our
friend had the interview.

The deal was not closed just then,
    for the president of the firm wanted more time to consider it.
A week passed by.
Then the offer came,
    with a very attractive salary.
But our friend was confused with the week's silence, so that he
was not sure that it was God's will that he take it.
Then came a telegram substantially raising the salary.
Finally, completely confused by side issues, he turned it down.

Now what was the result?

In the end he accepted a local position at half the pay,
    with an employer who had an ungovernable temper,
        and made his life completely miserable.
Now he clearly sees his mistake.

He had asked God to use a particular sign . . .
    namely, that the door would be closed, if it was God's will
    that he should not go to Michigan.
Instead of that,
    the door was opened very wide,
        and every inducement offered him to go ahead.

But apparently our friend simply couldn't believe that such was the case.

The result was that he spent the most miserable months of his life living out his mistake.

That is why I say praying is dangerous business.

Here again is a matter that many of us overlook when we ask God to do something.

We forget that God may require something of the one who prays.

Often He wants us to help answer the prayer.

The answer to a particular prayer may involve some real effort . . .
    maybe even some sacrifice.

I have yet to see a seriously threatened marriage in which all the blame was on one side.

Sometimes a wife, as she prays about her marriage, asks God to change her husband—

and is promptly shown something that *she* must change.

Prayer can help to make us clear-eyed about our own shortcomings.
    That isn't always pleasant.

You've got to be ready to be shown uncomfortable things
        to do your part
    to do anything God tells you,
if you really want your prayer answered.

God's method in answering almost any prayer is the head-on, straightforward approach.

It calls for courage, as well as faith.

It's the march-into-the-Red-Sea-and-it-divides method . . .
    or march-right-up-to-the-walls-and-they-fall-down technique.

You've got to have faith for that sort of venture . . .

and courage too.
That's why some prayers may be dangerous.

You set out, under God's guidance, on a course that seems almost
foolhardy . . .
But you keep going,
    if you really mean it . . .
and God works His wonderful works.

But there are times when you are "sweating it out," as they said
in the Air Force.

Yes, praying can be dangerous business. . . .
For God expects us never to question that He is a God of love . . .
Who loves us each one individually.

It is a wonderful idea, once it gets hold of you, that God loves *you*,
    whoever you are . . . for yourself.
You are precious to Him.
    He loves *you*.
        He wants you to be happy.
            He wants to give you good things.
It is His will for you that life should be full,
        abundant . . .
    and rich.

He expects us to believe that He holds us in the hollow of His hand,
    and that we are safe for all eternity.

This does not mean that no trouble shall come to us—
    or that we will never get sick—
        or that no sorrow shall ever touch us.

On the contrary, we are told very bluntly by Jesus Himself that
in this world we shall have trouble.

But then He says:
    "Cheer up! I have overcome the world.

357

My grace is sufficient for you.
I am with you alway, even unto the end of the world"
(Matthew 28:20).

In the words of Paul:
"We know that all things work together for good to them
that love God" (Romans 8:28).
God will not permit any troubles to come upon us, unless He has
a specific plan by which great blessing can come out of the difficulty.

To believe this calls for strong faith and no little courage . . .
but it shuts out all bitterness and rebellion against our
circumstances.
And when troubles come,
no matter what form it takes,
we can then turn it over to Him and ask Him to open the door
in the wall.

Nothing gives the Lord greater pleasure than to help His children.
But unless you really mean it,
praying can be dangerous business.

Inventions can never save mankind.
Redeeming grace will come
not from a laboratory . . . but from an altar,
in your home and in your heart.

"The hope of the world in this atomic age lies," as Mr. Oursler said,
"not in physics
but in prayer."

$E = MC^2$. . . .
Yes, that may be true.
But this is the truth that will save us all—Psalm 37:4 and 7:

"Rest in the Lord . . .
wait patiently for Him . . .
And He shall give thee the desires of thine heart."

Hear Us, Lord Jesus

Lord Jesus, Thou knowest the things that are trembling upon our lips, stirring in our hearts and along the corridors of our souls, walking on tiptoe across the cloistered spaces of our consciousness; conforming to the distant pealing of an angelus; looking expectantly upward; making prayers without words; breathing aspirations that have only wings.

Hear us, we pray Thee, as we call upon Thee for help, for strength, for peace; for grace, for reassurance, for companionship; for love, for pardon, for health, for salvation—for joy. Hear us, Lord Jesus. AMEN.

OTES

Chapter 2: *Under Sealed Orders*

   1. Matthew 6:33.

Chapter 3: *Singing in the Rain*

   1. On Sunday, October 2, 1927.

Chapter 4: *The Perils of a Young Preacher*

   1. *The Christian Observer*, Louisville, Kentucky. Used by permission.

   2. *The Oxford Book of English Verse*, p. 321, Oxford University Press, New York, 1918.

   3. Maxwell, Ted and Virginia, *The Key Note*, p. 3, Walter H. Baker Co., Boston, Mass. Used by permission.

Chapter 5: *The Halls of Highest Human Happiness*

   1. I was mistaken. Peter was actually thirty-one at the time.

Chapter 7: *The Preacher-Bridegroom*

   1. By this time, Westminster's balcony had been paid for.

Chapter 8: *The Country He Left Behind*

   1. It was she who had taken Peter under her wing in Georgia.

   2. Kipling, Rudyard, *The Five Nations*. Copyright 1903 by the author. Reprinted by permission of Mrs. George Bambridge and Doubleday & Co., Inc.

   3. Quoted by permission of Dodd, Mead & Company from *In Scotland Again*, by H. V. Morton. Copyright 1933 by Dodd, Mead & Company, Inc.

   4. *Road to the Isles*, words by Kenneth MacLeod, arr. by M. Kennedy-Fraser, Boosey and Hawkes, New York, 1917. Used by permission.

Chapter 9: *Washington—Opportunity Unlimited*

   1. *The Lutheran*, March 2, 1949. Used by permission.

Chapter 10: *The Man at Home*

   1. *The Washington Post*, Dec. 23, 1938. Used by permission.

   2. Mark 10:7–8.

Chapter 11: *Christianity Can Be Fun*

1. *An Eriskay Love Lilt,* words by Kenneth MacLeod, arr. by M. Kennedy-Fraser, Boosey and Hawkes, New York, 1908. Used by permission.

Chapter 14: *God Still Answers Prayer*

1. All Moffatt translations are from *The New Testament—A New Translation,* James Moffatt, Harper & Bros., New York, 1922, 1936, 1950. Used by permission.
2. See John 14:12.
3. Dr. Marshall used this same story in the sermon "Praying Is Dangerous Business." This is a good example of the vital link between his private life and his preaching.
4. He said in an article in *Presbyterian Life,* January 8, 1949.

Chapter 16: *Preacher's Workshop*

1. "Shepherd of the Senate," used by permission.
2. Ruskin, John, *Modern Painters,* Vol. III, Part IV, Chap. 16.
3. In his column "Day Book" in the *Washington Times-Herald,* Jan. 27, 1949. Used by permission.
4. Two paragraphs here are quoted from the *Pulpit Book Club Bulletin* for December 1949, "Sermon-Writing the Hard Way," by Catherine Marshall.

Chapter 17: *Valiant Heart*

1. Author of many books and pamphlets on prayer; *e.g., I Will Lift up Mine Eyes* and *How to Find Health through Prayer,* Harper & Bros., New York, 1937, 1940.

Chapter 18: *The Dominie*

1. Burkhardt, Robert, "The Solons' Shepherd," *The New York Times,* Jan. 11, 1948. Used by permission.
2. "A New Bite to Senate Prayers," *Chicago Sun-Times.* Used by permission.
3. *Life,* Feb. 7, 1949. Used by permission.
4. Harrington, Jeanette T., "Chaplain of the Senate," *Presbyterian Life,* March 17, 1948.
5. *The Washington Post,* Jan. 26, 1949. Used by permission.
6. For the *Fort Wayne Journal-Gazette,* Nov. 15, 1947.

Chapter 19: *Together*

1. *Time,* "Plain and Pertinent," Feb. 7, 1949. Used by permission.

Chapter 20: *See You in the Morning*

1. Dr. Clarence Cranford, the pastor of Washington's Calvary Baptist Church.
2. The *Washington Evening Star,* Jan. 25, 1949. Used by permission.
3. *The Lutheran, op. cit.,* p. 103.
4. *Mr. Jones, Meet the Master,* Fleming H. Revell Company, New York, 1949.

Gallery Christians

1. Edgar Goodspeed, *The New Testament: An American Translation* (Chicago: University of Chicago Press, 1931).

Sin in the Present Tense

1. *The British Medical Journal*, June 18, 1910.
2. From Dr. Swaim's presidential address (in 1942) presented before the American Rheumatism Association; published in the *Annals of Internal Medicine,* July 1943, American College of Physicians, Philadelphia.
3. From the column, "Pitching Horseshoes," by Billy Rose; published by the Bell Syndicate.

Letters in the Sand

1. Edgar Goodspeed, *The New Testament: An American Translation* (Chicago: University of Chicago Press, 1931), p. 294

Praying Is Dangerous Business

1. These paragraphs were also included in Fulton Oursler, *Why I Know There Is a God* (New York: Doubleday, 1950).
2. Starr Daily, *Recovery* (St. Paul, Minn.: Macalester Park), p. 91.
3. From the hymn "I'll Go Where You Want Me to Go," The Rodeheaver Hall Mack Company, Winona Lake, Ind.
4. From the hymn "Take My Life and Let It Be." Words by Frances Havergal.

A Man Called PETER

Filled with humor, wisdom and loving detail, the powerful story of Peter Marshall's life has touched the hearts and minds of millions of people. It is a book about love—the love between a dynamic man and his God, and the tender love between a man and the woman he married. It is also the gripping adventure of a poor Scottish immigrant who became chaplain of the United States Senate and one of the most revered men in America.

A Man Called Peter became the number-one best-seller when it was published in 1951, and around the world lives were changed by reading of the chaplain's remarkable faith. In the foreword to this book, Peter's son writes, "Even when [Dad's] words were preached 'secondhand'. . . in the movie version of *A Man Called Peter*, they had an amazing effect on people."

Through Peter's story and the compelling sermons and prayers included in *A Man Called Peter*, you will discover insight into God, man, and life on earth and hereafter. You will also be encouraged by the realization that "if God can do so much for a man called Peter, he can do as much for you."

Catherine Marshall (1914–1983), the widow of Peter Marshall, wrote more than twenty books, including the best-sellers *Christy, Beyond Our Selves* and *Something More.*

Biography/Autobiography
ISBN 0-8007-9311-0

9 780800 793111